Arabic–English–Arabic Literary Translation

Arabic–English–Arabic Literary Translation

Issues and Strategies

Ahmed Saleh Elimam

EDINBURGH
University Press

Edinburgh University Press is one of the leading university presses in the UK. We publish academic books and journals in our selected subject areas across the humanities and social sciences, combining cutting-edge scholarship with high editorial and production values to produce academic works of lasting importance. For more information visit our website: edinburghuniversitypress.com

Edinburgh University Press Ltd
The Tun – Holyrood Road
12 (2f) Jackson's Entry
Edinburgh EH8 8PJ

Typeset in 14/16 Myriad Arabic by
IDSUK (DataConnection) Ltd

A CIP record for this book is available from the British Library

ISBN 978 1 4744 8661 3 (hardback)
ISBN 978 1 4744 8662 0 (paperback)
ISBN 978 1 4744 8663 7 (webready PDF)
ISBN 978 1 4744 8664 4 (epub)

Contents

Figures and Tables

Acknowledgements

I would like to thank several colleagues and friends for their valuable suggestions and comments on the contents of this book. I would like to express my gratitude to H. Bryant, C. Cobham, A. Fletcher and S. Miah for their valuable comments and suggestions. I would also like to thank many of the MA in Translation and Interpreting students at the University of Leicester for their comments on different sections of this book which I have used as part of their learning material over the past few years.

Abbreviations and IJMES Transliteration System

ST Source Text
SL Source Language
TT Target Text
TL Target Language

The alphabet

ء	ʾ	ط	ṭ
ب	B	ظ	ẓ
ت	T	ع	ʿ
ث	Th	غ	Gh
ج	J	ف	F
ح	ḥ	ق	Q
خ	Kh	ك	K
د	D	ل	L
ذ	Dh	م	M
ر	R	ن	N
ز	Z	ه	H
س	S	و	W
ش	sh	ي	Y
ص	ṣ	ة	a
ض	ḍ	ال	al-

The vowels

Long	ا or يا	ā
	و	ū
	ي	ī
Short	ـَ	a
	ـُ	u
	ـِ	i

Doubled	يّ	iyy (final form ī)
	وّ	uww (final form ū)
Diphthongs	وَ	au or aw
	ىَ	ai or ay

Note that exceptions from this key will include published names of authors and literary titles.

INTRODUCTION

Translation as an academic discipline has become increasingly popular at both undergraduate and postgraduate levels, particularly since 1972 when Holmes published the Translation Studies map. By its very nature, Translation is an interdisciplinary field, which cuts across and draws on other relevant areas, including Cultural Studies (علم دراسة الثقافات), Cognition (علم الإدراك), Discourse Analysis (علم تحليل النصوص), Language (علم اللغة), Linguistics (علم اللسانيات أو اللغويات) and Sociology (علم الاجتماع). More attention is being paid in academia to translation not only in terms of how translators and interpreters should carry out their work, that is prescriptive translation studies (دراسات الترجمة التعليمية أو التوجيهية), but also in terms of how they actually do it, that is descriptive translation studies (دراسات الترجمة الوصفية). Therefore, bespoke Translation and Interpreting programmes have been set up in many universities around the world to teach Translation and/or Interpreting, hence the need for Translation textbooks, amongst other things.

The textbook at hand will help equip learners of translation, particularly literary translation, with the necessary background to be able to identify and deal with issues they come across when rendering texts of a literary nature between Arabic and English in particular. When a literary work is translated, it is the translator's job to recreate this work sensitively in the target language in a manner that serves the purpose of the translation, which, in a literary context, would often be to produce a rendering that is equally creative as the original. To do so, the target text should be as appealing in terms of its language and form to its readers as the original is to its own readers. In other words, literary translation is expected to reflect the original's salient characteristics to the target readers in order for them to appreciate the work and its author. This is a challenging process, particularly when translating famous writers or texts, since it involves an endless number of make-or-break decisions on how to deal with the source text's stylistic features (السمات الأسلوبية للنص الأصلي), and how to render those in a manner which does not rid the ST of its features in the translation, but at the same time does not make the translation a 'chore' to understand for the target readers. To produce a successful literary translation, therefore, a fine balance needs to be maintained between staying too close to the ST, on the one hand, or to the target language norms, on the other.

In the process of translation, the translator's role is twofold: he or she is a reader before being a writer. The translator needs to understand the source text, drawing on language resources and checking with the source text's author, if possible, in order to identify the correct meaning of the text before putting their "authoring" or "writing" hat on and attempting to render the original meaning into the target language, taking into account multiple considerations as will be elaborated throughout this guide. This is not an easy process, especially when the languages in question are as different grammatically and culturally as Arabic and English, which makes the translator's task all the more challenging.

In this context, some theorists argue that globalisation has made the lay reader aware of the peculiarities of other cultures and, therefore, translators can afford to keep these 'foreign' elements in their output. This is a strong assumption and needs to be examined on a case-by-case basis by translators. Identifying the target reader's level of knowledge and expectations is key to a successful reception of the translation.

With this in mind, this guide will provide to translation students and trainers the most common issues translators of literary texts between Arabic and English face, and the strategies available to deal with them. These issues and strategies can also be applied to translating not only other genres but also other language pairs. For this purpose, a back translation of the Arabic and English examples discussed throughout this coursebook is provided, when necessary, to make it accessible to other language users.

Furthermore, this guide adopts the view that the most two challenging factors in literary translation are style and context. In other words, it simultaneously adopts the linguistic and cultural approaches to rendering literary texts (see 1.4 in Chapter 1 and Chapter 6). Therefore, Chapter 1 provides an annotated table of some of the most significant linguistic components of style. These include diction, vocabulary, sentence structure, use of dialogue, tone, aesthetic qualities, figures of speech, tense, layout, and conventional and non-conventional writing. These components will be developed and illustrated through Chapters 2, 3, 4, 5 and 6 of this book. Note that the term 'context' (السياق أو السياق العام) is used as an umbrella term that covers all factors falling outside the text itself and influencing the process and/or producer of the translation in some way, shape or form. These include the translation approach (أسلوب الترجمة) and *skopos*, meaning purpose of the translation (الغرض أو الهدف من الترجمة), target readers' expectations (توقعات قارئ الترجمة), and the translator's ideology (معتقدات المترجم وأفكاره), to name but a few.

In short, this guide provides a systematic classification of the most common translation issues that can be encountered in any translation of a literary nature. It introduces theoretical issues and provides practical tools for the analysis of translation covering relevant translation theory and approaches. It also discusses the strategies available to deal with these translation issues, illustrating the discussion with plenty of examples to make the argument accessible to potential readers.

The translator's role

In rendering a literary work, the translator is expected to be able to understand the meaning of the original work and to be creative in maintaining the author's original style and offer the target readers a feel of it. Here, the translator needs to strike a balance between staying too close to the target language, bringing the work closer to the target readers at the expense of losing the work's authentic taste, and staying too close to the source language and culture, making the work a challenge to understand to target readers. A balance needs to be maintained between communicating the author's style and original culture of the source text and allowing the target readers to understand the translation and appreciate the original work. To draw on Venuti (1995, see also Chapter 2 of this coursebook), a balance between 'foreignising' (تغريب) the work, by maintaining all of its cultural references and idiosyncratic grammatical features, and 'domesticating' it completely (توطين), by ironing out all of these references and features, needs to be made. In other words, some level of what can be described as 'necessary foreignness' and/or 'necessary domestication' may need to be maintained in rendering literary works. Nevertheless, in some cases, 'completely' foreignised or 'completely' domesticated translations may also be required or expected. For instance, researching the original features of a source text by someone who does not know its respective language would call for an overwhelmingly foreignised translation.

The translator needs to understand that, as opposed to the area of technical translation, consistency in rendering some lexical items and structures in a literary work does not necessarily mean using the same translation throughout. Issues of co-text (سياق الجملة أو السياق اللغوي وهو الجمل السابقة و/أو اللاحقة للجملة المعنية), context (اختصارا السياق العام للنص وعملية الترجمة أو السياق) and style (أسلوب الكتابة أو أسلوب الكاتب), amongst other issues, play an important role in the selection of which rendering to use each time the same lexical item is encountered. In fact, as opposed to technical writing and translation, which feature a relatively high level of repetition of terms, literary writers and translators are expected to avoid repetition and to use synonyms to maintain an eloquent style. In short, a literary translator is expected to be as much of a creative writer as the author of the source text.

Book outline

This textbook is structured along the lines of the translation process. It starts with a definition of relevant terms necessary to the understanding of the translation process. Literary versus non-literary language is introduced, and then translation approaches are discussed, followed by an examination of translation issues and strategies at lexical, structural, textual and contextual levels, before providing examples of translation annotations to show the readers how the discussion of translation issues and strategies can be applied.

Chapter 1 identifies and defines the relevant concepts which guide the arguments elaborated throughout this textbook. These concepts are literature, translation, translation theory, style and context. Identifying whether the text being translated is literary or non-literary is essential in identifying, first of all, the overall translation approach to be adopted as well as the local translation strategies to be applied in dealing with translation challenges. Translation approach (أسلوب الترجمة) is used in this book to refer to the macro-level orientation that governs how we translate the whole text, e.g. foreignisation, domestication, communicative and formal versus dynamic equivalence (see Chapter 2 for definitions of these approaches). On the other hand, translation strategy (استراتيجية أو طريقة الترجمة) is used to imply micro-level procedures employed to deal with translation issues, for instance, direct, cultural or functional equivalent, transliteration, naturalisation or omission of lexical items. The choice of which strategy to use with a particular local translation issue is primarily guided by the overall translation approach adopted as is explained throughout this guide.

Secondly, understanding what 'translation' means as a product and process is key to proceeding to translate with full knowledge of what is required of the translator. Awareness of the advantages of translation theory helps the translator to maintain consistency throughout the translation process and gives him or her the ability to justify their choice of the translation approach and micro-level strategies. The concept of 'style' (أسلوب الكتابة أو أسلوب الكاتب) and its components are particularly important in the case of a literary work, considering that an author's style is his or her own linguistic identity, which needs to be communicated sensitively and accurately to the target readers to help them appreciate the original work. Finally, 'context' (السياق أو السياق العام لعملية الترجمة), as an overarching component of the process of translation, has an important role to play in both understanding why the source text is organised the way it is and in guiding the translator in his or her choice of translation approach. The following chapters, for ease of reference, divide and discuss translation issues and strategies into lexical issues and strategies, structural issues and strategies, textual issues and strategies, and contextual issues and strategies. It is worth mentioning here that this is a rough classification of translation issues and that there is a relatively large area of overlap between these types. For example, the issues associated with translating metaphor can occur at a structural (sentence) level or at the level of a whole text in the case of extended metaphor, for example, *Animal Farm* by George Orwell (1945).

Chapter 2 deals with the translation process itself and identifies the elements which should be taken into consideration by the translator. These factors relate to both the source text system (منظومة النص الأصلي) and the target text system (منظومة النص المترجم). This is because the translator is located on the interface between the two systems and his or her job is to negotiate relevant translation choices while taking a large number of considerations into account, as discussed in Chapter 2 in detail. The chapter then discusses the most common translation approaches which are supposed to guide the whole process: word-for-word translation, literal, faithful, semantic, communicative, idiomatic, free, adaptation, domestication, foreignisation, formal equivalence, dynamic equivalence and functional translation. As can be seen from the discussion in the chapter, some of these approaches are a better fit for certain contexts than others. For instance, some approaches are more source text-oriented, and others are more target text-oriented, meaning that they prioritise either the ST or the TT. Choice of which approach to choose depends on several factors, amongst which are the *skopos*, i.e. purpose, of the translation, target readers' expectations, the commissioner's preference, and the literary status of the ST or the ST author (see also Chapter 6 for more details).

Chapter 3 examines in detail the most significant lexical translation issues in literary translation. The issues examined represent the most commonly discussed issues by the relevant literature: Almanna (2016); Ghazala (2008/2014); Hatim and Munday (2004); Dickins et al. (2002); Fawcett (1997); Baker (1992/2011); Newmark (1988/2003); Vinay and Darbelnet (1958/1995). These issues include types of lexical meaning: denotative meaning (المعنى الإشاري أو الحقيقي أو المعجمي), connotative meaning (المعنى الضمني أو الكامن أو النفسي) and associated meaning (المعنى المتلازم أو المقترن أو المرتبط), complex lexical items (الكلمات أو الألفاظ المعقدة), context-dependent words vs context-free words (كلمات أو ألفاظ يعتمد معناها على السياق وكلمات أو ألفاظ معناها مستقل عن السياق), culture-specific words, alternatively called 'loaded words', (كلمات أو ألفاظ خاصة بالثقافة), a word's range of meaning (نطاق معاني الكلمات أو الألفاظ), use of a superordinate (استخدام لفظ شامل أو عام), that is a general word, use of a hyponym (استخدام لفظ مندرج أو خاص), that is a specific word, the difference in interpersonal or physical perspective, alternatively called 'modulation' (اختلاف المنظور الشخصي أو المادي أو"التعديل"), word formation (صياغة الكلمة), use of foreign/loan words (استخدام كلمات أجنبية أو مستعارة من لغات أخرى), false friends, or 'faux amis', (" أصدقاء مزيفون" وهي كلمات من لغتين أو أكثر تتشابه في الكتابة أو النطق وتختلف في المعنى), dialect and idiolect (اللهجة المحلية لمنطقة ما واللهجة الفردية), forms of address (صيغ المخاطبة أو استخدام الألقاب), neologism (الكلمات أو الألفاظ الجديدة أو المستحدثة), words with competing translations (كلمات ذات ترجمات متعارضة أو متباينة), gestures (الإشارات أو الإيماءات) and humour (الدعابة أو الفكاهة).

The chapter then provides, and illustrates with plenty of examples, the most commonly available translation strategies which can be used to deal with these issues. These strategies include using direct translation (الترجمة المباشرة أو المتداولة), that is frequently used to render the lexical item in question, through-translation, alternatively called 'literal translation' or 'calque' (الترجمة الحرفية), cultural equivalent, alternatively called 'cultural substitution' (المقابل أو المرادف أو البديل الثقافي), functional equivalent (المقابل أو المرادف الوظيفي), use of a superordinate, alternatively called 'use of a general word' or 'expansion' (استخدام لفظ شامل أو عام أو التوسع في نقل المعنى), use of a neutral or less expressive word, alternatively called 'reduction' (استخدام كلمة محايدة أو أقل تعبيرا عن المعني أو اختزال المعنى), paraphrase, sometimes called 'descriptive equivalent' (الشرح أو المقابل أو المرادف الوصفي), transliteration, alternatively called 'borrowing', 'loanword' or 'transference' (النسخ الصوتي أو استعارة الكلمات أو نقلها من لغة أخرى), naturalisation (تطويع أوتطبيع النطق أو الكتابة لقواعد لغة الترجمة), omission (الحذف), compensation (التعويض), in-text glosses (إضافة معلومات بين قوسين لتقريب المعنى), footnotes (حاشية سفلية) and use of two or more of these strategies simultaneously (استخدام استراتيجيتين أو أكثر معا).

Chapter 4 covers translation issues that can occur at a structural level, that is a phrase, clause or sentence. These are idiosyncratic grammatical structures, (التراكيب اللغوية) including word order variation, marked and unmarked word order in Arabic versus English (بناء الجملة أوالتقديم والتأخير), passive structure (أسلوب البناء للمجهول), *iḍāfa* (الإضافة), roughly translated as 'construct/genitive structure', grammatical gender (التذكير والتأنيث), grammatical number (الإفراد والتثنية والجمع), definiteness (التعريف والتنكير) and collocations (المتلازمات اللفظية). The discussion also covers the available translation strategies in each case, using relevant Arabic and English examples to illustrate the argument.

Chapter 5 focuses on the issues raised by dealing with textual features, used here to imply rhetorical or aesthetic features rather than the lexical and structural components. The chapter, therefore, examines the translation issues posed by, and the strategies available for dealing with the translation of, idioms and fixed expressions (الأقوال المأثورة والتعابير الاصطلاحية), metaphor (الاستعارة), simile (التشبيه), pun (التورية), and inter-sentential and intrasentential cohesion (سبكة النص أو تماسك النص). Here I adopt Halliday and Hasan's taxonomy (1976), which identifies the following as cohesion creating devices: reference (الضمائر), substitution (الإبدال), repetition (التكرار), ellipsis (الحذف), conjunction (حروف العطف) and lexical cohesion (التماسك اللفظي). The discussion is illustrated with relevant examples and their respective translations.

Chapter 6 deals with contextual, that is extra-textual, translation issues and strategies. Context (السياق العام للنص وعملية الترجمة أو السياق اختصارا) here is defined as an umbrella term referring to all extra-textual elements relevant to the ST, TT, the translator or the process of translation. There is a wide range of factors that can have an effect on the translation process or product. Some of these factors relate to the ST and its culture, while others relate to the TT and its readers. Some factors relate to the translator while others relate to the commissioner. This chapter will focus on some of the most important factors, namely, the translation approach, target readers' expectations, context of reception and translator's aim, the translator's ideology, the commissioner's influence, trends in academia or philosophy and register.

Chapter 7, building on the previous chapters, emphasises the importance of the practical issue of writing a translation commentary. It propounds that an annotation of a translation issue needs to cover the rationale for the selection of the particular issue, explanation of why it is an issue and how it was dealt with, drawing on the literature and using *meta* language of Translation Studies, or (مصطلحات علم الترجمة) in Arabic. Furthermore, the chapter provides many examples of actual annotations to further illustrate to the readers how to apply the discussion of translation issues and strategies elaborated throughout this guide in practice.

The section Final Remarks emphasises the need to look to the translation process as a whole and to consider the effect of each strategy you opt for on your output. It also stresses the importance of identifying your translation approach before writing annotations/commentary on translation issues which are usually a requirement for degrees in Translation and Interpreting Studies.

Features of this book

- Adopting a systematic bottom-up approach, this practical guide covers most of the issues that translators come across in dealing with literary texts and the strategies available to overcome them.
- To offer the readers a well-rounded background about the relevant literature, this guide draws upon the most popular coursebooks which deal with the practical issues of translation between Arabic and English.
- Illustrative examples are provided from both Arabic and English throughout the coursebook to clarify the points under discussion.
- Detailed explanations of relevant translation issues as well as back translations and glosses are provided to appeal to native speakers of both Arabic and English, whether students, trainers or professional translators or interpreters.
- Examples of annotations are also provided to help the students to translate and write commentaries on the translation as part of their coursework or dissertations.
- This guide includes practice exercises, drawn from Arabic and English literature, to allow the readers to put into practice the knowledge they gained after each chapter. Tips on how to deal with each exercise are also provided.
- The approach adopted, and the material included in this guide have been taught in several classrooms in UK universities, and feedback from students and peer reviewers has been taken into consideration in this guide in its current format.

How to read this book

There are at least two ways in which this book can be read. Firstly, the potential reader can read all the chapters in the order they are presented in this guide. This option presents a bottom-up approach which introduces micro-level translation issues and strategies as discussed in Chapters 3, 4 and 5, before illustrating how macro-level issues influence the translation process as illustrated in Chapter 6. Secondly, readers can also read the introduction, Chapter 1 and Chapter 2, then read Chapter 6 before going back to read Chapters 3, 4 and 5, followed by the commentary writing and example annotations provided in Chapter 7. Adopting a top-down approach, this reading will introduce the readers to the translation approaches discussed in Chapter 2 as well as the discussion and illustration of how they work in the translation process presented in Chapter 6, before discussing the micro-level translation issues presented in Chapters 3, 4 and 5. For maximum benefit, the exercises included at the end of each chapter should be undertaken by the reader.

CHAPTER 1
KEY CONCEPTS IN LITERARY TRANSLATION

1.1 Introduction

This chapter starts by introducing important definitions which are inevitably drawn upon throughout this book. Considering that the focus here is on literary translation, it is only natural that a definition of literary as opposed to non-literary writing is provided. This is followed by definitions of 'Translation' as both a process and a product, and Translation Theory, Style and Context, all of which are important concepts in this coursebook which focuses on the issues encountered and strategies used in literary translation. The discussion below does not intend to provide an exhaustive list of the arguments made in relation to these concepts but aims to provide the necessary background before engaging with the topic of working with literary texts and literary features in the area of translation.

1.2 Literature

There are several definitions of literary language (لغة الأدب أو اللغة الأدبية). I provide below some of the most salient ones which differentiate between literary and non-literary language. Identifying the type of text being translated is a prerequisite to selecting the most appropriate translation approach and, in turn, strategies, as will be elaborated below.

1. The inherency model:
   This model views literary language as distinct from the more 'practical' uses of language in that literary language itself is highlighted. Roman Jakobson 'referred to the poetic function of language, where there is a "focus on the message for its own sake." This property of language may also be termed self-referential' (Carter 2004: 10). For example, when someone reads poetry, he or she will unavoidably focus on the aesthetics, e.g. rhythmical and alliterative features, of the language as opposed to reading a technical report where the focus will be on the content itself.
2. The sociocultural model:
   This model sees 'literariness as socially and culturally determined ... conceptions of literature vary historically and culturally ... a text can be seen as literature if it is defined as such by institutions or if people read it as such' (Carter 2004: 10). A good example is

probably the genre of letter writing, which, historically, was not considered literary, but later this conception changed.

3. The cognitive model:

   This model relates literary language to mental processes: 'literary texts have an effect on the mind, helping us think in new ways and "refreshing and changing our mental representation of the world"' (Carter 2004: 11). For example, reading a poem or a short story refreshes our minds and makes us live a different reality.

4. The literary cline:

   According to this view, literariness is a matter of degree; creativity is used by different authors, whether in the area of literature or science. Therefore, the difference between literary and non-literary writing is a matter of quantity, meaning the quantity of literary/stylistic features used, rather than the quality of using these features. In other words, both types of writing share the same qualities of literariness but in different degrees. According to Carter (2004: 13–14), creativity binds people together and breaks the mould of language use as it allows people to think flexibly outside the moulds.

These definitions of what constitutes literary language are not necessarily exclusive or contradictory, but each of them applies in specific situations and in the relevant context. Furthermore, it is important for the translator to identify whether the text he or she is about to translate is literary or non-literary. This is key for the right selection of the overall translation approach as well as the local translation strategies to be used. For instance, non-literary language tolerates a great deal of repetition as opposed to literary language where synonyms, for example, are preferred to avoid repeating the same word (see also the role of the literary translator above). Finally, it is worth mentioning here that literature is a manifestation of cultural norms and that cultural norms are reflected in literature, making literary translation all the more challenging.

1.3 Translation: types and definitions

The term 'translation' (الترجمة) is used to refer to the process of rendering a ST into a TT and also to the product of this process. This is obviously a generic definition of the term, and the relevant literature abounds in more detailed and nuanced definitions. To elaborate, the relevant literature on Translation Studies provides a large number of definitions of Translation which are more or less context-based in the sense that each definition seems to focus on a specific aspect of the process of translation or the product thereof. I draw on some of these definitions below in order to contextualise this discussion.

First of all, the literature on Translation Studies proposes three types of translation as a process:

1. Intralingual translation:
   This is the process of rewording of signs in one language with signs from the same language; for example, paraphrasing a passage in the same language.
2. Interlingual translation:
   This refers to the interpretation of signs in one language with signs from another language. This is translation proper where knowledge of two languages is required to carry out this type of translation.
3. Intersemiotic translation:
   It refers to the transfer of the signs in one language to non-verbal sign systems (from language into art or music) (Jakobson 1959).

As can be seen, according to this view, rewriting a given source text written in one language in another variety of the same language is considered a translation by some theorists. For example, if a manuscript is rewritten into a more recent form of the same language for the benefit of modern readers, this is an act of translation. However, the most common type of translation is interlingual translation which involves working between two language systems and producing a target text which bears some kind of resemblance to another written in a different language and known as the source text.

Scholars offer variable definitions of Translation, each focusing on one or more aspects of the translation experience. To start with, Dubois et al. (1973: 22) explain that translation is 'the expression in another language (or target language) of what has been expressed in another language (referred to as the source language), preserving semantic and stylistic equivalence'. Adopting a linguistic approach to Translation (see 1.4 below), this definition assumes the existence of equivalent semantic and stylistic features across languages, overlooking the fact that each language has its own unique semantic and stylistic features. According to Wermer Koller (1995: 196), translation is

> the result of a text-processing activity, by means of which a source-language text is transposed into a target-language text. Between the resultant text in L2 (the target-language text) and the source text in L1 (the source-language text), there exists a relationship, which can be designated as a translational, or equivalence relation.

This definition views translation as a product and focuses on the argument that a target text needs to be 'equivalent' to the respective source text. Some recent Translation Studies literature considers the concept of 'equivalence' to be vague and, to disambiguate the term, features concepts such as cultural equivalence and functional equivalence. Qualifying the type of equivalence being discussed, e.g. functional or cultural, can unpack the concept and specify the type of equivalence being referred to.

To Roger T. Bell (1991: 1), translation is

> the process or result of converting information from one language or language variety into another . . . The aim is to reproduce as accurately as possible all grammatical and lexical features of the 'source language' original by finding equivalents in the 'target language.' At the same time all factual information contained in the original text . . . must be retained in the translation.

Although this definition focuses more on translation as a process, like the previous definition, it insists that a target text needs to be grammatically and lexically 'equivalent' to the source text. The main issue here is that there is an assumption that equivalent grammatical and lexical features exist across languages, which is not the case as will be discussed in the examples in the following chapters.

Mildred Larson (1984: 3) is of the opinion that translation

> consists of transferring the meaning of the source language into the receptor language. This is done by going from the form of the first language to the form of a second language by way of semantic structure. It is meaning which is being transferred and must be held constant. Only the form changes. The form from which the translation is made will be called the SOURCE LANGUAGE. Translation, then, consists of studying the lexicon, grammatical structure, communication situation, and cultural context of the source language text, analysing it in order to determine its meaning, and then reconstructing this same meaning using the lexicon and grammatical structures [style] which are appropriate in the RECEPTOR LANGUAGE and its context (original author's emphasis).

Larson's definition signals the importance of meaning rather than form. Although this is an important shift from some of the previous definitions which focus on equivalence, separation between form and content is not always possible as meaning is a combination of form and content. See how using marked as opposed to unmarked word order adds more meaning, for instance, emphasis (see 4.2.1 and 4.2.2).

Taking context into consideration, Vermeer (1987: 29) states that 'to translate means to produce a text in a target setting for a target purpose and target addressees in target circumstances', and, more recently, Christiane Nord (2007: 182) defines translation as 'the production of a functional target text maintaining a relationship with a given source text that is specified according to the intended or demanded function of the target text'. These definitions shift away from the concepts of equivalence, form and meaning to focus on the *skopos*, i.e. purpose, of the translation. According to this functional perspective of translation (see more below), the source text was organised the way it is for a specific function and the translation should, similarly, be organised in a manner that fulfils its own function. Note that the function of the target text may or may not be the same as that of the source text.

These definitions focus on specific aspects of translation as a process or a product. Some focus on reproducing the form, which can be the case when rendering poetry into rhymed prose, some focus on the meaning, for instance, rendering poetry in unrhymed prose format. Some focus on producing a translation which fulfils target readers' expectations, while others focus on staying close to the form of the ST in order to give the target readers a feel of its idiosyncratic features. These definitions and others are linked closely with the translation approach the translator opts for.

1.4 Translation theory

As a science, translation practice is always informed by translation theory (نظريات الترجمة). A translation theory aims 'to read an understanding of the process undertaken in the act of translation' (Bassnett-McGuire, 1980: 37). Bell (1991: 22) defines translation theory as 'the objective specification of the steps and the stages through which the translator works as the source text in the original language is transformed into the target language'. Similarly, Newmark (1988/2003: 21) defines translation theory as 'a large number of generalisations of translation problems'. Knowledge of translation theories and approaches enables the translator to, firstly, understand how the translation process works and become aware of its complexity and challenging nature. Secondly, it helps the translator to reflect on the translation product and be able to understand, explain and justify translation choices and decisions, instead of being intuitive about his or her choice of approaches or strategies. Thirdly, translation theory helps translators to understand the nature of equivalence and transfer in general and to identify 'equivalent' translations within the relevant context. Fourthly, translators become aware of the different translation methods/types and the implications of their use in terms of the gain and/or loss involved with each strategy. Fifthly, theories will enable translators to acquire the knowledge and the skills necessary to identify translation issues and make them aware of the options available to solve these issues, as well as when and how to use them. The result of this is understanding, confidence, consistency and being less intuitive, all of which are prerequisite for quality and professional translation (see Munday 2001).

Several translation theories have influenced the perception and practice of literary translation in particular. For example, the 1950s and 1960s saw the prevalence of a linguistic theory to translation which promoted the concept of equivalence, assuming a one-to-one correspondence between linguistic forms across languages. Within this paradigm, translations were judged on whether or not they are 'faithful' and 'accurate' against their respective originals. This approach also assumed there is a readily available 'equivalent' to express the same ideas or meanings in all languages. In the 1980s, another translation theory was proposed by Katharina Reiss and Hans Vermeer in the *Foundation for a General Theory of Translation*. According to this functionalist theory, the *skopos* (الهدف أو الغرض) of the target text, a German word meaning purpose, rather than linguistic equivalence, should be given primary attention by the translator (see Nord 1997; Reiss and Vermeer 1984; Vermeer 1987). In practice this meant more liberty for the literary translator who can no longer be obliged to stay close to the ST.

Another influential translation theory was expounded by Peter Newmark in the 1980s. He proposed a communicative approach for 'vocative' texts, i.e. poetic texts which appeal to the senses, while insisting that the translator should take the purpose of the translation, the nature of readership and text typology into account (see more in Chapter 2). Furthermore, the 1990s witnessed the appearance of the cultural turn in Translation Studies. Proponents of this approach consider translation to be primarily contextual and cannot therefore be assessed against the criteria of faithfulness and accuracy (Bassnett and Lefevere 1990: 3). According to this view, translation is a form of intercultural communication, giving rise to not only linguistic but also contextual issues. This means that translators would need to look for cultural rather than linguistic equivalents, especially for lexical items relating to food, fashion, folklore and narratives, while bearing in mind language-specific literary conventions (e.g. genres, literary devices and stylistic features). The cultural approach opened the door to drawing on other important theoretical developments, such as 'ideology', 'power' and 'discourse', and used them to redefine the contexts and conditions of translation (Bassnett and Lefevere 1990: 6). Another result of the cultural approach saw Translation Studies drawing on areas like sociology, see for example narrative theory (Baker 2006). And more recently, the technological development has led to disseminating literature through the mass digitisation of books and leading to a greater awareness – and perhaps curiosity – for foreign cultures and their literatures (Constantine 2020: 11, see also Cronin 2013). Neural machine translation systems, which are being developed using artificial neural networks and computational models, are even predicted to be able to produce masterful translations of literary texts (Constantine 2020: 13) or at least help literary translators produce them. Finally, computer-assisted translation tools are also being used widely now especially with technical translation. For more on this, see Elimam (2007).

1.5 Style

Style (أسوب الكتابة أو أسلوب الكاتب) can either be the standard of writing in a specific genre, like business writing, medical reporting and so on, or how an author or writer writes. Every writer has his or her own writing style. Style, as a personal way of writing, is not what an author writes, but the manner in which he or she writes it. It is an author's unique way of communicating ideas. One might say that style is the verbal identity of a writer. An author defines his or her style in their lexical choices, preferred syntax, thematic organisation of ideas, verb-tense choice, metaphoric language use, amongst other factors. Style is, therefore, an important concept to be examined in the context of literary translation where it is the focus of both authors and translators.[1] However, an author's style is not static; it changes and becomes refined with time and through exposure to other writing styles.[2]

Style has been the focus of increased interest amongst translation scholars in recent years. The concept no longer refers to the ST author's style only, but it has become widely accepted that translators also have their own writing styles: see Elimam 2013, Munday 2008, 2001; Parks 2007; Marco 2004; Millán-Varela 2004; Malmkjær 2004 and Baker 2000. Translation scholars also provide their definitions of style. For example, Boase-Beier (2006: 1) defines style as the outcome of choice and argues that the translator's style will inevitably influence the target text. Baker (2000: 245) defines style as 'a thumb-print that is expressed in a range of linguistic – as well as non-linguistic – features'. Baker further argues that style 'is a matter of patterning: it involves describing preferred or recurring patterns of linguistic behaviour, rather than individual or one-off instances of intervention' (ibid.).

Style and stylistic features, lexical, structural and textual, can be language-specific. In other words, what counts as a good stylistic feature in one language may sound awkward if rendered closely in another, making it read like a 'bad' translation. An example of this is word order variation between Arabic and English and how staying close to some Arabic word orders will produce an unnatural translation into English that is hard to read (see under 4.2.1 and 4.2.2). On the other hand, ironing out stylistic features of the source text or of the source text author will not offer the target readers a feel of how the source text reads. In literary translation in general, there is an emphasis on rendering the flavour of the original in an accessible manner to the target readers. In other words, there is a balance to be made between making the translation accessible to its readers at the expense of removing the idiosyncratic features of the source text, on the one hand, and staying very close to these features and producing a difficult read translation, on the other.

1.5.1 Elements of literary style

The list below covers some of the most salient components of literary style (**عناصر الأسلوب الأدبي**) (www.sthelens.k12.or.us).[3]

The different components of style listed above will be discussed and illustrated in detail in different chapters of this book based on the type of translation issues they relate to.

Table 1.1 Components of style

1. Expansive/ economical diction (الإيجاز والإسهاب)	*Is the writing tight and efficient, or elaborate and long-winded? When does the author use one or the other mode, and why?* Diction can shed light on the character's profile, including his or her socio-economic background and is, therefore, worth considering and reflecting in the translation.
2. Vocabulary (المفردات)	*Are the words simple or fancy? Are they technical, flowery, colloquial, cerebral, punning, obscure (and so on . . .)?* Like diction, lexical choices can reflect the character's level of education, amongst other issues, and help the readers piece together a mental picture of the character. In fact, lexical translation issues are the first level of problems which will be examined in this book.

3. Sentence structure (بناء أوتراكيب الجمل)	*Are the sentences long or short? Why do they change? Do they contain many subordinate clauses, or are they often fragments?* These elements are important since a succession of short sentences can reflect feeling agitated or excited on the part of the character, as opposed to long sentences, which usually reflect a composed and calm setting. *Are there any digressions or interruptions?* A character being interrupted all the time tells something about the character's lack of ability to hold his or her conversation turn and may be a lack of appreciation by other characters. *Is the word order straightforward or unconventionally crafted?* This is an important issue because, in Arabic, word order variation is used to signal the most important or salient elements in the sentence by foregrounding them to the sentence-initial position. Rendering this aspect into English is challenging due to its restrictions on word order. Rendering SL marked or unconventional word orders using TL unmarked or conventional word orders can result in the loss of nuances of ST meaning, or the functions thus realised in the ST, but still produces a smooth-reading TT. In other words, there is some kind of inevitable gain as well as loss involved in each choice of strategy.
4. Use of dialogue (استخدام الحوار)	*How often does dialogue tell the story? Do we see whole conversations or just fragments? Does the conversation use slang, or is it formal? Does it appear natural or contrived? Does the dialogue give a sense of pacing, of pauses, of the unsaid? How much does it substitute for narration?* How dialogues start and end is language-specific and needs to be considered in the translation process. Further, the level of formality or informality used can reflect the distance between the characters. Formality can be genre or language-specific and, therefore, an important issue to bear in mind while translating in order to make sure that not only the expressed but also the implied meanings are communicated to the target readers. Furthermore, flouting turn-taking rules may indicate rude or authoritative behaviour, and the right implication should be communicated to the target readers. In addition, identifying whether dialogue is used to move the story forward, build the characterisation or offer more information is important to establish and reflect to the target readers.

5. Tone (نبرة الكاتب أو الكتابة)	*What is the author's attitude? What is the mood of the story?* *Does the author seem sarcastic? Aggressive? Wistful? Pessimistic? In love? Philosophically detached? Hopeful? Ironic? Bitter? (And so on . . .) Whatever the tone, where is it visible in the narrative?* The author's tone needs to be identified and, similar to the source text, explicitly or implicitly communicated in a manner accessible to the target readers.
6. Aesthetic qualities (السمات الجمالية)	*How much does the language call attention to or depend on the quality of its sound, e.g. through alliteration, assonance, consonance, dissonance, rhythm, unusual word choice and so on?* Use of aesthetic qualities, especially sound-related ones, have a great effect on the readers' appreciation of the source text and of poetry in particular. Communicating sound-related effects can be challenging due to language norms. The translator needs to decide on how to deal with these qualities and whether he or she is going to focus on the meaning or on aesthetics.
7. Figures of speech (المجاز أو الصور البلاغية)	*Are there any metaphors, similes or symbols?* *Are there any other uses of figurative language (personification, metonymy and so on)?* The use of these stylistic features enhances our enjoyment of reading a literary work. According to the cognitive model discussed above, stylistic features can have a refreshing effect on the readers' minds. Furthermore, these features reflect a witty and sophisticated writing style and are therefore worth communicating to the target readers to give them a feel of the source-text author's style. In fact, the more sophisticated the style is, and the more established an author is, the more challenging the translation becomes because of this added pressure on the translator to find creative ways to produce this style for the target readers in an enjoyable manner.

8. Tense and chronology (الزمن والتسلسل الزمني)	*How has the author organised the chronology of events? To what effect? What is the work's structural 'rhythm'?* Is the flashback writing technique known to the target readers? Is it equally a writing convention in the target language, or will it confuse the readers? In a situation where a story written for adult readership using this technique is rendered for children in the target language, it is worth considering whether young readers will cope with the change in the chronological order of events.
9. Allusions and intertextuality (التلميحات والتناص أي إشارة النص إلى نصوص أخرى)	*How and how often does the author refer to other texts, myths, symbols, famous figures, historical events, quotations and so on?* The translator needs to consider whether the target readers will be able to figure out reference to these symbols, texts, figures and so on, on their own, or whether the information should be provided, based on expectations about the level of knowledge of the readers.
10. Layout (نسق النص)	*Are the paragraphs very short, or are they enormous blocks running across many pages? Are the chapters short or long? How many are there, how are they organised, and why is this important?* Layout is a stylistic issue. Modern English literary writing increasingly uses short paragraphs, for example, and it is the translator's job to decide whether this is worth communicating to the target readers or will this seem 'unacceptable' according to target language standards.
11. Conventional and non-conventional writing (الكتابة بإسلوب تقليدي/مألوف أو غير تقليدي/غير مألوف)	*Are there any unusual techniques, such as stream-of-consciousness, mixing styles and genres, unusual layout on the page, breaking rules of grammar and form, odd or unstable narrative perspectives, onomatopoeia and so on?* Modern English writing employs non-conventional writing techniques, including sentence structure, formal and informal expressions, short paragraphs, neologisms and so forth. These put a strain on the translator should he or she decide to reflect these features, or some of them, into the translation. Here too, the translator will decide whether to reflect the ST's idiosyncratic features in the TT or to smooth out these features so that the target readers can have an easier reading experience.

1.6 Context

Context (السياق العام للنص وعملية الترجمة أو السياق اختصارا) is an umbrella term that acts as an overarching component of the process of translation and has a great role to play in both understanding the source text and producing the target text (revisionworld.com).[4] Context relates to and affects the three main components of the translation process: the source text, the translator and the target text. The translator needs to identify when the source text was written since, for example, language use changes with time, and this is an issue to bear in mind while translating 'older' texts. Understanding what the society was like at the time the text was written can help understand the text. Identifying what or who influenced the writer and what political or social influences there would have been at the time of writing the source text and, more importantly, what influences there may have been in the genre that may have affected the writer can all help understand the source text better. The translator also needs to have an idea about target readers' expectations since the success or failure of the translation may well depend on the readers' reception of the work. This knowledge on the part of the translator will affect his or her choice of translation approach and translation strategies and, therefore, the overall quality of the product. The translator is under contextual factors which he or she may not be able to control: their ideology, including their belief system and understanding of the nature of the translation process and the world around them. All of these factors will have a conscious and/or unconscious effect on the translation process and product (see Melby and Foster 2010; Baker 2006; Gutt 2000).

1.7 Conclusion

To conclude, this chapter has introduced and defined five key concepts in the area of literary translation: Literature, Translation, Translation Theory, Style and Context. The discussion above has also produced an overview of the four main models of what constitutes Literature (Inherency, Sociocultural, Cognitive and Literary Cline). Identifying whether the language being translated is literary is key to successful rendering because stylistic features, one of the two important factors that shape the translation according to this textbook, with the second being Context, abound more in literary as opposed to technical writing, and because dealing with these features requires creativity on the part of the translator. The second concept covered in this chapter is Translation. Some of the most important, in fact classical, definitions of the term have been provided. The concept of Translation Theory and its importance to translators have also been explained. The discussion of the fourth concept, Style, covered some key significant stylistic features, and explained their relevance. Finally, the concept of Context as any extra-textual factors, consciously or unconsciously influencing the translation process or the translator, has also been explained. The following chapter will discuss the translation process and approaches to pave the way for the discussion of translation issues and strategies in Chapters 3, 4, 5 and 6.

1.8 Exercises

1.8.1 The following excerpt is from a short story entitled 'Victory Lap' by George Saunders, which was considered the best short story of the year by the *The New Yorker* (28 September 2009).[5] Read the passage carefully and identify the stylistic issues that you would encounter before translating it into Arabic. You may want to produce a draft translation at this stage until you have studied the following chapters.

Tips: Consider the stylistic issues which are particularly challenging to render from the English ST into Arabic, including sentence structure, sentence length, tone, internal dialogue, vocabulary and colloquialism, bearing in mind how Arabic writing is almost always associated with a formal writing style. In other words, will you attempt to communicate the colloquial tone across to the target reader, or will it be lost because of the Arabic language variety you opt for? You may want to revise this version of translation in light of the ideas you will cover in the following chapters.

> Three days shy of her fifteenth birthday, Alison Pope paused at the top of the stairs. Say the staircase was marble. Say she descended and all heads turned. Where was {special one}? Approaching now, bowing slightly, he exclaimed, How can so much grace be contained in one small package? Oops. Had he said *small package*? And just stood there? Broad princelike face totally bland of expression? Poor thing! Sorry, no way, down he went, he was definitely not {special one}.
>
> What about this guy, behind Mr. Small Package, standing near the home entertainment center? With a thick neck of farmer integrity yet tender ample lips, who, placing one hand on the small of her back, whispered, Dreadfully sorry you had to endure that bit Illustration by Quickhoney about the small package just now. Let us go stand on the moon. Or, uh, in the moon. In the moonlight.
>
> Had he said, *Let us go stand on the moon*? If so, she would have to be like, {eyebrows up}. And if no wry acknowledgment was forthcoming, be like, Uh, I am not exactly dressed for standing on the moon, which, as I understand it, is super-cold?
>
> Come on, guys, she couldn't keep treading gracefully on this marble staircase in her mind forever! That dear old white-hair in the tiara was getting all like, Why are those supposed princes making that darling girl march in place ad nausea? Plus she had a recital tonight and had to go fetch her tights from the dryer.
>
> Egads! One found oneself still standing at the top of the stairs.

> Do the thing where, facing upstairs, hand on railing, you hop down the stairs one at a time, which was getting a lot harder lately, due to, someone's feet were getting longer every day, seemed like.
> Pas de chat, pas de chat.
> Changement, changement.

1.8.2 The following excerpt is from a short story entitled (الصغيرُ يذهبُ إلى المخيّم) by Ghassan Kanafani.[6] Read the passage carefully and identify the stylistic issues that you would encounter before translating it into English. Like the previous exercise, you may want to revise your translation after reading the following chapters on translation approaches, issues and strategies.

Tips: consider the issue of the context in which the text is set and how important it is in understanding the meaning of some of the words used here. For example, (الاشتباك) and (العدو); how will you render these words into English? How will you render the dialogue between the author and the reader?

> الصغيرُ يذهبُ إلى المخيّم
>
> كان ذلك زمن الحرب. الحرب؟ كلا، الإشتباك ذاته. الالتحام المتواصل بالعدو لأنه أثناء الحرب قد تهب نسمة سلام يلتقط فيها المقاتل أنفاسه. راحة. هدنة. إجازة تقهقر. أما في الاشتباك فإنه دائماً على بعد طلقة. أنت دائماً تمرّ بأعجوبة بين طلقتين، وهذا ما كان، كما قلت لك، زمن الاشتباك المستمر!
>
> كنت أسكن مع سبعة أخوة كلهم ذكور شديدو المراس، وأب لا يحبّ زوجته ربما لأنه أنجبت له زمن الاشتباك ثمانية أطفال. وكانت عمتنا وزوجها وأولادها الخمسة يسكنون معنا أيضاً، وجدّنا العجوز الذي كان إذا ما عثر على خمسة قروش على الطاولة أو في جيب أحد السراويل الكثيرة المعلّقة مضى دون تردد واشترى جريدة، ولم يكن يعرف، كما تعلم، القراءة، وهكذا كان مضطراً للاعتراف دائماً بما اقترف كي يقرأ أحدنا على مسمعه الثقيلين آخر الأخبار!
>
> في ذلك الزمن – دعني أولاً أقول لك أنه لم يكن زمن اشتباك بالمعنى الذي يخيّل إليك، كلاّ لم تكن ثمة حرب حقيقية. لم تكن ثمة أي حرب على الإطلاق. كل ما في الأمر أننا كنا ثمانية عشر شخصاً في بيت واحد من جميع الأجيال التي يمكن أن تتوفّر في وقت واحد. لم يكن أي واحد منّا قد نجح بعد في الحصول على عمل، وكان الجوع – الذي تسمع عنه- همنا اليومي. ذلك أسميه زمن الاشتباك. أنت تعلم. لا فرق على الإطلاق!
>
> كنا نقاتل من أجل الأكل، ثم نتقاتل لنوزعه فيما بيننا، ثم نتقاتل بعد ذلك. ثم في أية لحظة سكون يخرج جدّي جريدته المطوية باعتناء من بين ملابسه ناظراً إلى الجميع بعينيه الصغيرتين المتحفّزتين، معنى ذلك أن خمسة قروش قد سرقت من جيب ما – إذا كان فيه هناك خمسة قروش – أو من مكان ما. وأن شجاراً سيقع. ويظل جدّي متمسّكاً بالجريدة وهو يتصدّى للأصوات بسكون الشيخ الذي عاش وقتاً كافياً للاستماع إلى كل هذا الضجيج والشّجار دون أن يرى فيها ما يستحق الجواب أو الاهتمام. وحين تهدأ الأصوات يميل أقرب الصبيان إليه (ذلك أنه لم يكن يثق بالبنات) ويدفع له الصحيفة وهو يمسك طرفها، كي لا تخطف.

Notes

1. <https://globalmysteriesblog.com/2012/08/16/literary-style-whats-that/> (last accessed 20 January 2019)
2. <http://nancycurteman.wordpress.com/2010/07/29/what-is-literary-style/> (last accessed 20 January 2019)
3. Adapted from <https://www.sthelens.k12.or.us/cms/lib05/OR01000906/Centricity/Domain/218/Elements%20of%20Literary%20Style.pdf> (last accessed 20 January 2019)
4. <https://revisionworld.com/gcse-revision/english/context-literature#sthash.RaQf6WsH.dpuf> (last accessed 1 April 2021)
5. <https://www.newyorker.com/magazine/2009/10/05/victory-lap> (last accessed 1 April 2020)
6. <http://www.adab.com/literature/modules.php?name=Sh3er&doWhat=shqas&qid=83686> (last accessed 5 April 2020)

CHAPTER 2
THE TRANSLATION PROCESS AND TRANSLATION APPROACHES

2.1 Introduction

The previous chapter has set the scene for this textbook by introducing the salient concepts that form the basis of literary translation in my view, namely Literature, Translation, Translation Theory, Style and Context. This chapter, first, will cover two of the major components of the translation process, namely the source text and the target text. The source text is the starting point of the translation process, and understanding it is essential to producing a successful target text, the ultimate aim of any translation process. Secondly, this chapter will explain the nature of Translation as a decision-making process and the stages of this process. Thirdly, the discussion will also cover the most important translation approaches expounded in the relevant literature as the choice of the global translation approach determines, to a large extent, the choice of local strategies throughout the process; these strategies will be examined in detail in the following chapters. Finally, this chapter will explain translation universals for their relevance to the understanding of the nature of translated texts.

2.2 From the source text to the target text

The translation process involves two systems: the source text system and the target text system. The source text system involves, first and foremost, the source text to be translated and without which there will be no translation process. It is important to understand that this ST was produced or commissioned by the source text writer (or producer) for a specific reader (or recipient) in mind and for a specific purpose at a given point in time. The source text reader, as well as the purpose and time of production, can and does shape the text and identifying these factors can help the translator to understand the text better, an essential step for successful translation. The source text is expressed in the source text language, which has its own grammar, structures and cultural context. These are likely to differ across languages, especially in the case of Arabic and English, as they belong to different cultural spheres and language families. The translation, on the other hand, usually bears some kind of resemblance to the respective source text. The level of this resemblance can differ based on the distance between the languages in question and the cultural contexts they are set in. Other factors which may also influence the translation, as both a process and a product, include *skopos* (purpose, see below) of the translation and the intended target readership whose expectations and assumed background must be taken into account by the translator for a successful translation. Furthermore, the translator, with his or her knowledge and background, plays a key role in this process since it is against his or her background that the source text is understood and subsequently rendered into the target language. The translator's ideology, value and beliefs system, education and training are all influential factors in the translation process as will be elaborated in Chapter 6 (see Elimam 2010; Newmark 1988/2003).

2.3 Translation as a decision-making process

Translation is a complex process; it is a continual process of decision-making on the part of the translator. Even what seems to be the most straightforward source text item requires a decision on how to render it. For example, people can argue until they become 'blue in the face' in English but until their faces turn 'red' in Arabic. Here, although a direct translation for the colour 'blue' exists in Arabic, it will not communicate the correct meaning in this context and is likely to cause confusion for the target readers. Going to work in London by public transportation is not an indicator of one's socio-economic status since the vast majority of Londoners do so. In Cairo, on the other hand, the use of public transportation, as opposed to driving or taking a taxi, is an indication of a low socio-economic status. Therefore, even though it is easy to find an equivalent translation to means of transportation between London and Cairo, the implication of meaning, that is the associated meaning (see Chapter 3), is not quite the same. In other words, the translator will be making decisions on all levels of the text throughout the translation process. The process of translation can be summarised as follows:

The Translation Process

Understanding the ST⟶ Brief analysis ⟶Translating ⟶Revision and editing

Figure 2.1 Stages of the translation process

The translator approaches the source text, first of all, as a reader: he or she attempts to understand the text and decode its meanings, bearing in mind the factors that influenced the ST production mentioned above. The translator may also be able to check his or her understanding of the source text or parts thereof with the source text author if this is possible. In this early stage of the process, the translator's background, education, ideology, training, amongst other factors, will also influence his or her understanding of the source text and, in turn, the final product. The translator will also try to identify potential translation challenges as he or she reads along, including SL idiosyncratic structures and other stylistic features, text type and genre (Reiss 1989). He or she then moves on to the second stage of the translation process. This stage starts off with the translator familiarising himself or herself with the Translation Brief, alternatively called 'translation instructions' (Nord 1991), provided by the commissioner, if applicable; otherwise, the translator will produce his or her own brief, which can be even 'mental'. The brief, actual or mental, identifies the *skopos* and the intended readership of the target text and, therefore, helps to identify other considerations, the most important of which is the translation approach to be adopted. In the third stage, the translation proper starts, and the translation strategies are selected in line with the chosen overall translation approach. In this stage, the translator can draw on language resources, including dictionaries, parallel texts – which are texts written on the same topic in both the source language and the target language – and other language users or translators for help and advice.

Here, special mention needs to be made of the unit of translation, a controversial topic in the relevant literature. According to Bell (1991), the unit of translation is the clause, to Newmark (1988/2003: 30–1), it is the sentence, and to Hatim and Mason (1997), it is the text. Like other theoreticians, I would argue that the unit of translation is the meaning whether this is communicated in a word, clause, sentence or a whole text. Translation is not about rendering lexical units or structures independently but about reproducing a meaningful whole, unless the purpose the translator sets out to achieve is to produce a literal or word-for-word translation of the source text. It is worth mentioning here that Arabic does not depend on the use of punctuation marks to delimit sentence boundaries but rather on meaningful chunks of sentences, short or long, unlike English where sentence boundaries are marked by the use of full stops. Furthermore, translators are expected to read the source text at least once before attempting to translate it; that is to make sure they understand the meaning of the whole text in general before starting to render the smaller structural units that build the whole.

Revision and editing are usually carried out at the final stage of the translation process in order to ensure the quality of the product. These can be carried out by the translator himself or herself and/or by a proofreader, especially if the translator is working out of his or her mother tongue into their second language. The translation commissioner, if different from the translator himself or herself, may also decide to have the translation proofread by a second translator, a proofreader or an editor.

2.4 Translation approaches

Focusing specifically on interlingual translation, that is translation between two different languages, the literature on Translation Studies discusses several general overarching translation approaches (أساليب الترجمة). Drawing on the literature, I provide below the most commonly discussed translation approaches by translation scholars. This is a non-exhaustive list, but it reproduces the most known and used approaches and, therefore, suffices in this context. It is worth noting that some of these approaches seem to prioritise different aspects of the source text or the target text. Some approaches prioritise the ST meanings over the ST form if both cannot be rendered simultaneously. Other approaches focus on the target language. Others still prioritise fulfilling target readers' expectations over other aspects.

Three points are in order here. First of all, the choice of which approach to use depends, amongst other factors, on what the translator or translation commissioner aims to achieve from the process. Secondly, and more importantly, choosing one of these approaches to be applied in a specific translation does not necessarily mean no other approach can be used at all, but it means it is the principal translation approach used. Translators may have to deviate from their main approach occasionally for textual and/or contextual reasons. An example of deviation for a contextual consideration would be a translation which adopts a ST-oriented approach but has to deviate in dealing with taboo terms to avoid offending the TT readers. Another example of deviation but for textual factors would be a deviation from staying close to the ST idioms because a close translation would be meaningless to the TT readers. This issue will be explained further and illustrated with examples in the following chapters. Finally, and as explained earlier, these approaches guide the whole translation process, and because it is not possible to illustrate with full texts, I provide below 'small scale' examples of how these approaches would influence the rendering of specific issues and give an idea about how the whole text would read. Note that even though these are overall approaches which guide the process as a whole, I use below some micro-level examples to illustrate how these approaches influence the process (see also Chapter 6).

2.4.1 Word-for-word translation

According to this word-for-word translation approach (الترجمة بإسلوب كلمة مقابل كلمة), 'the SL word order is preserved and the words translated singly by their most common meanings, out of context' (Newmark 1988/2003: 45–6). This is alternatively called 'interlinear translation' (Dickins et al. 2002: 16). This approach can be used to give the TT readers a close-up picture of the ST style, for example, in translating manuscripts and in explaining grammatical structures especially for the purpose of studying how they differ between the ST and TT. Some of the available translations of the Qur'an into English adopt this approach, serving as dictionaries which help the readers to understand how words are constructed in Arabic and what they mean in English. Some readers find these translations helpful in giving them a clear idea about the structure of the ST. The following example also demonstrates how this approach is used to translate a pre-Islamic poetic verse (معلقة لبيد), 'Labid's hung up poem'.

Ex 2.1: عفت الديار محلّها فمقامها بمنى تأبد غولها فرجامها

Dickins et al.'s translation: Disappeared the-camping-grounds alighting-places-their and-stopping-places their//

in-Minā become-desert Ghaul-its and Rijām-its. (2002: 16)

2.4.2 Literal translation

According to Newmark (1988/2003: 46), in the literal translation approach (الترجمة الحرفية), 'the SL grammatical constructions are converted to their nearest TL equivalents, but the lexical words are again translated singly, out of context'. Similarly, Dickins et al. (2002: 16) agree that literal translation involves grammatical transposition. They state that literal translation implies 'the replacement or reinforcement of given parts of speech in the ST by other parts of speech in the TT'. They describe this approach as 'the practical extreme of SL bias' (Dickins et al. 2002: 16). The example below is a translation of the above poetic verse using the literal translation approach to show clearly how the results of applying the two approaches differ from each other.

Ex 2.2: عفت الديار محلّها فمقامها بمنى تأبد غولها فرجامها

Dickins et al.'s translation: The camping grounds have disappeared their alighting places and their stopping places/

at Minā; its Ghaul and its Rijām have become deserted. (ibid. 16)

2.4.3 Faithful translation

The faithful translation approach (الترجمة الأمينة) also prioritises the ST features. It attempts

> to produce the precise contextual meaning of the original within the constraints of the TL grammatical structures. It 'transfers' cultural words and preserves the degree of grammatical and lexical 'abnormality' (deviation from SL norms) in the translation. It attempts to be completely faithful to the intention and the text-realisation of the SL writer. (Newmark 1988/2003: 46)

In other words, Newmark uses the term 'faithful' to imply loyalty to the ST features by staying close to the ST. This approach is similar to Venuti's concept of 'foreignisation' (see below).

Recently, however, the concept of 'faithfulness' has become considered as a vague term in the area of Translation Studies as it raises more issues than it resolves. The reason is that if interpreted to mean staying close to the ST, faithfulness may not necessarily lead to producing a meaningful translation or a translation that is fit for purpose.

Ex 2.3: إياك نعبد وإياك نستعين (Qur'an 1: 5)

Proposed faithful translation: You we worship and You we seek assistance from.

The proposed translation above faithfully mirrors the word order of the Qur'anic verse. It reflects the preposing of the object 'You' in both clauses and the ensuing structural parallelism, thus allowing the readers access to the structural specificity of the verse. However, this translation does not read as smoothly as other possible alternatives, see under semantic translation below.

2.4.4 Semantic translation

Although similar to 'faithful translation', Semantic translation (الترجمة الدلالية التي تركز على نقل جمال وطبيعة النص المصدر) is a source text-oriented approach, which

> takes more account of the aesthetic value of the SL text, compromising on 'meaning' where appropriate so that no assonance, wordplay or repetition jars the finished version. It may translate less important cultural words by culturally neutral third or functional terms but not by cultural equivalents and it may make other small concessions to the readership. (Newmark 1988/2003: 46)

In other words, the semantic translation approach allows little room for flexibility in dealing with the ST in order to reproduce its formal features as much as possible. Newmark (1993: 1) proposes using this approach to translate authoritative texts, which are 'texts where the content and style, the matter and the manner, the thought and the words in their structures are equally important'. These texts, according to Newmark (ibid.), include serious imaginative literature and religious texts. He proposes translating these at 'the author's level'. In my opinion, this sounds similar to Venuti's foreignisation approach described below.

Along the lines of this approach, I can propose the following translations of the verse above:

Proposed semantic translation 1: You do we worship and You do we seek assistance from.

Proposed semantic translation 2: You alone we worship and You alone we seek assistance from.

These translations communicate the propositional meaning of the verse, reproduce its parallel structures and unpack the function of the unmarked word order of the verse by using the emphasis carrier 'do' or the restrictive item 'alone'. In other words, it reflects the aesthetic, i.e. structural uniqueness of the original, to the target readers (see more on word order variation under 4.2.1).

2.4.5 Communicative translation

A communicative translation approach (الترجمة التواصلية وتركز على نقل المعنى السياقي للنص الأصلي) attempts 'to render the exact contextual meaning of the original in such a way that both content and language are readily acceptable and comprehensible to the readership' (Newmark 1988/2003: 47). According to Dickins et al. (2002: 15–16), there is a vague 'correspondence between the textual units of the ST and those of the TT' produced using this approach. Furthermore, this approach involves the ST using an SL expression standard for a specific situation and the TT using a TL expression standard for an equivalent target culture situation (ibid. 17). Along these lines, the colloquial expressions 'you alright' or 'what's up', used by some speakers to replace many greetings, can be rendered into Arabic as (صباح الخير) (good morning) or (كيف حالك) (how are you), depending on the context of usage. Newmark (1993: 1) explains that this approach adopts natural usage at the level of target readers and is used for non-authoritative texts. He adds that 'the translation has to be well written, whether the original is or not, but linguistically and culturally it may have to be adapted to suit' the target readership (ibid.). It is worth noting that this approach may not be commonly used with famous literary texts as the main translation approach, which usually require a more ST-oriented translation approach to deal with them. However, it can be used in conjunction with other more source-text oriented approaches, to deal with translation challenges which cannot be rendered closely due to structural, linguistic or cultural issues.

2.4.6 Idiomatic translation

Idiomatic translation (الترجمة الاصطلاحية) refers to achieving a target text that sounds natural in the target language, using idiomatic expressions when possible and/or appropriate. According to Newmark (1988/2003: 47), this target text-oriented approach 'reproduces the "message" of the original but tends to distort nuances of meaning by preferring colloquialisms and idioms where these do not exist in the original'. In other words, it attempts to sound smooth in the TL at the expense of communicating some of the ST meanings. Note, however, that this definition is at odds with the common, non-academic understanding of the term which implies using a smooth-reading TL which does not follow the form of the ST but communicates all of its meanings, nonetheless. This approach can probably be used to translate popular literature in general. However, the issue it raises with Arabic translation is that Arabic is written in a standard formal tone and colloquialism is restricted to the spoken mode.

2.4.7 Adaptation

The adaptation approach (الترجمة الملائمة أو المعدلة) is described as 'the freest form of translation, and is used mainly for plays (comedies) and poetry; the themes, characters, plots are usually preserved, the SL culture is converted to the TL culture, and the text is rewritten' Newmark (1988/2003: 46). I argue, however, that 'free translation' rather than 'adaptation' is the freest form of translation. The reason is that there is still a relatively stronger affinity between the ST and the TT produced through this approach as opposed to free translation. Adaptation is a common translation approach in converting novels or stories into films where the story needs to be presented in a, more or less, two-hour long film. This involves cutting out non-essential characters and reducing the number of conversation turns that the main characters are assigned in the novel. For instance, *Oliver Twist* is 373 pages long but the film itself is only two hours and ten minutes long. Another example is how Shakespeare's *Romeo and Juliet* was adapted, intralingually, for child viewers specifically. The translation, although abridged, 'modernises the play, with guns replacing swords and the opposing families having rival business empires'.[1] Furthermore, Shakespeare's *A Midsummer Night's Dream* was translated by adaptation in Egypt by Fatima Yusuf under the title (زهرة الحياة) 'Life's Flower' (2005).

2.4.8 Free translation

A free translation approach (الترجمة الحرة) 'reproduces the matter without the manner, or the content without the form of the original. Usually, it is a paraphrase much longer than the original, a so-called "intralingual translation," often prolix and pretentious, and not a translation at all' (Newmark 1988/2003: 46–7). In a similar vein, Dickins et al. describe this approach as featuring maximum TL bias: here there is a vague 'correspondence between the textual units of the ST and those of the TT' (2002: 17). Due to the comparatively higher level of liberty the translators enjoy according to this approach as opposed to adaptation, free translation is sometimes called 'creative translation'. Free translation and adaptation approaches can be used to render adult literature for child readership since this process may involve significant reworking of the plot and themes to make them child-friendly.

2.4.9 Domestication

Domestication (توطين الترجمة) and foreignisation (تغريب الترجمة) (see below) are dichotomous translation approaches which were originally proposed by Schleiermacher (1813) and developed later on by Venuti (1995). According to Venuti (1995: 20), the domestication approach refers to an ethnocentric reduction of the foreign text to target language cultural values, bringing the author back home. This approach brings the source text closer to the target readers by reducing, rather than completely eliminating, the foreignness of the TT. In other words, domestication designates the type of translation in which a transparent, fluent style is adopted to minimise the strangeness of the foreign text for target language readers. This seems to be the approach used for translating into English. In other words, translation into English fulfils target readers' expectations of what they should find in translated literature. Many theorists, including Venuti (1995), have issues with this approach and see it as a sign of the hegemony English is exercising over the other languages and therefore 'foreignisation' has been proposed as an approach to translating foreign literature into English. This approach seems to be similar to the target-oriented translation approaches, including adaptation, communicative and idiomatic translation, mentioned above. Adopting this approach in translations into Arabic allows the translator to rid the TT of taboos and ST cultural items which would not appeal to the target readers if they were rendered closely.

2.4.10 Foreignisation

This foreignisation approach is the opposite of the previous one and is defined as an ethnodeviant pressure on those (cultural) values to register the linguistic and cultural difference of the foreign text, sending the reader abroad (Venuti 1995: 20). The target text produced according to this approach deliberately breaks target conventions by retaining something of the foreignness of the original text (see Shuttleworth and Cowie 1997: 59). Venuti proposed foreignisation as an approach that can restrain the violently domesticating cultural values of the English language world (Munday 2001: 147). In other words, this approach is a revolt against the hegemony of the dominant Anglo-American culture over other non-Western dominated cultures. Foreignisation produces a non-fluent translation aiming to make visible the presence of the translator and the source text culture by protecting it from the ideological dominance of the target culture (ibid. 147). Readers should have the feeling that they are in the presence of the foreign, and translations should be allowed many strategies which would not be allowed elsewhere. This approach seems also similar to the source-text oriented translation approaches, including literal, semantic and faithful translation, mentioned above.

It is worth noting here that many students apply these foreignisation and domestication approaches outside the main contexts for which they were proposed originally, namely translating foreign literature into English, and adopting 'domestication' in rendering English texts into other languages in order to produce target texts which read smoothly in the target languages. Also note that both approaches can be adopted simultaneously in translating the same text, however, one of them needs to be the main approach and the other only used when necessary. For example, if your overall translation approach is foreignisation, some ST cultural references would not make much sense if rendered closely, therefore a domestication approach may well be used to avoid alienating the target readers.

2.4.11 Formal equivalence

Formal and dynamic equivalence are another set of dichotomous translation approaches which were proposed by Nida (1964/1995, see also Nida and Taber 1969/1982), a Bible translation expert. Formal equivalence (الترجمة الشكلية أو التكافؤ الشكلي) focuses attention on the message itself, in both form and content. It is a means of providing some insight into the lexical, grammatical or structural form of a source text, which is similar to source-text oriented translation, including faithful translation, in Newmark's terminology and foreignisation in Venuti's terminology. In other words, the main focus here lies on communicating the form and meaning of the ST at the expense of sounding 'foreign' in the TL. This approach does not seem to be a great fit for literary translation between Arabic and English due to the large cultural and linguistic gap between the two languages.

2.4.12 Dynamic equivalence

Nida's second approach, dynamic (functional) equivalence (الترجمة التأويلية أو تكافؤ التأثير), is based on the principle of equivalent effect, that is the relationship between the receiver and message should aim at being the same as that between the original receivers and the source language message (1964/1995: 118, see also Nida and Taber 1969/1982). In other words, 'the readers of a translated text should be able to comprehend it to the point that they can conceive of how the original readers of the text must have understood and appreciated it'. Therefore, the aim of this approach is to produce a translated text that allows the target readers to understand and appreciate it in essentially the same manner as the original readers of the source text (ibid.). This approach, in turn, seems, to some extent, similar to Newmark's target-oriented translation approaches and Venuti's domestication approach.

One issue with Nida's concepts is that they were derived out of the context of Bible translation, and he did not illustrate how they work in translating other genres. Secondly, the same meaning may not reproduce an equivalent effect across cultures, and the concept of 'equivalence' itself is quite vague and hard to establish. For example, one turns 'green' with envy in English, but 'yellow' in Arabic. Here, the colours can be directly translated between the two languages, but their implications differ (see also the examples of using public transport mentioned above).

2.4.13 *Skopos* (functional) translation

Skopos is a Greek word meaning 'purpose' (الهدف من الترجمة). According to this theory, the ST was organised in a specific manner to achieve its purpose and, therefore, the translation should also be produced in such a way that achieves its own purpose, which can be the same as, or different from that of the ST. According to Nord (1997: 27–8) and Hatim (2001: 74), the *skopos* can be the general purpose of the translator himself or herself, for example, gaining reputation or adding to their cultural capital, the communicative purpose of the translation, such as informing or persuading, or the purpose of the translation approach, which implies the reason for choosing one approach over another. Thus, the *skopos* of a translation may well be determined by the translation brief, which usually specifies the purpose of the translation. Note that, according to this approach, the success of a translation depends on whether or not it fulfils its *skopos*, rather than remaining close to the original or to ST or TT culture. The purpose of the translation is the criterion against which it is judged rather than whether or not the TT is 'equivalent' to the corresponding ST. Note that the aesthetic function of a literary ST should be maintained in the TT. Literary texts may also have passages with different purposes embedded in them, such as a political speech delivered by a character for the purpose of persuasion. This, however, does not alter the overall purpose of the literary text. Even though some see that the main *skopos* of a literary text is to entertain, this does not contradict the argument that the main function of literature is aesthetic. This is because literature can entertain through aesthetic, engaging the readers' senses with both the content and the form of the literary work.

Notes on translation approaches

Translation approaches represent the overall translation orientation that relates to the whole text and, therefore, informs the choice of translation strategies which are used at the level of sentence and the smaller units of language (see also Newmark 1988/2003: 81). Regardless of the approach used, the TT will be an approximation of the ST in some respects rather than a photographic image of it. This is because translation loss is inevitable even at the most basic level of translation. For example, (أوتوبيس) (باص) or (حافلة) are considered as direct Arabic 'equivalents' (see Chapter 2) of the word 'bus' in English. However, this is only the tip of the iceberg. A bus in London, for example, has its distinctive colour and shape (red double-decker and twin buses) as opposed to buses in other countries and cities. In other words, the image that the word 'bus' conjures up in the minds of readers in the context of London differs from that which the Arabic readers, for instance, would think of. In addition, as mentioned above, it is normal for people in London to travel using public transport. This does not tell much about their social status or economic conditions. In most Arabic countries, on the other hand, taking public transportation implies anything but a high social status or good economic condition. That is to say, the cognitive effect and the associated meaning differ across the two cultures. In short, a translation, any translation, aims to make available in the

TL an 'image' that bears some resemblance to the corresponding ST to give those who cannot access the ST due to language barriers some kind of idea about its content and/or form.

For some, the success, or otherwise, of a translation mainly depends on it realising its purpose or *skopos* rather than being 'equivalent', 'faithful' or 'accurate' in comparison with the ST, terms which have become increasingly controversial and ambiguous. For example, a recipe written for adults that is being translated for children readership will require several changes. For instance, where an adult reader of the ST is instructed to put something in the oven or to turn the cooker on, the translation will ideally instruct the child target reader to ask an adult, usually their mum or dad, to do this for them. Although in this particular example the ST information can be 'closely' rendered, a successful translation keeps the intended requirements and expectations of the target audience in mind. This example emphasises the importance of taking target readers' expectations into consideration and the relative meaning of 'accuracy' and 'faithfulness'. The example also accentuates the role of the translator as a decision-maker who may, in this case, decide to employ 'adaptation' or even 'free translation' approaches.

Finally, assuming a binary approach to translation is problematic and looking at these dichotomies as a continuum, one where the translator may and does slide from one side to the other, may be more helpful. For example, even a free translation can feature cases where the literal translation of some items, structures, metaphors and so on, can be seen. In other words, even the identification of one translation approach as the principle approach does not necessarily exclude all other approaches completely since there may well be occasions within the same text which justifiably call for a deviation from the main approach.

2.5 Features of translated texts: translation universals

Research on the difference between translated and untranslated texts in the same language has identified some characteristic differences between the two genres. According to the literature, a number of features have been identified as characteristics of translated texts in general. These are: simplification, explicitation and normalisation. According to Baker (1993: 243), translation universals are 'linguistic features which typically occur in translated rather than original texts and are thought to be independent of the influence of the specific language pairs involved in the process of translation'. These universals seem to be intrinsic to the translation process itself and do influence the product of this process.

2.5.1 Simplification

As opposed to original writing, translated texts seem to feature three types of simplification (تبسيط): lexical, syntactic and stylistic. Lexical simplification (تبسيط الألفاظ) involves the use of superordinate, that is general terms, an approximation of the source text concepts, use of familiar synonyms, use of functional target equivalents and use of paraphrase (see

Malmkjær 2011; Baker 1992/2011). Syntactic simplification (تبسيط التراكيب) involves the use of simplified syntax by, for example, breaking up long source text sentences into smaller sentences or chunks. Stylistics simplification (تبسيط الأسلوب) includes reducing or omitting repetitions and omitting or modifying phrases and words (see Mauranen and Kujamäki 2004). Elimam (2013; 2020) concludes that some translators of the Qur'an tend to smooth out intricate grammatical structures to produce TT featuring regular, and simpler, sentence structures in English at the expense of losing ST unique sentence structure.

2.5.2 Explicitation

Translated texts seem to feature explicitation (وضوح أو توضيح) of meaning compared to the corresponding source texts. Translators do this by inserting additional words or phrases which make the meaning clearer, and the translations more expanded than the originals. They also split up longer sentences into shorter ones. Vanderauwera (1985, quoted in Laviosa-Braithwaite 2001: 289) identifies several explicitation techniques including

> the use of interjections to express more clearly the progression of the characters' thoughts or to accentuate a given interpretation, expansion of condensed passages, addition of modifiers, qualifiers and conjunctions to achieve greater transparency, addition of extra information, insertion of explanations, repetition of previously mentioned details for the purpose of clarity, precise renderings of implicit or vague data, the provision of more accurate descriptions, the explicit naming of geographical locations and the disambiguation of pronouns with precise forms of identification (see also Murtisari 2016).

Note here that the techniques mentioned under 'simplification' above can also result in the explicitation of meaning.

2.5.3 Normalisation

Vanderauwera (1985, quoted in Laviosa-Braithwaite 2001: 289–90) examines translated texts and identifies shifts in 'punctuation, lexical choice, style, sentence structure and textual organization' compared to the relevant source texts, which are all evidence of a 'tendency towards textual conventionality', i.e. normalisation (تعديل أو تطبيع أو تنميط), to appeal to target readers' expectations by making the text sound 'normal'. Some strategies include adaptations of cultural references and source language-specific expressions, standardisation of unusual punctuation, completing unfinished source text sentences and use of standard idiosyncratic source text structures (Laviosa-Braithwaite 2001).

With these characteristics in mind, one can expect a translation, any translation, more or less, to be relatively longer than its respective source text. In fact, it is reported that a translation is typically 30 per cent longer than the relevant source text. In other words, adopting the tendencies mentioned above, more unintentionally than intentionally, as they are intrinsic to the translation process, results in a target text that is more explicit, less ambiguous, simpler to process and, therefore, longer in terms of word count than the corresponding source text. This is especially true in the case of literary texts, which, by their very nature, pack a lot of meanings that may need to be unpacked for the benefit of the target readers. Think, for example, of how cultural references and stylistic features, including metaphors and idioms, to name but a few, will need to be 'paraphrased' to communicate the correct meaning to the TT readers. The cumulative effect of this kind of translation will reflect the translation universals discussed above.

2.6 Conclusion

This chapter has discussed the translation process, emphasising that decision-making is part and parcel of the whole process from beginning to end, even what seems to be a direct translation still requires some kind of decision on the part of the translator. For example, the translation of 'bus' discussed above foregrounds the importance of taking associated meaning into consideration before deciding on how to render a source text unit, as simple as it may seem. The chapter has also discussed the various translation approaches commonly discussed and used by translation theorists and practitioners. The decision on which translation approach to adopt rests with the translator himself or herself or the commissioner of the translation project. In either case, the approach adopted will certainly influence the strategies used to deal with local translation issues at word, sentence and text levels, and ultimately the product of the process, meaning the translation or TT. Further, the same source text can be translated using different translation approaches, one at a time, in order to fulfil a specific *skopos* each time. For instance, a Shakespearean play can be rendered using a source text-oriented approach to give the target readers a feel of the original author's style. Adopting a free or an adaptation approach can result in a translated text that makes Shakespeare's work more accessible to target readers. Furthermore, this chapter has also explored how translated texts seem to share some common features, namely, simplification, explication and normalisation, regardless of the language pair in question. These tendencies seem more of an unintentional result of the translation process than anything else. Research also confirms that a translation is longer in terms of word count than its counterpart.

2.7 Exercises

2.7.1 Translate the following stanza, which is part of a long poem entitled (أنشودة المطر) 'The rain song', by Badr Shakir Alsayab, into English. Produce more than one version of the translation adopting a different translation approach each time. Note which approach you choose and justify your selection.

Tips: Note that the poet is a well-known modern Arab poet, with a sophisticated writing style, and that this is his most famous poem. Note also that the rhyming scheme is quite acoustic. Will a literal/faithful translation approach be possible? Will you attempt to reproduce the rhyming scheme or use a communicative translation to render the meanings without the aesthetics? In other words, will you attempt to produce a prose format which communicates the meaning and loses the aesthetics of the poem or a rhyming verse format which attempts to mirror the aesthetics, particularly the ST rhyme and rhythm but considers the meaning secondary to the stylistic features of the poem? Note that each approach should be guided by the *skopos* of your translation, which in turn will be based on who your intended audiences are.

أنشودة المطر

عيناكِ غابتا نخيلٍ ساعةَ السحَرْ،
أو شُرفتان راح ينأى عنهما القمر.
عيناك حين تبسمان تورق الكرومْ
وترقص الأضواء . . . كالأقمار في نهَرْ
يرجّه المجذاف وهْناً ساعة السَّحَر
كأنما تنبض في غوريهما ، النّجومْ . . .
وتغرقان في ضبابٍ من أسىً شفيفْ
كالبحر سرَّح اليدين فوقه المساء،
دفء الشتاء فيه وارتعاشة الخريف،
والموت ، والميلاد ، والظلام ، والضياء ؛
فتستفيق ملء روحي ، رعشة البكاء
ونشوةٌ وحشيَّةٌ تعانق السماء
كنشوة الطفل إذا خاف من القمر !
كأن أقواس السحاب تشرب الغيومْ
وقطرةً فقطرةً تذوب في المطر . . .
وكركر الأطفالُ في عرائش الكروم،
ودغدغت صمت العصافير على الشجر
أنشودةُ المطر . . .
مطر . . .
مطر . . .
مطر . . .

2.7.2 The following is one of Shakespeare's most famous poems ('Shall I compare thee to a summer's day?'). Translate it into Arabic; which approach (or approaches) would you adopt?

Tips: Note that an Arabic translation of this particular stanza exists. You may, therefore, want to familiarise yourself with this translation. Consider which approach (or approaches) you would opt for to produce your own translation of the poem and why. Are you, for example, going to use a literal/semantic translation approach and stay close to the SL or are you going to domesticate your translation in dealing with a cultural concept like 'summer's day', considering the cultural difference between how summer is viewed in the UK and in Arab countries? (See example 6.7 in Chapter 6.)

Shall I compare thee to a summer's day?
Thou art more lovely and more temperate.
Rough winds do shake the darling buds of May,
And summer's lease hath all too short a date.
Sometime too hot the eye of heaven shines,
And often is his gold complexion dimmed;
And every fair from fair sometime declines,
By chance, or nature's changing course, untrimmed;
But thy eternal summer shall not fade,
Nor lose possession of that fair thou ow'st,
Nor shall death brag thou wand'rest in his shade,
When in eternal lines to Time thou grow'st.
So long as men can breathe, or eyes can see,
So long lives this, and this gives life to thee.

2.7.3 The following is the introductory passage from (خاوية) 'Empty', a novel by Ayman Al-Otoom, discussing the human suffering that followed the revolutions which started in 2011and spread across the Arab countries.[2] Decide which approach (or approaches) would be suitable to render this passage into English.

Tips: This is an expository passage that sets the scene for telling the story of the Arab revolutions which started in 2011. Familiarising yourself with the story of the novel is a prerequisite to selecting the appropriate translation approach. Although the setting of the story is local, taking place in Syria and Jordan, it connects together personal stories with events of a revolution which are well known around the world. Therefore, source-text oriented approaches may well be appropriate since most English readers would know the tragic results of war, any war.

ما أسهل الحديث عن الصبر عندما لاتكون المصيبة مصيبتك

كان لابد من الحزن ؛ الطريق الطويلة ليست محفوفة بالأمل، ولا بالورود! لاتصدقوا، كانت مليئة بالشوك، والحفر، وكانت مظلمة ومخيفة، وكان على البائسين أن يعيشوا كل الآلام الفظيعة التي تحز القلب بسكين صدىء، وكان عليهم أن يحزنوا وحدهم لأن قصصهم الرهيبة ولدت منسية ! !

لم نكن شجعانا؛ لاتصدقوا هذه هي الكذبة الأخرى، كنا جبناء، ووحدنا. وكان علينا أن نسير فسرنا، وكان علينا أن نعبر الجسر المهدم وعبرناه، وكان علينا أن نقضم الحجر ونسف التراب ففعلنا..!!

ولكن لماذا رضينا كل ذلك؟! هربا من الموت؟! بلى. هربا من الجنون؟! بلى. هربا من أنفسنا؟! بلى بلى. كنا نهرب من أنفسنا لأنها أسوأ ما واجهناه في هذه الحرب الطويلة، في منتصف الموت تقف الروح اليائسة على أقدامها تنادي عليه أن يعجل، وتستغيث به أن يأتي سريعا.

2.7.4 The following is a short story for kids entitled 'Is There Anyone Like Me?', written by Fred Strydom, Jess Jardim-Wedepohl and Stephen Wallace (n.d.).[3] Translate it into Arabic.

Tips: The main and only character in this story is a donkey, which is not considered an endearing animal in Arabic, a cultural issue that needs to be dealt with carefully in the translation. Would you maintain a direct translation of this particular animal or replace it with another more loveable animal like a cat or a rabbit in the target text? Do you think a target-oriented translation approach that takes the expectation of the children target readers into account is more appropriate than staying close to the source text?

Is there anyone like me?
I wonder if there's another me somewhere in the world.
Who looks the same.
And talks the same.
And even has my curls.
Someone with my eyes my ears.
Who even has my laugh.
Who can do what I can do . . .
. . . and can't do what I can't.
I've looked and looked everywhere to find another me.
I went down to the park and looked behind the trees.
I looked around, up and down . . .
. . . at every single face.
I couldn't find another me in any single place.
There's only one me in the world!
I'm special, oh it's true!
But not just me, don't you see?
There's only one of *you*! (5 min Bedtime Stories)

Notes

1. <https://www.independentschoolparent.com/school/top-5-shakespeare-films-to-introduce-children-to-the-bard/> (last accessed 3 August 2022)
2. <https://www.noor-book.com/en/ebook-%D8%AE%D8%A7%D9%88%D9%8A%D9%87--pdf> (last accessed 3 August 2022)
3. <https://storyberries.com/is-there-anyone-like-me/> (last accessed 3 August 2022)

CHAPTER 3
LEXICAL TRANSLATION ISSUES AND STRATEGIES

3.1 Introduction

The previous two chapters introduced key concepts and discussed the translation process and translation approaches. In this chapter, as well as in Chapters 4 and 5, I examine stylistic translation issues at lexical, structural and textual levels and propose strategies to deal with the relevant issues. Chapter 6 will then deal with the contextual factors which influence the translation as both a process and product. This classification is adopted for ease of reference only because in some cases the same translation issue can occur at two or more different levels. For example, a metaphor can be discussed at lexical level, sentence level or even textual level in a given literary text, as in the case of extended metaphors. Another issue to bear in mind is that the concepts of style, covered in Chapters 3, 4 and 5, and context, covered in Chapter 6, are not mutually exclusive, for literary style can be seen as a reflection of the relevant context – and context, in its wider sense, can be examined in terms of its effect on the literary style of the author. However, I treat style as a linguistic representation of an experience in the form of a literary source text and a target text, and context as extralinguistic factors with influence on this experience. One further problem is that this classification may also give the wrong impression that translation is carried out at these four levels (lexical, structural, textual and extra-textual) independently, which is not the case, as will be clarified throughout the rest of this textbook.

3.2 Lexical translation issues (مشكلات الترجمة علي مستوى الكلمات)

This textbook aims to be as comprehensive and thorough as possible in its coverage of translation issues and strategies which occur in literary translation. With this in mind, I will first discuss the types of translation issues that occur at lexical level before I proceed to discuss the possible translation strategies. Therefore, the first section below produces the most common translation issues which can occur at word level, based on my own experience in teaching literary translation and on a number of coursebooks written on the topic of translation problems: Almanna (2016); Ghazala (2008/2014); Hatim and Munday (2004); Dickins et al. (2002); Fawcett (1997); Baker (1992/2011); Newmark (1988/2003) and Vinay and Darbelnet (1958/1995). The most common issues that literary translators may face at word level from the source language perspective include the following sixteen issues. Note that all the examples and translations are mine, unless otherwise indicated.

3.2.1 Types of lexical meaning (أنواع المعنى)

There are several types of meaning that a word may have, and this can occasionally be a challenge to render into the TL. Of relevance to the current discussion of lexical translation issues is denotative meaning, connotative meaning and associated meaning.

1. The denotative meaning (المعنى الإشاري أو الحقيقي أو المعجمي):
   This type of meaning is alternatively called 'referential' or 'propositional meaning' by Baker (1992/2011: 11); see also Newmark (1988/2003: 16). This is, more or less, the dictionary meaning of a word, or what a word refers to in the world, e.g. table, car, door. The denotative meaning of a word can be challenged by the receiver of the message since there is a kind of agreed semantic range of the meanings of a particular word which the receiver can fall back on in order to evaluate the correct usage of the word. One exception to this rule may be what is known as 'poetic licence', which allows poets to deviate from the rules of common usage to produce poetic effects. Another exception may be creating neologisms based on the use of existing words with new meanings or senses, especially in the areas of science and technology. The issue of creating neologisms will be discussed in detail below. On the other hand, finding SL and TL corresponding words with the same denotative meanings can sometimes be difficult to achieve. This is not to say that translation issues can only occur at connotative rather than denotative meaning. In fact, both types of meaning are a potential candidate for translation issues, but one less so than the other, see below.
2. The connotative meaning (المعنى الضمني أو الكامن أو النفسي):
   This type is alternatively called the 'expressive' meaning by Baker (1992/2011: 11) and the 'attitudinal' meaning by Dickins et al. (2002: 66–7). In contrast to denotative meaning, that is the dictionary or primary meaning of a word, connotative meaning relates to a speaker's feeling or attitude as can be seen in the manner in which he or she uses a particular word. According to Baker (1992/2011: 11), this type of meaning cannot be challenged by the reader or receiver of the message because it relates to the personal way in which a particular word is used. The challenge, in this case, is how to render the connotation of the SL word into the TL. Words can be positive, negative or neutral in one language while their TL equivalents are not. This can relate to the way in which a culture or language views the relevant concept. In languages and cultures as different as English and Arabic, this can be of particular concern to the translator. Newmark (1988/2003: 16) argues that, in a literary text, connotations of words should be given precedence over their denotations, while the opposite is true in non-literary texts. Note that understanding and reproducing connotative

meaning in literary translation clearly, if the same level of implicitness cannot be maintained, will result in a more explicit TT.

Ex 3.1: 'The police' and 'the boys in blue' are synonyms in terms of the denotative meaning (الشرطة) but have different connotative or attitudinal meanings. According to Dickins et al. (2002: 67), the first is neutral while the second is more affectionate. These connotations should not be ignored in the translation process and may need to be communicated clearly if considered important in the ST context, especially if a close rendering, which maintains the same level of implicitness of meaning, does not communicate these particular connotations to the TT readers.

3. Associated meaning (المعنى المتلازم أو المقترن أو المرتبط):
This type of meaning is defined by Dickins et al. (2002: 68) as 'that part of the overall meaning of an expression which consists of expectations that are – rightly or wrongly – associated with the referent of the expression'.

Ex 3.2: 'Nurse': this word is automatically associated with the female gender by most people (Dickins et al. 2002: 68), that is (ممرضة). I would also say that this is the case with 'nursery teacher' (مُدرسة روضة). The associated meaning in these two examples applies to both Arabic and English.

Ex 3.3: 'Crusade' (حملة صليبية) has positive associations in English but, understandably, not in Arabic (ibid.). The translator in this case will need to make clear to the target readers the difference in the associated meaning of the SL term and its translation using one or more of the strategies discussed below.

Ex 3.4: 'Homosexuality' may sound neutral to some English speakers. The Arabic equivalent, however, of this particular term is (اللواط), which translates as 'sodomy', (شذوذ), which implies 'deviation' or 'perversion', and (مثلية), which roughly means 'same-sex attraction'. All three translations pack negative associations and there is no equally neutral way of expressing this particular ST term in Arabic since the types of relationships allowed between sexes is firmly entrenched in the language and the culture due to the influence of Islam which only allows a male-female relationship in wedlock. Although Baker (1992/2011: 11–12) discusses this example under attitudinal meaning, I find it an example of associated meaning since the negative overtones are part of the meaning of the word rather than in the way it is being used.

Ex 3.5: (غيرة) *'ghaira'*, meaning 'jealousy', is an example of an Arabic word which has a positive connotation, especially in the context of the husband-wife relationship, where each of them is expected to have this feeling of *ghaira* for the other. On the other hand, the idea of 'jealousy' seems to have negative connotations in English. The possible translation of this word into English as 'protective jealousy' is far from being as positive as the Arabic word is and the strategies discussed below should be navigated carefully in order to communicate this difference to the target readers.

3.2.2 Complex lexical items (الكلمات أو الألفاظ المعقدة)

The term 'complex lexical item' focuses on the SL, describing a ST word which refers to a complex phenomenon or concept, for example, which does not have a direct TL correspondence. Looking at this from the TL perspective, there is a 'lexical gap', referring to the lack of a corresponding TL equivalent to the SL word (see Bolinger and Sears 1968: 114; Baker 1992/2011: 19). This can be the case with cultural words in particular (see below).

Ex 3.6: 'Incapacitated' is an example of an English word with such a complex meaning that it cannot be reproduced into Arabic in an equally concise manner, especially when referring to a holder of an official position or job. The dictionary meaning of this word in a political context is (غير قادر على القيام بمهام منصبه),[1] which means 'to be unable to carry out the duties of one's work'. Translators should not shy away from using more than one TL word to communicate the SL meaning. There is no rule that dictates this one to one word approach to render lexical items.

Ex 3.7: (الشهادة) (*al-shahāda*, literally, 'to testify or bear witness') is an Arabic term which refers to the verbal action of someone reciting a statement known as 'the declaration of faith', especially by individuals wishing to 'convert' to Islam from other religions. (Note that some use 'revert' instead, as it implies coming back to Islam, considering that the Islamic belief is that everyone is born Muslim, meaning a believer in God, and is, therefore, a term preferred in the relevant context, especially by new Muslims, over 'convert'). This statement reads as follows: 'I bear witness/testify that there is no god except Allah and that Muhammad is the Prophet of Allah.' This complex SL word does not really have a direct corresponding English translation and has to be explained, or rather 'paraphrased' in the TT. There are several ways in which a complex terms like this one can be rendered, as will be discussed below. See also the discussion of cultural terms below.

Ex 3.8: (البسملة) '*al-basmala*', or *bismilla*' as commonly referred to in English, is an expression which refers to reciting a verse from the Qur'an, namely, (بسم الله الرحمن الرحيم) 'in the name of Allah, most Gracious, most Merciful' (Qur'an 1: 1). This is a widely used expression while offering a prayer or outside of prayers. Here too, there is no equivalent in English for this complex SL concept whose meaning may need to be paraphrased (see below) or replaced by a functionally equivalent target text expression, or none at all, depending on the translation approach adopted. See under strategies below.

3.2.3 Context-dependent vs context-free words (كلمات أو ألفاظ يعتمد معناها على السياق وكلمات أو ألفاظ معناها مستقل عن السياق)

Context-dependent words are the type of words whose meanings depend on the context in which they occur, while context-free words do not change meaning based on their context of occurrence, generally. Some scholars describe context-dependant words as 'polysemous' because they can have multiple meanings. The translator needs to understand the context of use before deciding which meaning to render.

Ex 3.9: 'Appreciation' is a context-dependent word, which, in a general context, implies recognition of the quality, value, significance, or magnitude of people and things; a judgment or opinion, especially a favourable one; an expression of gratitude and awareness or delicate perception, especially of aesthetic qualities or values. For example, 'She was grateful for the help and baked them a cake as a token of her appreciation'[2] can be rendered as (كانت ممتنة للمساعدة وأعدت لهم كيكة كدليل على تقديرها لهم.). However, in a business text, and in particular with exchange rates, 'appreciation' implies 'a rise in value or price, especially over time.'[3] For example, 'the U.S. currency has appreciated versus major rivals'[4] can be translated as (ارتفعت قيمة العملة الأمريكية مقابل العملات المنافسة). Understanding the context of occurrence, in this particular case, is key to producing a correct translation.

Ex 3.10: 'Table' is also a word which derives its meaning from the context in which it occurs. It can imply many meanings including: 'a piece of furniture', 'food provided in a restaurant or household', 'a meeting place or forum for formal discussions', 'a flat, typically rectangular, vertical surface', amongst several other meanings.[5] The translation of this word as (طاولة), (مائدة), (جدول), etc., will certainly differ according to its contextual meaning.

Ex 3.11: 'Carrot' (جزر) is a word that does not change meaning based on its context of occurrence and can, as such, be considered context-free.

Ex 3.12: (عين)[6] is a context-dependent word. It can mean 'an eye', 'a spy', 'an army leader' and 'a water spring', amongst other meanings.

Ex 3.13: (قص)[7] is also a context-dependent word which can mean 'to cut', 'to snip', 'to tell (a story)', 'to narrate' and 'to follow the tracks of someone'.

3.2.4 Culture-specific words (alternatively called 'cultural words' or 'loaded words') (كلمات أو ألفاظ خاصةبالثقافة)

Culture is defined as 'the customary beliefs, social forms, and material traits of a racial, religious, or social group',[8] and as 'the way of life and its manifestations that are peculiar to a community that uses a particular language as its means of expression' (Newmark 1988/2003: 94; see also Baker 1992/2011: 18; Strelkova 2012). Culture has a great influence on how people view the world and everything in it and, in turn, how they express their views, opinions and ideas. Language is part of its culture; it contains all kinds of cultural deposits in its grammar and lexis. Therefore, the translation of cultural words between languages which are culturally different, such as Arabic and English, can be a challenge. Note that cultural terms can also be seen as complex lexical items as discussed above.

In translating a literary work, a task that mostly requires communicating the flavour of the source text in the translation, leaving in too many cultural references may weaken the translation and lose the target readers as it may be difficult for him or her to cope with such an abundance of references. A balance between removing all ST cultural references and keeping some, and considering explaining them, needs to be made. The latter case is not devoid of challenges either since the translator will have to decide on how to add the necessary explanations: in footnotes, in-text glosses or glossaries, for example.

Newmark (1998/2003: 95–102) proposes five categories of cultural references. I provide below a more focused discussion of these categories, which I illustrate with English-Arabic examples.

1. Environmental references (كلمات خاصة بالبيئة):
   Local geographical features, names of winds, seasons, rains, plains, forests, bushes and so on (see Newmark 1998/2003: 96–7).

   Ex 3.14: 'The Highlands' refers to a mountainous region in the north of Scotland, an area known for its beautiful landscape. A close translation is possible, (الأراضي المرتفعة) or (الجبال), but it does not communicate the implied meaning.

   Ex 3.15: 'The Peak district' is a nature reserve known for its beauty in England. Here too, a close rendering, (منطقة القمم), may not communicate the implied meaning of natural beauty.

2. Life style references (كلمات خاصة بأسلوب الحياة):
   Food, clothes, houses and means of transport are prime examples of this category. Also included under this sub-category are types of art, names of museums, theatres, exhibitions and so on. Words which relate to these types can be too specific to find

an equivalent in another language. This category further includes trades, crafts, shops, shopping and leisure activities (see Newmark 1998/2003: 97–8).

Ex 3.16: (جلباب) refers in Arabic to a type of outfit worn by both men and women that is long, loose and wide. Since there is no similar outfit in English, rendering this word will depend on various contextual factors, including the purpose of the translation and the TT readers' expectations and assumed knowledge about Arabic culture. For example, 'cloak' can be used in some contexts.

Ex 3.17: 'After lunch' is an English expression which refers to a specific time during the day as employees usually finish their 'lunch' break, around 13:00 to 14:00. A direct translation of this term into Arabic, where the time of lunch differs from that time period, can be misleading unless the translation approach selected is a source-text oriented one in line with the aim of the translation.

3. Historical references (كلمات ذات دلالة تاريخية):
   This category covers references to past local events including wars, floods, celebrations and so on (see Newmark 1998/2003: 101).

   Ex 3.18: 'Guy Fawkes Night' or 'Bonfire Night' (ليلة الألعاب النارية) dates back to 5 November 1605 when Guy Fawkes was arrested while guarding explosives placed beneath the House of Lords. In the UK people continue to commemorate the event with fireworks. This reference is unlikely to be known to most Arabic readers.

   Ex 3.19: (النكبة), meaning the 'catastrophe', refers to the 1948 fall/occupation of Palestine which may not have the same effect on the English language readers due to their understanding of the events.

4. Religious references (كلمات ذات دلالة دينية):
   Local and specific religious terms, for example, Islamic religious terminology, can be challenging to translate into English since the terms either do not exist in English or the available or direct translations do not quite communicate the ST meaning.

   Ex 3.20: (مواعيد الصلاة) or 'Muslim Prayer times' is a good example of a religious reference. The use of the five daily prayers in Arabic to specify time can be challenging to render into English for two reasons: the Prayer itself may not be known to the TT readers and the time itself differs depending on the change of seasons since prayer times are determined by the position of the sun in the sky. In the UK, the 'Maghrib' (sunset) prayer can be offered at around 16:00 in winter but at about 21:00 in summer, for instance.

5. Organisational references (كلمات ذات دلالة تنظيمية):
   A country's institutional set-up reflects its political and administrative organisation. This category includes names of ministries and other official institutions, names of official documents, political parties and political concepts (see Newmark 1998/2003: 99–101).

   Ex 3.21: 'Speaker of the House of Commons' is an English concept which is rarely understood by people from other cultures, according to Baker (1992/2011: 18). The Speaker acts as an independent person who maintains authority and order in Parliament. It can be translated as (رئيس مجلس العموم أو النواب).

   Ex 3.22: 'The Treasury' in the UK administrative system means the Ministry of Finance in other countries, (وزارة المالية) in Arabic.

   Ex 3.23: 'Home Office' in the UK implies the Ministry of Interior (وزارة الداخلية) in Arab and European countries.

   Ex 3.24: 'Foreign Office' in the UK means the Ministry of Foreign Affairs in Arabic (وزارة الخارجية البريطانية).

Words under the above categories can cause some of the most prominent challenges that translators have to deal with. The reason is that rendering them into the TL requires not only background knowledge on the translator's part of what the word actually means in its cultural context but also on how to make the rendering accessible to the TT readers.

3.2.5 A word's range of meaning (نطاق معاني الكلمات أو الألفاظ)

This issue has to do with the range of semantic meanings that a word covers in the language. In other words, the ranges of the TL and SL word meanings may not map onto each other (see also Baker 1992/2011: 19), causing a translation loss or gain.

Ex 3.25: (خالة) literally means maternal aunt, while (عمة) means paternal aunt. This distinction in meaning is lacking in the corresponding English word 'aunt' alone. The use of the expression 'my maternal aunt' or 'paternal aunt' in English may be used only when the speaker finds it important to make this distinction.

Ex 3.26: 'Uncle' refers to both maternal and paternal uncles. Arabic, on the other hand, makes a distinction between the two types of relationships, with a different word for each: (خال) refers to maternal uncle and (عم) to paternal uncle.

3.2.6 Use of a superordinate (or a general word) (استخدام لفظ شامل أو عام)

The dictionary meaning of a 'superordinate' is as follows: 'a word that denotes a general class under which a set of subcategories is subsumed'.[9] Lack of a TL equivalent superordinate may be a challenge for the translator (see also Baker 1992/2011: 17).

Ex 3.27: 'Cousins' is also a superordinate that covers sons and daughters of uncles and aunts. An equivalent superordinate does not exist in Arabic, which has specific terms, that is hyponym (see below), for each relationship and the gender of the cousin. For example, a cousin can be (ابن عمي) 'son of my paternal uncle' or (بنت خالتي) 'daughter of my maternal aunt'. Understanding what relationship 'cousin' holds in the ST can help decide on the correct translation. Some translations use (أبناء العمومة), literally 'sons of paternal uncles' or (أطفال العائلة) 'family's kids' to render 'cousins'.

3.2.7 Use of a hyponym (or a specific word) (استخدام لفظ مندرج أو خاص)

This is the converse of the previous issue. A 'hyponym' is defined as 'a term that denotes a subcategory of a more general class'[10] (see also Baker 1992/2011: 19–20). In other words, lack of an equivalent TL hyponym is a translation challenge.

Ex 3.28: 'Pasta' is an Italian word, originally from Greek, which acts as a superordinate for different types of *pasta*, fresh and dry, covering many hyponyms, such as *cannelloni* and *spaghetti*. These hyponyms are used in English as loan words. Arabic lacks these hyponyms and usually uses the equivalent superordinate loan word, either (مكرونة *makarūna*) or (معكرونة *ma'karūna*), to refer to most types and shapes of pasta.

Ex 3.29: There are several types of houses in English including bungalow, cottage, chalet, hut, manor house and villa. Baker (1992/2011: 20) discusses the examples of the types of houses and how different they can be, requiring a specific hyponym for each type. Arabic lacks equivalents for some of these types due to the way in which houses are built across the Arab world. Therefore, some of these types are transliterated (see under strategies below) into Arabic, for instance, 'chalet' (شاليه) and 'villa' (فيلا).

3.2.8 Difference in interpersonal or physical perspective (alternatively called 'modulation') (اختلاف المنظور الشخصي أو المادي أو"التعديل")

According to Baker (1992/2011: 20), this issue relates to how different cultures and, therefore, different languages view things. Vinay and Darbelnet (1958/1995) discuss this issue under what they consider as 'modulation' and define it as 'a change of viewpoint, of perspective ... and very often of category of thought'. In other words, cultures can and do view the world and many things in it differently and, understandably, express these views differently.

Ex 3.30: 'Night' (ليلة) can be confusing while translating between English and Arabic since the latter considers that, in a 24-hour cycle, the night-time precedes daytime. Along these lines, 'Friday night' (ليلة الجمعة), for example, refers to the period starting from sunset on Thursday till sunrise on Friday morning, while in English it implies the night-time from sunset of Friday till sunrise on Saturday morning. Expressions like this one can cause confusion if translated directly without consideration of the relevant perspective.

Ex 3.31: 'Deliver a baby' is a more common expression in English than 'deliver a woman'. In Arabic, the second expression (توليد المرأة) is used more often since the focus is on the mother more than the baby.

Ex 3.32: 'Couple' implies two people living together regardless of their marital status. In Arabic, the direct translation as (زوج) refers to a husband and wife living together in wedlock only due to the influence of Islam. Similarly, 'marriage', rendered as (زواج), refers in Arabic to a legal relationship that holds between a man and a woman only.

3.2.9 Word formation (صياغة الكلمة)

English words are formed through the use of syllables while Arabic derives words from a cluster of three (and occasionally more) consonants. If English uses suffixes and/or prefixes to imply approval or disapproval, for example, the Arabic translator has to try to reproduce the meaning through the use of words derived, more likely than not, from different clusters, occasionally losing the connotation of English prefix (بادئة أو حروف تضاف إلى بداية الكلمة) and/or suffix (لاحقة وهي حروف تضاف إلى آخر الكلمة) (see Baker 1992/2011: 21; Newmark 1988/2003: 85; Vinay and Darbelnet 1958/1995).

Ex 3.33: 'Retrievable' and 'drinkable' end in the suffix 'able'. 'Retrievable' may be translated as (قابل للاسترجاع أو ممكن استرداده),[11] which means 'can be retrieved or returned', while 'drinkable' may be translated as (صالح للشرب أو يمكن شربه),[12] that is 'good for drinking or can be drunk'. As is clear from the translations, the English suffix 'able' is translated differently in each case, i.e. *qābil*, *mumkin*, *ṣāliḥ* and *yumkin*, due to the Arabic word's morphological rules.

Ex 3.34: 'Legalese' is defined as 'the specialized vocabulary of the legal profession, especially when considered to be complex or abstruse'[13] (see also Baker 1992/2011: 21). The connotations of complexity and difficulty in understanding this type of language, which is implied through the suffix 'ese' is lost in the close Arabic translation (اللغة القانونية), that is 'the legal language'. Therefore, paraphrasing (see under strategies) the lost nuance of meaning can communicate the meaning better: (اللغة القانونية المعقدة) 'complex legal language'.

Ex 3.35: (بسم الله الرحمن الرحيم) (*bism i-llah i-raḥāmn i-raḥīm*) is usually translated as 'in the name of Allah, most Gracious, most Merciful'. The consonant root system in Arabic allows, in addition to the repetition of consonants, for part of the meaning to be shared by all the words derived out of the same root. Assonance, the repetition of vowels, or consonance, the repetition of consonants, produce a particular rhythm which will inevitably be lost when translated into English. Such issues feature in the translation of the words (الرحمن, *al-raḥmān*) and (الرحيم, *al-raḥīm*) above, which both come from the same root (ر ح م) (r ḥ m), which means 'mercy'. Each of the words has a particular meaning: *al-raḥmān* implies God's mercy which encompasses all creations, whilst *al-raḥīm* implies a type of God's mercy which is reserved for those who believe in Him (Elimam 2013: 40–1).

Ex 3.36: (صيغ التصغير) 'diminutive forms of nouns' are used in Arabic to denote a small example of something or with 'caritative or pejorative overtones, depending on the context' (Holes 1995/2004: 160, see also Strelkova 2012). To elaborate, according to Arabic grammar,[14] diminutives can be used (لتقليل ذات الشيء أو كميته), 'to belittle something or someone', (دُرَيْهمات) 'few Dirhams' and (رُجَيل) 'little man', and to approximate time and space, (قُبيل العصر) 'a little before ʿ*Asr* (i.e. late afternoon)', (بُعَيد المغرب) 'a little after sunset', (وفُوَيق الفَرْسخ) 'a little more than a league'. Diminutive address forms, such as (أُخَيَّ) (*'ukhaiyy*, little brother) and (أُخَيَّة) (*'ukhaiyya*, little sister), are usually terms of endearment in Arabic (Holes 2004: 160). The same applies to proper names too. For instance, (أُحيمد *'uḥaimid*) is diminutive from (أحمد Ahmed), and means 'little Ahmed'. The same forms of words can be used disparagingly and the correct function of the form needs to be established by the translator in each case. Furthermore, a character may use a term of endearment, including diminutives, before making a request or asking for a favour. The literary translator needs to figure out the motivation behind the use of the diminutive to be able to render it accurately and creatively into English.

Ex 3.37: The gerund in English is created by adding the suffix *ing* to the verb, which can then be used as a noun. For instance, 'playing' is a gerund and can be used as a noun rather than a verb or part of a verbal group. This form does not have a direct Arabic equivalent, and different forms may be used to translate it instead. 'Playing' as a noun is rendered into the noun (اللعب *al-laʿib*, literally, the-playing), while 'playing' as a verb is rendered as (يلعب *yal'ab*, he-plays or he-is-playing). (Note here that Arabic conjugates a verb for tense, number and gender and that there is no basic form of a verb as such, but a verb properly conjugated for all three aspects.) This strategy is described as a 'shift' by Catford (1965/1978: 3) and as 'transposition' by Newmark (1988/2003: 85).

Ex 3.38: Nominalisation (استخدام التراكيب الاسمية) is common in English. A nominalisation is a 'noun phrase that has a systematic correspondence with a clausal prediction which includes a head noun morphologically related to a corresponding verb' (Quirk et al. 1985: 1288, see also Dik 1997 and Jackendoff 1972). These structures, for example, 'take a bath' as opposed to 'bathing', can form a particular challenge to translators into Arabic, a language which prefers verbal structures (التراكيب الفعلية) under normal circumstances of usage. In this particular example, Arabic can reproduce both structures: (يستحم) can be rendered as 'bathe' and (يأخذ حماما) as 'to take a bath', (which seems to have come to Arabic through literal translation from English). However, in 'to take a shot' and 'to shoot', Arabic would render them both as (يطلق النار) 'to shoot'. This may inevitably lead to the loss of some stylistic aspects, particularly in literary and sacred texts.

Ex 3.39: The suffix 'ish' is added to many English words, colloquially, to imply 'sort of.' For instance, something can be 'reddish' in colour (محمر) or (من درجات الأحمر), the latter meaning 'one shade of red'. Someone or something can be 'okayish', meaning (جيد لحد ما), that is 'okay/fine to some extent'. Arabic does not have an equivalent suffix and therefore paraphrases its meaning in translation.

3.2.10 Use of foreign/loan words (استخدام كلمات أجنبية أو مستعارة من لغات أخرى)

This is an issue of particular relevance to English, which features the use of many foreign/loan words. The challenge here is not only to find an equivalent TL word but also, and perhaps more importantly, to reproduce the implication of using the loan word in the ST which can be to emphasise the speaker's knowledge of foreign languages (see also Baker 1992/2011: 22).

Ex 3.40: 'Bon appétit' is a French expression which is used by some English speakers to wish someone a good meal (English speakers can also use 'enjoy'). This can be rendered into Arabic as (بالعافية) 'with health', amongst other renderings. The issue with this Arabic translation is that it renders the meaning but loses the connotations of the use of a loan word in the ST, especially if it is used to show off or highlight the speaker's knowledge of French. This can be an important issue to communicate in the translation if it relates to the characterisation or the development of the plot.

3.2.11 False friends (”أصدقاء مزيفون“ وهي كلمات من لغات مختلفة تتشابه في الكتابة أو النطق وتختلف في المعنى)

Some languages, especially those belonging to the same language family, for example, English and French, may share the use of some words which may be similar in their pronunciation or spelling, but remain different in their usage or meaning. For example, 'adepte' in French means 'member' or 'enthusiast', while 'adept' in English means 'competent' or 'expert'.[15] Although this is not an issue which affects Arabic-English translation to a great extent because they belong to different language families and are written in different scripts, it is a challenge that translators need to be aware of (see Baker 1992/2011: 22 Newmark 1988/2003: 72–3).

Ex 3.41: 'Professor' is an academic title, which, in the UK, comes only after being a lecturer and a senior lecturer at a university, generally speaking. The close-sounding 'professore' in Italian and 'professeur' in French are titles used by secondary school pupils to address their teachers and by university students to address their lecturers, regardless of their respective academic rank. 'Professor' is transliterated into Arabic as (بروفيسور), and is used to refer to a university professor only, although other translations exist, namely, (أستاذ دكتور) (أستاذ جامعي).[16]

Ex 3.42: (دكتور) is a title used to address university lecturers, regardless of their academic rank, amongst other things, in Arabic speaking countries. The direct English equivalent, 'doctor', seems to be reserved for medical doctors, at least in British English. Although the SL and TL words sound very similar, they seem to be applicable in different contexts. Note that the pronunciation of the English word is naturalised (see under strategies below) as '*duktūr*' in Arabic.

Ex 3.43: (مراقب): This word has a direct translation as 'observer'. However, it can be used in Arabic to refer to someone who 'invigilates' or 'proctors' exams, in which case the right meaning needs to be communicated. This word can also be considered polysemous.

3.2.12 Dialect and idiolect (اللهجة المحلية لمنطقة ما واللهجة الفردية)

A 'dialect' is defined as 'a regional or social variety of a language distinguished by pronunciation, grammar, or vocabulary, especially a variety of speech differing from the standard literary language or speech pattern of the culture in which it exists: Cockney is a dialect of English'.[17] An 'idiolect' is 'the speech of an individual, considered as a linguistic pattern unique among speakers of his or her language or dialect'.[18] Some people have distinctive features in their language; these would be part of their idiolect; their individual linguistic choices and idiosyncrasies. These two concepts are quite important in helping the receiver of a literary work build an image of the character concerned. One can give away information as to whereabouts he or she is from, his or her level of education, sociocultural background, amongst other factors, from his or her dialect and/or idiolect. This can be of particular importance for characterisation in a novel, for example (see also Newmark 1988/2003: 194–5). According to Paul (2009: 43),

> [t]ranslating a book written in a particular style (baroque, for example), even when written by contemporary authors, poses its own problems. Do translators 'update' the text to refresh it and make it accessible, thereby losing distinctive use of vocabulary and turn of phrase, or do they labour to match it?

Ex 3.44: 'Lift' vs 'elevator' and 'pavement' vs 'sidewalk', the use of either word can probably help identify whether the speaker is, say, British or American, respectively.

Ex 3.45: 'Jersey' vs 'jumper', the use of either word may help identify the speaker's social class, where 'jersey' is probably associated more with higher classes than is 'jumper'.

Ex 3.46: 'To be upset', in some English dialects, means 'to cry' rather than the dictionary meaning of being 'unhappy', 'disappointed' or 'worried'. The challenge is rendering this word not only to understand the meaning correctly but also to communicate to the readers/listeners the nuances of meaning implied in its usage.

Ex. 3.47: (ج) '/j/' is pronounced as /g/ in some Arabic dialects, e.g. Egyptian and Yemeni, and can therefore help locate the speaker.

Ex 3.48: (إيش لونك), (شو الجو) and (إزيك) are all dialect versions of (كيف الحال), meaning 'how are you' in standard Arabic. Using one version rather than the others can help the reader or listener place the speaker in a certain part of the Arab world.

It is also worth mentioning at this point that the challenge in rendering colloquialisms, in other words, slang words, is not only in finding an equivalent for them, but also in the fact that they change meaning quickly, making the timeliness of rendering a slang source text word by an equivalent target text word a challenging issue. Finally, taboos, or swear words, are equally challenging considering that swearing is against the cultural norms in Arabic, generally speaking. In most cases, translators, for consideration of target readers' expectations, end up either euphemising (that is 'toning down') the swear word or omitting it completely.

3.2.13 Forms of address (صيغ المخاطبة أو استخدام الألقاب)

The use of the first name, as opposed to a title (اللقب), when addressing people can be indicative of the social distance, or rather lack thereof, between the speakers involved. This is true of Arabic where titles, formal and informal, are used more often than in English in dealing with elders as well as those the speaker is not friends with. The misuse of the correct title while addressing people can be interpreted as disrespectful. Further, the use of titles and/or honorific statements in Arabic is particularly observed before the names of the Prophets and their companions. On the other hand, the use of the first name to address people in English is no longer indicative of familiarity or 'closeness', but a marker of informality which seems to be filtering through to many areas where formality had been maintained and practised. For example, university students in British universities call the lecturers by their first names and without titles. This issue relates to a much wider issue of formality versus informality as a cultural issue with linguistic realisation (see Ghazala 2008/2014: 20). Choice of whether or not to 'insert' titles in translations from English into Arabic, or to remove them if the translation is into the opposite direction, is a decision that needs to be taken carefully in line with the aim of the translation, amongst other considerations.

3.2.14 Neologism (الكلمات أو الألفاظ الجديدة أو المستحدثة)

This concept implies the coining (or use) of new words, expressions, terms and phrases. In other words, the term refers to newly coined, made-up or invented words.[19] This is another area which potentially causes problems for translators either because the new word itself or its meaning is unknown to them. This is particularly important in non-literary translation. The following discussion on how neologisms are coined in English is based on Newmark's classification of neologism (1988/2003; see also Sayadi 2011), with illustrative examples from Arabic and English. New words are needed to refer to new concepts, ideas, inventions and products.

1. Coinage through the use of old words but with new meaning:
   This is called 'euphemism' or (التلطف في التعبير) by Newmark (1988/2003: 141–2) as is clear from Ex 3.49 below. However, I argue that euphemism can be realised through any of the methods of coinage discussed below.

   Ex 3.49: 'Challenged' is now used euphemistically in combination with other words to describe a type of physical incapacity. 'Vertically challenged' is used to refer to someone who is either too short or too tall. 'Visually challenged' is used to describe a (semi)blind person. Arabic uses (ذوي الاحتياجات الخاصة), which means 'people with special needs'. In a religious context, a translation along the lines of (مبتلى في بصره) 'plighted/tested in his eyesight' can be used. This translation is based on the Islamic belief that life and whatever happens in it is a kind of test from Allah, so eyesight, or lack of it, is a test, and people will be rewarded, or otherwise, on the day of judgement based on how they used the blessings of Allah in this world and how patient they were in the face of calamities.

Ex 3.50: 'Partner' is now used in English to refer to someone living with another out of wedlock. The closest Arabic translation which can be used to render this term is (شريك حياة) 'life partner', which implies husband and wife.

2. Coinage through the creation of new words:

   Ex 3.51: 'Selfie' is a new informal coinage referring to a photograph that one has taken of oneself. This has been rendered literally and used also equally informally in Arabic as (سيلفي *silfi*).

   Ex 3.52: 'Smurfs' is the title of a popular TV children's cartoon. This title has been rendered into Arabic through an equally new coinage: (سنافر *sanāfir*).

   Ex 3.53: (طائرة *ṭāʾira*) is an example of a new coinage in Arabic. The word (طائرة), meaning aircraft, was coined from the closely related word (طائر *ṭāʾir*), which means 'bird-male', via the addition of the feminine suffix to the word.

3. Coinage of new collocations:
   New collocates (المتلازمات الفظية) can be challenging to translate between languages as sometimes they are language-specific (Ibrahim 2003; Newmark 1988/2003: 145).

   Ex 3.54: 'Domino effect' is a relatively new collocation that is usually closely translated into Arabic as (سقوط أحجار الدومينو),[20] that is 'the fall of domino pieces', which may not reproduce the meaning clearly, or more communicatively as (شيء يؤثر على شيء) 'something which influences/affects something else'.

   Ex 3.55: 'Cold calling' is a new collocation and can be translated into Arabic in different ways. For instance, it can be rendered as (إجراء مكالمات مبيعات غير مطلوبة),[21] 'making unsolicited sales calls', (اتصال غير مرتب), 'unplanned phone call', and (المكالمات أو الزيارات المفاجئة), 'surprise phone calls or visits'. The Arabic translations are rather a paraphrase (see under strategies below) of the meaning of the SL collocations.

4. Coinage through eponymy:
   Eponymy (صفة النسبة أو مسمى على اسم) refers to the coinage of words from proper names (Newmark 1988/2003: 146) as can be seen from the following two examples.

Ex 3.56: 'Hallidayan' and 'Thatcherism' are coinages which are based on proper names, 'Halliday' and 'Thatcher', respectively. These two examples can be rendered as (هاليدية) and (تاتشرية) (*hālidiyya* and *tātshariyya*, respectively). Translating eponyms relates to the issue of word formation and how different the SL and TL are.

Ex 3.57: (محمدية *muḥamadiyya*) is an eponym which is derived from 'Muhammad'. In other words, like English, Arabic makes use of this coinage procedure too.

5. Coinage through the use of phrasal verbs:
   A phrasal verb (الأفعال المركبة) is defined as 'an idiomatic phrase consisting of a verb and another element, typically either an adverb, as in "break down", or a preposition, for example, "see to", or a combination of both, such as "look down on"'.[22] Finding an equivalent, which captures the difference between the meaning of the verb alone and of its meaning in combination with a preposition and/or an adverb, is no easy task. More challenging is reproducing the stylistic difference between the phrasal verb and the equivalent word, as in the following example (see Newmark 1988/2003: 147 and Ghazala 2008/2014: 134ff.).

   Ex 3.58: 'Work out' is a phrasal verb which means 'to exercise', amongst other meanings.[23] The Arabic rendering, (يتدرب، يتمرن), 'to exercise/train', does not reflect the morphology of the SL phrase and simply unpacks its meaning.

6. Transferred words:
   Transferred words (كلمات منقولة من لغات أخرى) are lexical items which have found their way to common usage in one language from another, and Arabic and English are no exception. Newly transferred words may keep only one sense of their foreign nationality (see also use of foreign/loan words above). They are words whose meanings are least dependent on their contexts, and they are likely to refer to everyday rather than technological concepts (Newmark 1988/2003: 147).

   Ex 3.59: 'Tandoori' refers to an Indian dish which can be made with chicken or meat, has been adopted into the English menu. Arabic uses a close rendering of this word: (تندوري *tandūrī*). The challenge in translating this word from English into Arabic consists of reflecting the foreign origin of the ST word in the TT.

7. Acronyms:
   The use of acronyms (الاختصارات) is quite common in English literary and scientific writing for reasons of brevity (الإيجاز) or euphony (عذوبة الصوت) 'agreeableness of sound, pleasing effect to the ear'.[24] For example, in science, letters can be joined up to

form a word which will stand for the scientific concept behind it and occasionally the newly formed word may become an internationalism (for instance, 'laser') (Newmark 1988/2003: 148). English literary genres also feature the use of acronyms to refer to places, buildings, and even people. Arabic literary genres, on the other hand, hardly use acronyms, especially when the letters cannot be used to form a word.

Ex 3.60: 'UN' is an acronym, which, like many others, is always translated into Arabic in full as (الأمم المتحدة), 'the United Nations'.

Ex 3.61: 'IMF' is also written out in full in Arabic (صندوق النقد الدولي) that is (International Monetary Fund).

Both these examples have to be rendered in full in Arabic since the abbreviations cannot be pronounced as a word, as opposed to the following example which can be pronounced as a word in Arabic.

Ex 3.62: FAO is translated into Arabic as (منظمة الأغذية والزراعة التابعة للأمم المتحدة) الفاو. As opposed to the previous two examples, this one can be pronounced and, therefore, rendered into Arabic as a word with or without full translation.

Ex 3.63: 'Covid 19' is a recent abbreviation for 'Coronavirus Disease 2019'. This is commonly translated into Arabic as (فيروس كورونا المستجد) or 'the new corona virus'. However, some specialist Arabic writings have rendered the abbreviation closely as (كوفيد 19). This latter translation may not be accessible to the lay reader.

However, when the acronym refers to a character in a novel, Arabic translations can transliterate the letters; for instance, 'CJ' can be transliterated as (سي جيه '/si jei/'). This is because character names are almost always transliterated in translation and acronyms used as names are no exception.

3.2.15 Words with competing translations (كلمات ذات ترجمات متعارضة أو متباينة)

This is another potentially challenging area of translation because it implies that the translator has to be 'on either side of the fence' by selecting one of two or more competing words used to refer to the same thing or concept. This will be discussed further under 'Ideology' as a contextual issue in Chapter 6. However, the examples below will illustrate the issue for now.

Ex 3.64: 'Palestine' vs 'Israel' is a relevant example. Using either name places the translator firmly on either side of the two competing parties. The use of Palestine is a recognition of the authentic right of the indigenous population of Palestine to their land, while the use of 'Israel' is a recognition of the occupiers who came from Europe and beyond to take the land away from its original owners. This also applies to the use of both names simultaneously by some speakers who want to sound neutral.

Ex 3.65: 'Arabian Gulf' vs 'Persian Gulf' is another relevant example. Here too, choosing one translation over the other places the translator on either side of the fence.

Ex 3.66: 'Return of refugees' (إعادة اللاجئين) is an expression used by some host countries to imply the 'refusal of entry of refugees' (رفض دخول اللاجئين) from the refugees' perspective.

3.2.16 Gestures (الإشارات أو الإيماءات)

These can be problematic to translate between different languages as the meaning of the same gesture, for example, can differ across cultures (see also Newmark 1988/2003: 102).

Ex 3.67: 'Pointing' (الإشارة بالإصبع) while talking is not seen as a negative gesture in Arabic, where speakers arguably use hand movement more than English speakers.

Ex 3.68: Giving 'the victory sign' (إشارة النصر) with the back of the hand facing outward, usually to signal the number 'two' is not rude in Arabic, but it is in English.

3.2.17 Humour (الدعابة أو الفكاهة)

Humour can present a problem for translators because one thing can be really funny in one language but not another. Explaining why something is funny in the source text might not be a valid option since it can reduce the humour involved in the source text item. That is why most jokes get lost in translation. The other issue here is that if humour is part of the characterisation, this can result in a change in the plot of a literary work. In fact, in conference interpreting situations, and in recognition of the difficulty of translating jokes, when a speaker makes a joke, the interpreter often says to the audience 'the speaker is telling a joke, please laugh' without actually translating the joke. For instance, Trevor Peacock, who acts Jim Trott in the *The Vicar of Dibley*, a British sitcom, has a tendency to stutter 'no' repeatedly whenever questioned until he finally says his truthful answer which is usually 'yes', confusing the other characters and making the audience laugh.[25] The Arabic translator needs to consider whether or not maintaining the repetition of 'no' would have the same effect on the Arabic audience.

3.3 Translation strategies for lexical issues (استراجيات الترجمة على مستوى الكلمات)

The above section has explored the most frequent types of translation issues which may occur at a lexical level, although, admittedly, some of these issues can occur at other levels too. For example, the difficulty of translating neologisms can occur at a sentence level if the coinage involves a multi-word term. Dealing with these challenges requires knowledge of the available translation strategies in order to achieve accuracy and consistency in one's output, in line with the translation *skopos*. As has been mentioned, I use 'strategies' here to imply micro-level procedures, reserving 'approach' to describe macro-level guiding translation orientation. As such, the following section offers an examination of the most common types of translation strategies discussed in the relevant literature and/or used by professional translators in dealing with the word-level translation issues discussed above. It is worth mentioning that some of the strategies discussed here can also be used to deal with some of the other level issues discussed in later chapters. Note also that the translator may not know what the lexical item means, i.e. knowledge gap, or how to render it, i.e. linguistic gap. This is because words can be used in their material physical, figurative, technical or colloquial sense and the translator needs to establish which usage features in the ST before attempting to translate (see Newmark 1988/2003: 33).

3.3.1 Direct equivalent (الترجمة المباشرة أو المتداولة)

Unless there is a good reason for doing otherwise, this is the first strategy a translator opts for if a TL equivalent or corresponding item is available for the SL word. In other words, established equivalents of ST words as evidenced by the frequency of using one to render the other should be used. Deviation from using direct equivalents, unless strongly justified, can be frowned upon.

Ex 3.69: 'History' can be translated directly into Arabic as (التاريخ), and 'book' as (كتاب).

Ex 3.70: (سيارة) is translated directly into English as 'car' and (قلم) as 'pen'.

3.3.2 Literal translation (alternatively called 'through-translation' or 'calque') (الترجمة الحرفية)

This micro-level lexical translation strategy involves the literal translation of words, names of organisations, acronyms of international organisations and so on (Newmark 1988/2003: 84). This strategy, which is called 'calque' by Vinay and Darbelnet (1958/1995: 32), is a very common strategy in translating terms, especially in the areas of business and technology from English into Arabic. Titles of films and TV shows are generally rendered via this method of calque, especially if they are short. In literary translation, character names, cultural references to places and events, and some idioms and metaphors are usually rendered in this manner. This strategy can also be over-used, which suggests that signs of 'translationese' can be seen in the TT.

Ex 3.71: 'House of Commons' is translated literally as (مجلس العموم) (see also under cultural equivalent below).

Ex 3.72: 'House of Lords' is translated as (مجلس اللوردات) (see also under cultural equivalent below). Note that there is some kind of naturalisation involved in this rendering in how Lords was translated into Arabic (see naturalisation below).

Ex 3.73: 'Spiderman' is rendered into Arabic using the through-translation strategy as (الرجل العنكبوت).

Descriptive titles of literary works can be rendered closely (Newmark 1988/2003: 57). However, according to Paul (2009: 42), who draws on literary translators' opinions about how to render literary titles, '[l]iteral translations of titles will often fail to grab the prospective audience for the book. Sometimes complete change is required to make the book sellable.' It probably is the translator's job to decide whether a close translation can render the meaning of the title or if changing it is necessary. It seems, however, that the literal translation of titles is quite common in Arabic translation.

Ex 3.74: *A Tale of Two Cities*, a title of a famous novel by Charles Dickens, is translated literally as 'قصة مدينتين'.

Ex 3.75: *Pride and Prejudice* by Jane Austin, is translated literally as 'كبرياء وتحامل'.

3.3.3 Cultural equivalent (alternatively called 'cultural substitution') (المقابل أو المرادف أو البديل الثقافي)

The strategy of 'cultural equivalent', alternatively called 'cultural substitution' by Baker 1992/2011: 29), can be used where a literal rendering can distort the meaning of the SL word, especially if it is a cultural reference. In other words, an SL word is rendered with a TL cultural equivalent (Newmark 1988/2003: 83).

Ex 3.76: 'Wedding reception' is an English cultural term, which can be translated by the Arabic cultural equivalent (فرح *faraḥ*) or (عرس *'urs*).

Ex 3.77: 'Breast milk' is rendered by the culturally acceptable translation (حليب الأم), which literally means 'mother's milk'.

Ex 3.78: 'Coffee' is a word that can be directly translated into Arabic as (قهوة); in fact the origin of the English word is from Arabic *qahwa*, which passed into English via Turkish *kahveh*. However, the translator may decide to substitute 'tea' for 'coffee', considering how common drinking 'tea' in Arab countries is. This solution serves the purpose of bringing the TT closer to readers' expectations.

Ex 3.79: 'Tea' is another example which may also be a source of confusion. Some English speakers use the word 'tea' to imply dinner, especially when used late in the afternoon. In that case, the appropriate Arabic translation may well be (العشاء), that is dinner or supper, if confusion is to be avoided. Further, English 'tea' is usually with milk or cream while Arabic 'tea' (شاي) is usually black and with sugar. One can, however, order 'tea with milk' specifically.

Ex 3.80: 'Pasta' can be translated into Arabic as (مكرونة *makarūna*) or (معكرونة, *ma'karūna*). Note that 'macaroni' itself is a subtype of 'pasta', but it is used in Arabic in a more generic sense than it is in Italian or English.

Ex 3.81: A-level: (الثانوية العامة *al-thānawiyya al-'āma*) in Egypt or (البكالوريا *bakālūrya*) in Levant countries. The translation involves some kind of loss since the British education system, and hence A-levels, are not the same as in Arab countries.

Ex 3.82: '*Othello*' has been translated into the nearest Arabic name, which is similarly uncommon in Arabic, (عطيل *'uṭail*).

Ex 3.83: 'The Tube' and 'the Underground' have the Arabic cultural equivalent (مترو الأنفاق), that is *mitrū* of the tunnels. As can be seen, the first word 'metro' is used as a loan word which has been naturalised and became common usage, followed by a descriptive term to differentiate this type of 'metro' from the overground 'metro', which is used in some Arabic cities, like Cairo.

Names of institutions are directly translated if they are descriptive enough or replaced by a cultural equivalent if they are not.

Ex 3.84: 'Treasury', as has been discussed above, is used in Britain to refer to the Ministry of Finance. It can be translated into Arabic by the most common cultural equivalent as (وزارة المالية) or the less common equivalent may sound quite ambiguous (وزارة الخزانة), literally 'ministry of the treasury'.

Ex 3.85: 'Home Office', which is also used in Britain to refer to the 'Ministry of Interior'. This institutional name is usually translated by the common Arabic cultural substitution (وزارة الداخلية), 'the ministry of interior'.

Ex 3.86: 'House of Lords' can be rendered using the cultural equivalent (مجلس الشورى) while the 'House of Commons' can be rendered as (مجلس النواب) or (مجلس الأمة).

3.3.4 Functional equivalent (المقابل أو المرادف الوظيفي)

This strategy implies the use of a TL equivalent of the function of the ST-specific word to disambiguate it to the target readers. Newmark argues that 'for impact and for neatness, but not for accuracy, a TL cultural equivalent of an SL cultural term is always more effective than a culturally free functional equivalent, but it may be particularly misleading for legal terms' (1988/2003: 100). The use of both functional and cultural equivalence is common in dealing with many lexical issues in translating popular texts or for general readerships as they bring the ST closer to the readers, while academic texts and educated writing make more use of strategies which produce features of the ST into the TT.

Ex 3.87: '10 Downing Street' refers to the headquarters of the British government, and since it may not be known to the target readers, a functional equivalent can be used to make the meaning accessible to them, (مقر الحكومة البريطانية) that is (the headquarters of the British government). In a legal document, however, it may be more appropriate in the setting to use both transference and functional equivalent.

Note that a technical term which has no TL equivalent can be rendered using a functional equivalent (Newmark 1988/2003: 83). Dickins et al. (2002: 32), on the other hand, argue that

> where precise terms are important, one solution for the translators is to add a glossary at the end of the book or to use footnotes or endnotes. Alternatively, whether the translator decided that for some reason it is necessary to retain an SL term, but also make it plain to the reader roughly what is meant, it is sometimes possible to insert an explanation, or partial explanation, into the TT alongside the cultural borrowing, normally as unobtrusively as possible!

Note: All of the strategies mentioned in the above quote are explained and illustrated below.

3.3.5 Use of a superordinate (alternatively called 'use of a general word' or 'expansion') (استخدام لفظ شامل أو عام أو التوسع في نقل المعنى)

Use of a superordinate can create a translation issue, as has been explained under 3.2.6 above. It can, however, be used as a solution too. According to Baker (1992/2011: 23), using a general word to render a ST item is a common translation strategy, particularly in the area of propositional meaning. She further adds that this strategy works well in most languages since the hierarchical structure of semantic fields is not language-specific. Vinay and Darbelnet (1958/1995) name this strategy 'expansion'.

Ex 3.88: 'Apply cream on your skin' is translated into Arabic as (استخدمي الكريم علي بشرتك) 'put/use the cream on your skin'.

Ex 3.89: 'Shampoo your hair' poses an interesting translation challenge, which also relates to the issue discussed above under 'word formation'. In English, it is common for the same word to be used as either a verb or noun, which is not the case in Arabic, where nouns and verbs have different formation patterns. The word 'shampoo' poses an issue since it is used as a verb and Arabic does not have a ready equivalent for it. Here the solution may be the use of a general word such as (اغسل شعرك بالشامبو) 'wash your hair with shampoo' or (يغسل الشعر بالشامبو) 'the hair is washed with shampoo' (adapted from Baker 1992/2011: 24).

3.3.6 Use of a hyponym (alternatively called a 'neutral word', 'less expressive word', or 'reduction') (استخدام لفظ مندرج أو خاص أو كلمة محايدة أو أقل تعبيرا عن المعني أو اختزال المعنى)

The use of a hyponym or specific word can create a translation issue as explained under 3.2.7 above, but can also be used as a translation strategy. This strategy, called 'use of a more neutral/less expressive word' by Baker (1992/2011: 25) and 'reduction' by Vinay and Darbelnet (1958/1995), involves some kind of translation loss but is effective in rendering at least part of the meaning.

Ex 3.90: 'Archaic' can mean (عتيقة), which probably reflects the same strength of the English word. It can, however, be translated as (قديم), which means 'old', if need be in order to avoid the slightly negative implication of the SL word and its close translation.

Ex 3.91: 'Sexual relationships' can be directly translated into Arabic as (علاقات جنسية) which, based on the context in which it is used, may sound 'obscene', and a less expressive alternative (علاقات حميمية), meaning 'intimate relationships', may be used instead. This can also be seen as a case of euphemism (see above).

Ex 3.92: 'Ugly' is directly translated into Arabic as (قبيح), but it can be toned down to (غير جذاب) 'non-attractive'. Similar to the previous example, this rendering can be seen as a case of euphemism.

Ex 3.93: 'Mumble' means 'to utter words in a low confused indistinct manner'[26] and as such does not have a positive meaning. It can be rendered directly into Arabic as (غمغم) or (تمتم). It can also be toned down through the use of the more positive (يهمس), that is 'whisper', meaning 'to speak softly with little or no vibration of the vocal cords especially to avoid being overheard'.[27]

3.3.7 Paraphrase (sometimes called 'descriptive equivalent') (الشرح أو المقابل أو المرادف الوصفي)

In my view, this is one of the most common strategies, but one that comes at the cost of losing stylistic brevity. Elimam (2010) surveys cases in which this strategy seems to be the only available translation procedure and cases in which it is an optional strategy. Newmark calls this strategy 'descriptive equivalent' and explains that it involves the use of a translation that describes the ST word or concept to the readers. This strategy can be used when a description is more relevant or important than the function of the SL item (Newmark 1988/2003: 83–4, see also Baker 1992/2011: 36–9). I prefer to use 'paraphrase' over 'descriptive equivalent' since it is difficult to use the term 'equivalence' in a situation where the level of description can vary from one translator to another. Additional information, which is of interest to readers, according to Newmark (1993: 5), should be incorporated in the TL text rather than in a footnote.

Ex 3.94: 'Too' can be used in English as an adverb to imply 'to an excessive extent or degree; beyond what is desirable, fitting or right'.[28] 'Too' seems to lend itself easily to this particular strategy. For instance, 'investors who are too risk-averse to invest directly in shares' is translated as (المستثمرون الذين يتجنبون المخاطر بشكل كبير لدرجة أنهم لا يستثمرون في الأسهم) which can be back-translated as 'investors who avoid risks to a great degree, to the extent that they do not invest directly in shares', which features paraphrasing the meaning of 'too'.

Ex 3.95: 'The tea is too hot to drink' is translated as (الشاي ساخن لدرجة أنني لا أستطيع أن أشربه) 'the tea is hot to the extent that I cannot drink it'.

Ex 3.96: 'Unfortunately, this hope is more hogwash than Hogwarts' can be translated as (للأسف هذا الأمل كلام تافه أكثر منه تأثرا بسحر مدرسة هوجوارتز لتعليم السحر والشعوذة) which back-translates as 'unfortunately this hope is more nonsense than being influenced by the magic of the Hogwarts school for teaching magic and sorcery'. 'Hogwarts' is the school of magic which Harry Potter joins, which may not be known to the Arabic reader and, therefore, a paraphrase is necessary. In other words, paraphrasing unpacks for the TT reader what 'Hogwarts' is.

Ex 3.97: 'Samurai' (الساموراي) describes the Japanese aristocracy from the eleventh to nineteenth centuries whose function was to provide officers and administrators. Which equivalent is more salient in a given context is a decision that the translator will have to make (see Newmark 1988/2003: 84).

3.3.8 Transliteration (alternatively called 'borrowing', 'loanword' or 'transference') (النسخ الصوتي أو استعارة الكلمات أو نقلها من لغة أخرى)

This strategy is discussed by different scholars under different names. It is called 'transference' (النقل) (Catford 1965/1978: 35) or 'transliteration' (النسخ الصوتي) and 'transference' (النقل) by Newmark (1988/2003: 81, 84) and 'borrowing' (استعارة) by Baker (1992/2011: 33). This strategy involves writing the source language word using the orthography of the target language. Another variation of this procedure is to use a loan word or transliteration plus a classifier (تصنيف), alternatively called 'explanation' (وصف) (see Baker 1992/2011: 33; Vinay and Darbelnet 1958/1995). Note that the addition of a classifier is particularly helpful in enabling the target reader to identify what is being talked about.

Notwithstanding the terminology issue, this is a common procedure in literary translation, especially for the translation of peoples' and street names, titles (e.g. lord), areas (e.g. London), institutions (Islamic Aid), newspapers (Aljazeera), and so on. It is particularly common in journalistic as well as technical genres. This strategy is used when the TL features a lexical gap with respect to the SL item, or when the ST word is not familiar to the target readers. The use of a 'classifier' or 'explanation' depends on how unfamiliar the loan word sounds in the TL. See the following examples.

Ex 3.98: Names of periodicals and journals can be rendered in this manner (Newmark 1988/2003: 82). *The Guardian* is the name of an English national newspaper, which may not be well known to the target readers. It can be transliterated/transferred into Arabic, usually within quotes or brackets, as (الجارديان) or with a classifier/explanation as in (صحيفة الجارديان) '*The Guardian* newspaper', if the translator does not consider the word familiar enough to the target readers. The use of a 'classifier' (Newmark 1988/2003: 35), namely 'newspaper', here can help familiarise the readers with the SL word.

Ex 3.99: Geographical areas which do not have direct established translations can be translated with this strategy. For instance, 'Zealandia', the newly discovered continent, is transliterated as (زيلانديا).

Ex 3.100: Newly independent countries, for example, most countries formed after the dissolution of the USSR in 1991, are transliterated into Arabic: (جورجيا) 'Georgia' and (كازاخستان) 'Kazakhstan', 'Azerbaijan' (أذربيجان), 'Estonia' (إستونيا) and 'Moldova' (مولدوفا).

Ex 3.101: 'Cannelloni' can be transliterated as (الكانالوني), or transliterated together with a classifier as (طبق الكانالوني) or (طبق مكرونة الكانالوني), 'cannelloni dish' or 'cannelloni pasta dish', respectively, if the translator assumes it is not familiar to the target readers.

Ex 3.102: Titles of untranslated literary works can be transliterated, pending the appearance of an 'authorised' translation of the work. This is particularly useful in the context of discussing potential literary works to be translated, writer nominations for prizes and so on. For example, *The Removed*, title of a novel by Brandon Hobson (2021), can be transliterated as (ذا ريموفد) until an official or a published translation of the work appears.[29]

Ex 3.103: Some cultural words can be transliterated in the literary text for flavour, to attract target readers' attention or to create a bond between the TT and TT readers. For instance, the use of the word *hammam* in English rather than 'public bath' serves the purpose of retaining the flavour and distinctiveness of the SL word. According to Newmark (1988/2003: 82), cultural words can be transferred in some novels, essays and advertisements in order to 'give local colour, to attract the reader, to give a sense of intimacy between the text and the reader – sometimes the sound or the evoked image appears attractive'.

Ex 3.104: Flora (المجموعة النباتية) and fauna (المجموعة الحيوانية) are local and culture-specific and as such can be borrowed or transliterated into the TL unless the species are known by other names in the receiving culture, in which case direct translation or cultural substitution can be used.

Ex 3.105: Types of means of transport have become internationally known. Car brands are to be transliterated or borrowed only. For instance, 'Toyota' is transliterated into Arabic as (تويوتا).

Ex 3.106: Local historical and/or religious terms can be rendered by transliteration alone or together with a classifier. For instance, (الله أكبر) can be rendered as (the Islamic expression '*Allah-u Akbar*'). The use of a classifier, 'the Islamic expression', helps the target readers understand what kind of expression they are reading. In other contexts, a translation can also be provided: 'Allah is Great'.

Ex 3.107: Abbreviations of international organisations which can be read as words are transliterated into Arabic. For instance, UNESCO and FAO are transliterated as (يونسكو) and (فاو), respectively. Abbreviations which cannot be read out as words are spelt out in full in Arabic.

Ex 3.108: Proper names are usually transliterated into the TL. If there is a standard or a published spelling of a particular name, it should be used. If there is not, the translation commissioner should be consulted to confirm which spelling to use. Alternatively, the translator will have to do his or her best transliterating the SL proper names into the TT. For instance, (أحمد) is transliterated as either 'Ahmed' or 'Ahmad'. On some occasions, proper names are translated for no apparent reason. For instance, (ابن سينا) is known in English as 'Avicenna' rather than ibn sīnā, and (ابن رشد), pronounced as /ibn rushd/, as 'Averroes'. Proper names given as titles of fictional works need also to be transliterated: *Pamela* and *Shamela*, (باميلا) and (شاميلا), respectively.

On the other hand, transliteration of proper names, especially in literary works where peoples' names can help with the characterisation, may involve loss of the implied meaning of the name. Someone's name can possibly tell something about the person's socio-economic background. In an Arabic novel, *Zuqaq al-Midaq*, one of the main characters is called (كرشة) '*kirsha*'. This name can be easily transliterated into English, but a great deal of meaning will be lost. This name literally means 'animals' intestines' and using it as a person's name implies a poor and uneducated character, which indeed is the case in the novel. Along these lines, Newmark (1993/2003: 15) argues that '[i]n literature it has to be determined whether the name is real or invented'.

Ex 3.109: New coinages in English can be transliterated into Arabic. For example, 'Internet', 'Facebook' and 'Instagram' are transliterated, without a classifier, as they are known to the Arabic readers, as (إنترنت) (فيسبوك) and (إنستجرام), respectively.

Ex 3.110: (مكة) is the name of the holiest city in Islam. It is not only transliterated into English as 'Mecca', but is also used to mean 'a place that attracts people to it'.[30]

Ex 3.111: (حجاب) is also transliterated into many English dictionaries as *hijab*, meaning an Islamic head covering.

3.3.9 Naturalisation (تطويع أوتطبيع النطق أو الكتابة لقواعد لغة الترجمة)

This strategy implies adapting the SL word, whilst transliterating it, to the normal TL rules of pronunciation, morphology and/or orthography (Newmark 1988/2003: 82) as in the following examples.

Ex 3.112: 'Laptop' (لاب توب pronounced as */labtob/*), as well as other words featuring the letter 'p', which have been naturalised into Arabic, is pronounced with a 'b' instead since Arabic does not have the letter 'p'.

Ex 3.113: 'Vagabond', and similar English words featuring the letter 'v', which does not exist in Arabic, are transliterated with the closest Arabic letter, namely (ف) 'f', (فاجابوند / fagabond/). Note, however, that some Arabic speakers pronounce the letter 'v' as /v/ but they write it down as 'f'.

Ex 3.114: (برقع) features a letter which does not exist in English, (ع /ʿ/), and, therefore, the word is naturalised as 'burqa', meaning an Islamic face cover.

Ex 3.115: (الكحول) features the letter (ح /ḥ/), which also does not exist in English, and, therefore, it gets naturalised as 'alcohol'.

Ex 3.116: (الصُفة) is pronounced as */alṣuffa/*, referring to 'a raised, carpeted platform on which people sat',[31] and has been naturalised into English as 'sofa'.

3.3.10 Omission (الحذف)

This strategy can be particularly useful in dealing with SL words which do not really add to meaning or in producing target-oriented translations. Lexical candidates for translation by this strategy include: 'instead', 'otherwise', 'rather than', and 'though'.

Ex 3.117: 'A-Can I borrow your pen? B-Which one though?' can be translated as (أ- هل أعرتني قلمك؟ ب - أيهم/أي قلم؟), which back-translates as 'which one/pen'. This translation omits 'though' and sounds natural in Arabic.

Ex 3.118: 'The collection is already creating interest' can be translated as (المجموعة لاقت اهتماما) 'the collection is creating interest' (adapted from Baker 1992/2011: 43). 'Already' does not add to the meaning as such and can be omitted in favour of producing a smooth-reading translation.

Ex 3.119: 'Real-life detail' can be translated into Arabic as (بالتفصيل) 'in detail' (adapted from Baker 1992/2011: 42).

Ex 3.120 'Take a shot' is rendered into Arabic as (يصوب) 'to shoot', a translation which omits 'take', but sounds natural in Arabic. See the discussion of nominalisation and verbalisation above.

Ex 3.121: 'I am a teacher' is rendered into Arabic as (أنا مدرس) which can be back-translated literally as 'I teacher', featuring the omission of 'am' and 'a'. This is because verb 'to be' in the present tense (alternatively called 'copular be') should not be rendered since it is implied in the Arabic verb conjugation and Arabic nouns do not need an article before them.

Similarly, omission can be used, in the right context, to deal with idioms which are too culture-specific or too complex to be understood by the TT readers if rendered closely, provided the gain realised from omitting the idiom, for example achieving a fluent TT, outweighs the ensuing loss of meaning.

3.3.11 Compensation (التعويض)

This strategy can be used to make up for the loss of SL meaning, sound-effect, metaphor, pragmatic effect, or stylistic effect, amongst others (see also Newmark 1988/2003: 90). This will be illustrated in the following examples.

Ex 3.122: Referring back to the example of (كرشة/*kirsha*/), the translator, if he or she decides to transliterate it into English, may consider compensating for the lost nuance of meaning through some other means, for instance, by unpacking the reference of this name in the body of the text, for example, in a footnote, or as an in-text gloss.

Ex 3.123: (إِنِ الْحُكْمُ إِلَّا لِلَّهِ عَلَيْهِ تَوَكَّلْتُ وَعَلَيْهِ فَلْيَتَوَكَّلِ الْمُتَوَكِّلُون) (Qur'an 12: 67)

Gloss: Indeed judgement is for none except Allah, <u>in-Him</u> I-put-my-trust, and <u>in-Him</u> let-those-who-trust put-their-trust.

Bewley and Bewley's translation: 'for judgement comes from no one but Allah. In Him I put my trust, and let all those who put their trust, put it in Him alone.' (1999/2005: 224)

Al-Bayḍāwī, a classical commentator of the Qur'an, is of the opinion that the object (عَلَيْهِ) 'in Him', underlined above, is foregrounded in the last two clauses of the Qur'anic verse above before (تَوَكَّلْتُ) 'I put my trust' and (فَلْيَتَوَكَّلِ الْمُتَوَكِّلُونَ) 'let those who trust put their trust' for specification: people should rely on Allah specifically. Bewley and Bewley use regular, unmarked word order and a lexical item, namely alone, to compensate for the verse's stylistic function: (وَعَلَيْهِ فَلْيَتَوَكَّلِ الْمُتَوَكِّلُونَ) is rendered as 'and let all those who put their trust, put it in Him *alone*' (2005: 224, my emphasis).

3.3.12 In-text glosses (إضافة معلومات بين قوسين لتقريب المعنى)

This translation strategy features the insertion of extra, but essential, information, which does not exist in the ST, usually between brackets by the translator to explain SL terms or concepts, disambiguate meaning, or provide comment on linguistic issues, amongst other considerations. This strategy, which can be used together with any of the strategies discussed above, can be distracting, like footnotes, but it depends on the overall approach adopted by the translator and the expectations of the target readership. For instance, Hilali and Khan's English translation of the Qur'an features a considerable number of both footnotes and in-text glosses in which they refer to hadith (Prophetic traditions) and provide other relevant information to the readers (1977/1998). In addition, the translators specifically use in-text glosses to use some honorific phrases such as (صلى الله عليه وسلم) 'May God's peace and grace be upon him' and (عليه السلام) 'May God's peace be upon him', following Prophets' names, as well as 'رضي الله عنه/عنها/عنهم' (May Allah be pleased with him/her/them), after the names of the Prophet Muhammad's companions and some other figures whose names or stories are mentioned in the Qur'an. It is worth noting that mentioning these phrases after names of the Prophets and other individuals mentioned in the Qur'an or hadith is standard Muslim practice, whether in oral or written forms of communication. But it is noteworthy also that the expressed translation approach of Hilali and Khan is 'paraphrastic', which allows them to add extra information whether in the form of in-text glosses or footnotes (see the figure below).

3.3.13 Footnotes (حاشية سفلية)

This strategy can be used on its own or together with any of the strategies discussed above for the addition of extra information considered by the translator to be important for the understanding of the TT. Some theorists and translators argue that footnotes, however, should be kept to a minimum since they can be distracting to the readers and may only be supplied when absolutely necessary. For example, Hilali and Khan's translation features elaborate footnotes quoted from a number of Islamic resources, namely, (الطبرى) *Al-Ṭabarī*, *Al-Qurṭubī* (القرطبي), *Ibn Kathīr* (ابن كثير), *Sahīh Al-Bukhārī* (صحيح البخاري), to provide exegetical notes on the relevant verses (see the figure below). It is interesting to note that in another research

Sūrat 2. Al-Baqarah 14 Part-1

***Sūrat Al-Baqarah* (The Cow) II**

In the Name of Allāh,
the Most Gracious, the Most Merciful.

1. *Alif-Lām-Mīm.* [These letters are one of the miracles of the Qur'ān and none but Allāh (Alone) knows their meanings.]

2. This is the Book (the Qur'ān), whereof there is no doubt, a guidance to those who are *Al-Muttaqūn* [the pious and righteous persons who fear Allāh much (abstain from all kinds of sins and evil deeds which He has forbidden) and love Allāh much (perform all kinds of good deeds which He has ordained)].

3. Who believe in the *Ghaib*(1) and perform *As-Salāt* (*Iqāmat-as-Salāt*),(2) and spend out of what we have provided for them [i.e. give

(1) (V.2:3): *Al-Ghaib*: literally means a thing not seen. But this word includes vast meanings: Belief in Allāh, Angels, Holy Books, Allāh's Messengers, Day of Resurrection and *Al-Qadar* (Divine Preordainments). It also includes what Allāh and His Messenger ﷺ informed about the knowledge of the matters of past, present, and future, e.g., news about the creation of the heavens and earth, botanical and zoological life, the news about the nations of the past, and about Paradise and Hell.

(2) (V.2:3): *Iqāmat-as-Salāt* إقامة الصلاة : The performance of *Salāt* (prayers). It means that:

a) Every Muslim, male or female, is obliged to offer his *Salāt* (prayers) regularly five times a day at the specified times; the male in a mosque in congregation and the female at home. As the Prophet ﷺ has said: "Order your children to perform *Salāt* (prayers) at the age of seven and beat them (about it) at the age of ten." The chief (of a family, town, tribe) and the Muslim rulers of a country are held responsible before Allāh in case of non-fulfillment of this obligation by the Muslims under their authority.

b) One must offer the *Salāt* (prayers) as the Prophet ﷺ used to offer them with all their rules and regulations, i.e., standing, bowing, prostrating, sitting, as he ﷺ has said: "Offer your *Salāt* (prayers) the way you see me performing them." (See *Sahih Al-Bukhāri, Hadīth* No. 631 and 7246.) [For the characteristics of the *Salāt* (prayer) of the Prophet ﷺ see *Sahih Al-Bukhāri, Hadīth* Nos. 735, 736, 737, 766, 823, 824].

Sūrat 2. Al-Baqarah 15 Part-1

Zakāt,(1) spend on themselves, their parents, their children, their wives, and also give charity to the poor and also in Allāh's Cause — *Jihād*].

4. And who believe in (the Qur'ān and the *Sunnah*)(2) which has been sent down (revealed) to you (Muhammad ﷺ) and in that which was sent down before you [the Taurāt (Torah) and the Injīl (Gospel)] and they believe with certainty in the Hereafter. (Resurrection, recompense of their good and bad deeds, Paradise and Hell).

5. They are on (true) guidance from their Lord, and they are the successful.

6. Verily, those who disbelieve, it is the same to them whether you (O Muhammad ﷺ) warn them or do not warn them, they will not believe.

7. Allāh has set a seal on their hearts and on their hearing, (i.e. they are closed from accepting Allāh's Guidance), and on their eyes there is a covering. Theirs will be a great torment.

8. And of mankind, there are some (hypocrites) who say: "We believe in Allāh and the Last Day" while in fact they believe not.

(1) (V.2:3) *Zakāt* زكاة : A certain fixed proportion of the wealth and of every kind of the property liable to *Zakāt* of a Muslim to be paid yearly for the benefit of the poor in the Muslim community. The payment of *Zakāt* is obligatory as it is one of the five pillars of Islām. *Zakāt* is the major economic means for establishing social justice and leading the Muslim society to prosperity and security. [See *Sahih Al-Bukhāri*, Book of *Zakāt*, No. 24]

(2) (V.2:4) Narrated Ibn 'Umar رضي الله عنهما: Allāh's Messenger ﷺ said: Islām is based on (the following) five (principles):

1. To testify that "*Lā ilāha illallāh wa anna Muhammad-ur-Rasūl Allāh*" (none has the right to be worshipped but Allāh and that Muhammad ﷺ is the Messenger of Allāh).
2. *Iqāmat-as-Salāt*: to perform the five (compulsory congregational) *Salāt* (prayers).
3. To pay *Zakāt*.
4. To perform *Hajj* (i.e. pilgrimage to Makkah).
5. To observe *Saum* (fasting) during the month of Ramadan.

(*Sahih Al-Bukhāri, Hadith* No. 8).

Figure 3.1 Hilali and Khan's use of in-text glosses and footnotes to provide extra information about the meaning of Qur'anic verses (1977/1998)

I found out that most readers of the translations of the Qur'an prefer editions featuring in-text glosses and footnotes to provide extra information about relevant verses (see Elimam 2017). Whether readers of translated literature share the same opinion or not, it needs to be established.

3.3.14 Use of two or more strategies simultaneously (استخدام استراتيجيتين أو أكثر معا)

The translator may decide to use more than one strategy at a time due to different contextual factors or because he or she considers one strategy not enough to reproduce a rendering which fulfils the translator's aim. When translating from English into Arabic, and probably other languages, the translator may decide to render specific words or concepts, for example, via transliteration and translation. For instance, see the discussion of 3.3.12 and 3.3.13 above. This strategy is common with new scientific terms which do not yet have established Arabic translations, or cultural words which need to be communicated to the readers as closely as possible (see Newmark 1988/2003: 91).

Ex 3.124: 'Requirements Engineering' is translated into Arabic as 'Requirements Engineering (هندسة المتطلبات)' (Elimam 2008). This translation features the use of the terms in English, a loan translation, in addition to a literal translation of the term into Arabic.

3.4 Conclusion

This chapter has explored the most common lexical issues that translators come across and analysed and illustrated the strategies available to deal with them. As has been made clear in the discussions above, there are numerous lexical issues that the translator may face while rendering literary texts between Arabic and English and, indeed, any other language pair. Identifying the issue in question is a prerequisite to selecting the suitable translation strategy. It was also emphasised throughout the chapter that the selection of which strategy to use needs to be in line with the overall translation approach, which is itself a direct result of establishing the *skopos* of the translation. Note also that literal translation does not result in what some translators, particularly newly qualified ones, consider as 'faithful' translation, and that deviation from a close translation approach may indeed be the best approach in the relevant context. Below is a summary of these issues and strategies.

Lexical translation issues

1. Types of lexical meaning
2. Complex lexical items
3. Context-dependent vs context-free words
4. Culture-specific words (alternatively called 'loaded words')
5. A word's range of meaning
6. Use of a superordinate (or a general word)
7. Use of a hyponym (or a specific word)
8. Difference in interpersonal or physical perspective (alternatively called 'modulation')
9. Word formation
10. Use of foreign/loan words
11. False friends
12. Dialect and idiolect
13. Forms of address
14. Neologism
15. Words with competing translations
16. Gestures
17. Humour

Translation strategies for lexical issues

1. Direct equivalent
2. Literal translation (alternatively called 'through-translation' or 'calque')
3. Cultural equivalent (alternatively called 'cultural substitution')
4. Functional equivalent
5. Use of a superordinate (alternatively called 'use of a general word' or 'expansion')
6. Use of a hyponym (alternatively called a 'neutral word' or 'less expressive word' or 'reduction')
7. Paraphrase
8. Transliteration (alternatively called 'borrowing', 'loanword' or 'transference')
9. Naturalisation
10. Omission
11. Compensation
12. In-text glosses
13. Footnotes
14. Use of two or more strategies simultaneously

It is worth mentioning that the same word-level issue may be dealt with in several different ways through the use of some of the strategies above. Choice of which strategy is more appropriate ultimately rests with the translator, based on the overall translation approach, target readers' expectations, the purpose of translation and so on. Here is an example that lends itself to several renditions.

'A-levels': this is a term which refers to a stage in the British education system which does not match the education system adopted in Arab countries. This can be translated as follows:

Use of a loan translation: *A-levels*.

Use of transliteration and naturalisation: (إيه ليفل), since the Arabic alphabet does not have the letter 'v', the closest Arabic letter 'f' is used.

Use of a cultural equivalent: (الثانوية العامة) 'high/secondary school'.

Use of a paraphrase: (عامين من الدراسة بعد المرحلة المتوسطة وقبل الالتحاق بالجامعة) 'two years of study after secondary school and before joining university'.

Use of functional equivalent: (امتحانات التأهيل للجامعة) 'university qualifying exams'.

Use of transliteration alone or in addition to any of the versions above.

Use of literal translation in addition to any of the versions above.

Note that translation aims at communicating the meanings of texts, not individual words, and that it is always difficult to translate a word out of context. Note also that concrete words may be easier to render than abstract words. Attention should also be paid to context-bound words since those require deciphering the relevant meaning each time the translator comes across them. Finally, the issue of multiplicity of terms used in the relevant literature to refer to the same translation issue and strategy needs to be taken into consideration when writing annotations or commentary on translation. That is why I have tried to provide as many of these terms as possible to spare readers potential confusion that could result from reading other coursebooks.

3.5 Exercises

3.5.1 The following text, entitled 'Three Culture Vultures Hit the Tracks', was used by the EU Commission in their annual competition to reward the best young translators in the European Union (2018).[32] Read the text carefully before translating it into Arabic. Note that translating this text would pose many of the lexical challenges discussed in this chapter. Identify as many challenges as possible and consider which translation strategies you would use to deal with them. It will also be a good idea to explain why you would choose one strategy rather than the other, especially for university students who will be required to write commentaries on their translation.

Tips: Before translating the text, decide, first of all, which translation approach you are going to use, bearing in mind that this will influence your choice of translation strategies throughout the process. For example, consider the informal tone in which the text is written and think whether you will be able/want to communicate it into Arabic and how: how will you render the informal greeting 'hi' and all the contractions of the auxiliary verbs, which are all markers of informality? Think how you would translate the foods and drinks mentioned in the text.

Note that the strategies you need to deal with some of the issues you will come across in the text below, for example, translating idioms and cohesive devices are discussed in later chapters. Therefore, for now, try to focus on the issues that you encounter at a lexical level only.

> Three Culture Vultures Hit the Tracks
>
> Hi there Katy and Anna,
>
> Usually when my Dad is banging on about the 'good old days', I just pretend to be listening. But he's had a tempting idea about how we could celebrate finishing our A-levels when we leave school, before we all go our separate ways. He suggested we take a leaf out of his book – it turns out that when he was eighteen, he bought an Interrail pass with a couple of his friends and travelled by train from place to place in Europe. This would have been in the 1980s, when half of Europe was

behind the Iron Curtain, shrouded in mystery for teenagers from the West. To travel to quite a few countries you needed to apply in advance for a visa, which meant jumping through several hoops. Their idea was to glimpse some European culture, though I can't help but wonder how much culture he did actually get to see.

It's funny what sticks in your mind, my Dad said, vividly describing how they spent a night on the floor of a train station in Nice. Apparently the youth hostel was full and there was nowhere left for Dad and his friends to go. You need to keep in mind that this was ages before we all became glued to our smartphones, and instead they got all their travel info from a single paper guidebook, which pretty much says it all. That must have been kind of insane, don't you think?

Then there was the time when Dad and his mates were in Budapest, and they decided on a big splurge of a meal with goulash, chocolate pancakes – the works (and probably a glass or three of red wine too, knowing Dad). They tried to give the waiter a tip at the end of the meal by leaving some money on the table when they left, but the waiter chased after them to give them their tip back. I can't imagine that happening anywhere now!

I asked him: 'So Dad, what about all those museums and galleries you were supposed to be visiting?'

He said that after Nice they took a train to Padua in Italy. They walked in the heat of the afternoon to a chapel that had a good write-up in their guidebook. Inside the chapel it was cool and dark and on the walls, illuminated, were the most marvellous frescoes painted by Giotto of the Last Judgement and other scenes, in the brightest blue and orange and purple. There was something about the way the painter handled perspective that drew you into the frescoes and made you feel, Dad said, sort of 'part of them'. It turns out that all those years ago Dad did find some culture after all!

So, girls, what do you say? Are you up for going Interrailing this summer?

3.5.2 The following short story aims to boost children's self-confidence as the title clearly indicates, (الثقة بالنفس). Translate it into English while paying attention to the lexical translation challenges discussed above.

Tips: After deciding on a translation approach, identify the most challenging issues rendering this text would pose at a lexical level. For example, do you think (بعد تصحيحها و إعطاء الدرجات) include some kind of repetition which can be eliminated in the translation in line with English translation norms? Note that the issue of grammatical gender, for example, (المعلمة) 'female teacher' and (طالب) 'male pupil', will be discussed in Chapter 4.

الثقة بالنفس

في يوم من الأيام كان هناك طالبا بالمرحلة الابتدائية لا يثق بنفسه ولا بقدراته إذ أنه في يوم جاءت مدرسة الفصل لتوزع ورقة الإجابة بعد تصحيحها وإعطاء الدرجات، وبمجرد أن استلم ذلك الطالب ورقته وجد نفسه لم يحصل إلا على درجتين من عشرين، لم يكن هم الطالب إلا إخفاء درجته لكيلا يعلمها والداه فقام برسم ديناصور كبير في منتهى الجمال شمل الورقة كليا. وخبأ أسفله الأسئلة والإجابات عنها وأيضا درجته التي استاء منها.

هنا لاحظت المعلمة ما فعله الطالب وبراعته في الرسم، فأخبرت جميع طلاب الفصل بأنهم في إمكانهم تحسين درجاتهم وقسمت الفصل إلى مجموعات، ولكنها لاحظت أن الطالب لا يهتم لأمرها ولا إلى ما تقول على الرغم من أنها تفعل كل ذلك من أجله، رفعت صوتها ونادت عليه باسمه وأخبرته بمجموعته وبعنوان مشروعهم، وقد كان عن الوحوش المفترسة.

خاف الطالب من النطق بأية كلمة حينما كان بقية طلاب مجموعته كلا منهم يبدي رأيه ويتحدث عن فكرته على حده، جلس صامتا لا يبدي أي رأي، هنا لاحظه طالبا من مجموعته وأخبره ببعض الكلمات التشجيعية محفزا إياه ولكنه مازال خائفا ولا يثق في نفسه ذرة واحدة حتى اقتربت منه المعلمة وسألته إن كان يحتاج إلى مساعدة، تلعثم الطالب المسكين في الكلام، سألته المعلمة برفق عن إمكانيته في إبداء أي فكرة وكل شيء في دنيانا قابل للصواب وللخطأ أيضا؛ أخبرها الطالب أنه لا يعرف أي معلومات عن الوحوش، ثم صمت لبرهة وسألها هل بإمكانه رسم ديناصور، أجابته المعلمة فرحة: " نعم يمكنك فعل ذلك فالديناصور من الوحوش."

لم يتبقَ من الوقت إلا دقائق معدودات، أمسك الطالب بورقته الفارغة على الفور وبكل همة ونشاط وجد واجتهاد بدأ في رسم ديناصوره، والمعلمة ترقبه من بعيد، وما هي إلا دقائق قليلات حتى أنهى الطالب رسمته الجميلة التي من شدة روعتها وبراعته في رسمها كادت أن تنطق، لقد لونها بالألوان الزاهية التي تتيح لها إمكانية ككونها حقيقية.

سُر كل من رآها، حقا لقد كانت في روعة الجمال والكمال، فخر طلاب المجموعة من كونه معهم، وتحاوط عليه الطلاب من كل اتجاه يبتغون رؤية رسمته التي شهد لها الجميع، لم يشهد الطالب مشهدا رائعا كهذا طوال فترة تعليمه، استعاد بها ثقته في نفسه التي كان قد فقدها من فترة طويلة.

3.5.3 The following is the introductory paragraphs of *The Power and the Glory* by Graham Green (1940). Translate it into Arabic.

Tips: This is the introduction of one of Graham's most famous novels which revolves around the feeling of inadequacy and psychological torture. This passage is quite descriptive as it sets the scene for the novel. Make sure that your translation communicates the detailed description to the target readers. Consider how you will render colloquial words, e.g. 'shabby' and 'tiny', and loan words, e.g. 'Buenos días', into Arabic. Similar to the other exercises in this chapter, some translation issues, for instance, the metaphoric expression 'he wasn't carrion yet', will be dealt with in later chapters.

> MR. TENCH went out to look for his ether cylinder: out into the blazing Mexican sun and the bleaching dust. A few buzzards looked down from the roof with shabby indifference: he wasn't carrion yet. A faint feeling of rebellion stirred in Mr. Tench's heart, and he wrenched up a piece of the road with splintering fingernails and tossed it feebly up at them. One of them rose and flapped across the town: over the tiny plaza, over the bust of an ex-president, ex-general, exhuman being, over the two stalls which sold mineral water, towards the river and the sea. It wouldn't find anything there: the sharks looked after the carrion on that side. Mr. Tench went on across the plaza.
>
> He said 'Buenos días' to a man with a gun who sat in a small patch of shade against a wall. But it wasn't like England: the man said nothing at all, just stared malevolently up at Mr. Tench, as if he had never had any dealings with the foreigner, as if Mr. Tench were not responsible for his two gold bicuspid teeth. Mr. Tench went sweating by, past the Treasury which had once been a church, towards the quay. Half-way across he suddenly forgot what he had come out for—a glass of mineral water? That was all there was to drink in this prohibition state—except beer, but that was a government monopoly and too expensive except on special occasions. An awful feeling of nausea gripped Mr. Tench in the stomach—it couldn't have been mineral water he wanted. Of course, his ether cylinder ... the boat was in. He had heard its exultant piping when he lay on his bed after lunch. He passed the barbers' and two dentists' and came out between a warehouse and the customs onto the river bank.

3.5.4 Below is a prose excerpt from a recent collection of Arabic texts by different authors (ألم يَجدكَ يَتيمًا فآوى) 'Did He not find you an orphan and give refuge?' a Qur'anic verse, (93: 6).[33] The passage is entitled (يتيمة الحرب) 'War's Orphan'. In line with the title, the main theme of the story is the struggle of orphans. With this in mind, translate this passage into English using appropriate translation strategies and an overall approach.

Tips: The volume focuses on the struggle of the orphans and the passage below stresses the role of war in aggravating their feelings of loneliness and emotional deprivation. Your aim should be to communicate these feelings to the target readers. Therefore, your adopted translation approach, for instance, a domesticating or communicative translation approach, should help you express the nuances of meaning packed in the source text. Consider also how you are going to deal with the rhyming of some of the sentences, for instance, (الإرادة), (الحجارة) and (الخلابة) end in /ha/, and whether or not you are going to mirror the layout and the punctuation of the passage into English.

يتيمة الحرب

رأيتها بين الركام نائمة مسلوبة القوة والإرادة.
،أبعدت عنها تلك الحجارة
وكان التراب قد غطى ملامحها الخلابة..
صغيرة جدا على الهلاك!

سحبتها برفق خوف أن تتكسر عظامها
وأبعدت عن وجهها كل التراب، لكنها مازالت نائمة تلك
الملاك . . .
انتابني خوف دفين، فالموت يرهب مهما كان حق اليقين.
وضعت أذني على صدرها؛ فسمعت نبضات وأنين.
كان حزني بقدر فرحتي، وصراخي أيقظ جميع النائمين!
سقيتها ماء باردا من قنينتي وأحسست أنها زهرة لم ترتو من سنين!
لكن صدمتي كبرت عندما فتحت عينان كالسماء الزرقاء في الصباح!
كلمات قليلة نطقت بها: - أين أمي وأبي وكل عائلتي؟
ماذا أقوا لطفلة؟ هل أخبرها أنها الوحيدة التي بقيت على قيد الحياة؟
لم أستطع ذلك فأخبرتها أنهم ذهبوا لإحضار الغداء.

أحلام طه حسين

Notes

1. <http://www.almaany.com/en/dict/ar-en/incapacitated/> (last accessed 20 January 2021)
2. <https://dictionary.cambridge.org/dictionary/english/appreciation> (last accessed 21 January 2021)
3. <http://www.thefreedictionary.com/appreciation> (last accessed 20 January 2021)
4. <https://www.marketwatch.com/story/why-the-u-s-dollar-continues-to-rise-defying-a-2021-consensus-trade-11616701621> (last accessed 20 January 2021)
5. <http://www.thefreedictionary.com/Table> (last accessed 10 June 2021)
6. https://www.almaany.com/ar/dict/ar-ar/%D8%B9%D9%8A%D9%86/ (last accessed 10 June 2021)
7. <https://www.almaany.com/ar/dict/ar-ar/%D9%82%D8%B5/> (last accessed 10 June 2021)
8. <https://www.merriam-webster.com/dictionary/culture> (last accessed 10 June 2021)
9. <http://dictionary.reference.com/browse/super+ordinate> (last accessed 10 June 2021)
10. <http://dictionary.reference.com/browse/hyponym%20?s=t> (last accessed 10 June 2021)
11. <http://www.almaany.com/home.php?word=retrievable> (last accessed 10 June 2021)
12. <http://www.almaany.com/home.php?language=arabic&word=drinkable&lang_name=English&type_word=0&dspl=0> (last accessed 11 May 2021)
13. <http://www.thefreedictionary.com/legalese> (last accessed 11 May 2021)
14. <https://al-maktaba.org/book/11243/105> (last accessed 10 July 2021)
15. <http://french.about.com/od/vocabulary/a/fauxamis-a.htm> (last accessed 20 June 2019)
16. <https://www.almaany.com/ar/dict/ar-en/professor/> (last accessed 10 July 2021)
17. <http://www.thefreedictionary.com/Dialect> (last accessed 10 July 2021)
18. <http://www.thefreedictionary.com/idiolect> (last accessed 10 July 2021)
19. <http://www.merriam-webster.com/dictionary/neologism> (last accessed 11 May 2021)
20. <http://www.wordreference.com/enar/domino%20effect> (last accessed 10 July 2021)
21. <http://www.wordreference.com/enar/cold> (last accessed 10 July 2021)
22. <http://www.oxforddictionaries.com/definition/english/phrasal-verb> (last accessed 7 August 2021)
23. <http://www.merriam-webster.com/dictionary/work%20out> (last accessed 7 August 2021)
24. <http://www.dictionary.com/browse/euphony> (last accessed 7 August 2021)
25. <https://vicarofdibley.fandom.com/wiki/Jim_Trott> (last accessed 7 August 2021)
26. <https://www.merriam-webster.com/dictionary/mumble> (last accessed 7 August 2021)
27. <https://www.merriam-webster.com/dictionary/whisper> (last accessed 7 August 2021)
28. <http://dictionary.reference.com/browse/too> (last accessed 7 August 2021)
29. <https://www.goodhousekeeping.com/life/entertainment/g34931305/best-books-2021/> (last accessed 7 August 2021)
30. <https://www.vocabulary.com/dictionary/mecca> (last accessed 7 August 2021)
31. <https://www.indy100.com/article/arabic-english-words-roots-same-etymology-learn-language-amazing-7624371> (last accessed 5 Febuary 2020)
32. <https://ec.europa.eu/info/sites/info/files/education/events/documents/juvenes-translatores_2018_text_en_english_0.pdf> (last accessed 7 August 2021)
33. <تحميل كتاب ألم يجدك يتيما فآوى PDF - مكتبة نور (noor-book.com)> (last accessed 19 August 2022)

CHAPTER 4
STRUCTURAL TRANSLATION ISSUES AND STRATEGIES

4.1 Introduction

The previous chapter dealt with lexical translation issues and the strategies available to deal with them (مشكلات الترجمة علي مستوى الكلمة واستراتيجياتها), depending, as always, on the *skopos* of the translation, the translation approach and target readership, amongst other factors. Focusing on the structural level (phrase, sentence and clause), this chapter continues the micro-level discussion, focusing on structural translation issues and available strategies (مشكلات الترجمة علي مستوى الجملة واستراتيجياتها). Grammar rules determine how lexical items are combined to form phrases, clauses and sentences in order to express meaning. Jakobson (1959: 235–6) argues that 'the grammatical pattern of a language (as opposed to its lexical stock) determines those aspects of each experience that must be expressed in the given language'. Some of these grammatical rules are universal and therefore do not cause problems in translation; others, however, are language-specific. This latter category can be particularly challenging to deal with when the languages in question are very different grammatically as is the case with Arabic and English. Further, 'differences in grammatical structures of the source and target languages often result in some change in the information content of the message during the process of translation' (Baker 1992/2011: 95). This situation is further accentuated by the necessary chunking and rechunking of structures, particularly at sentence level, which often results in loss, addition or variation in the information content being communicated to the target readers. Below I expound the most common issues that occur at structural level while translating literary texts between Arabic and English, namely, word order variation (بناء الجملة أو التقديم والتأخير), passive structure (أسلوب البناء للمجهول), (الإضافة *iḍāfa*) structure, grammatical gender (التذكير والتأنيث), grammatical number (الإفراد والتثنية والجمع), definiteness (التعريف والتنكير) and collocations (المتلازمات اللفظية).

4.2 Word order variation (ترتيب الجملة)

Both Arabic and English have regular word order for declarative sentences (الجمل الإنشائية أو الخبرية) which are used in normal circumstances. In some cases, however, users of both languages can, and do, deviate from regular, unmarked word order to use marked word order, albeit more so in Arabic than English, which helps them emphasise and place focus on a specific element in the sentence. I provide below a detailed account of this notion of markedness in both Arabic and English for its effect on meaning and hence its relevance to translation.

4.2.1 Marked word order in Arabic (التقديم والتأخير)

Arabic features two types of sentence structures, verbal and nominal (الجملة الفعلية والجملة الاسمية). The verbal sentence is the default type (when there is a verb in the sentence), and its unmarked word order is verb-subject-complement (al-Makhzūmī 1966). To elaborate, a verbal structure starts with a verb or part of a verbal group, followed by a subject and/or complement. The subject of a verbal sentence may be free-standing (a noun or an independent pronoun), or dependent (consisting of one or more bound morphemes which form part of the verb). Note that a single orthographic word in Arabic may realise both verb and subject or verb and object. Similar to English, the complement in Arabic can be an object, adjective/adjectival phrase, adverb/adverbial phrase, or prepositional phrase. A sentence may also have more than one of these types of complement, or none at all.

The second type of sentence in Arabic is the nominal sentence. This typically begins with a noun or nominal group followed by a predicate (al-Makhzūmī 1966: 148ff., see also Elimam 2020, 2013 and 2009). Unlike the subject of a verbal sentence, the subject of a nominal sentence must be free-standing (whether a noun or pronoun). The predicate can be a noun, pronoun, adjective/adjectival phrase, adverb/adverbial phrase, prepositional phrase or verb. The nominal sentence may or may not have a verb since Arabic does not use the copular 'be' in the present tense (Elimam 2020: 2–3; 2013: 54–5).

In Arabic, a verbal structure is used as default and when the speaker or writer considers the action denoted by the verb more important than the doer himself or herself. For example, to tell a story, the speaker is more likely than not to start with the element which orients the audience as to the way the story is structured. If the story is about a certain character, then the character's name, as well as pronominal references to it, are likely to occur in sentence-initial position, while if the actions around which the story evolves are more important, verbs are likely to come in sentence-initial position for importance rather than emphasis (ibid. 68–9). English, on the other hand, features only a nominal sentence structure: subject-verb-complement; see under 4.2.2 below. As such, the subtleties of the verbal structures can be challenging to reproduce while translating from Arabic into English.

To elaborate this issue further, the unmarked order of either a nominal or a verbal sentence may be altered for grammatical necessity, in which case foregrounding will either be (واجب *wājib*) 'obligatory' (see Cantarino 1974: 8ff., 42ff.; Ibn Hishām 1963: 124f., 184f.), or because the writer wishes to prepose a certain element before another to achieve a certain discursive function, in which case it is called (جائز *jā'iz*) 'optional'. This variation of word order allows for an element to be preposed to a marked position in either type of sentence. Grammarians consider a sentence starting with a noun nominal even if the predicate contains a verb. Scholars of (البلاغة *al-Balāgha*) 'the art of Arabic literary eloquence', who also adopt a similar distinction between the two types of sentence, attempt to describe the function of each structure and offer an explanation of why a nominal sentence rather than a verbal sentence is used. Further, Arabic marks words for case – case is signalled by the use of vowel markers, or diacritics, at the end of the word or by morphemes, which form part of the word. These intricate verb inflection and case-marking systems allow for flexibility of word order since the grammatical meaning does not depend completely on the position of the words in a sentence, but rather on case-marking (Elimam 2020: 2–3; 2013: 55–6).

Drawing on the works of renowned Arabic *al-Balāgha* scholars, Lāshīn (1978: 217) explains that every word has an unmarked position in the linear order of a sentence, depending on its linguistic function; a verb precedes a subject in a verbal sentence, and a subject precedes a predicate in a nominal sentence. He also explains that there may be reasons for foregrounding a specific constituent within a sentence. Deviation from unmarked word order (that is structures other than subject-predicate in nominal sentences and subject-verb-complement in verbal sentences) may realise a number of functions, including: specification (الاختصاص أوالتخصيص), restriction (الحصرأو القصر), emphasis (التوكيد أو التأكيد), importance (الأهمية أوالاهتمام), attention-setting (تنبيه أو إثارة انتباه السامع), denial (الإنكار), preserving parallelism (الحفاظ على النظم) and preserving rhyme (الحفاظ على القافية) (see Elimam 2020: 3; 2013: 56; 2009).

Ex 4.1: سعد فر من الميدان (Lāshīn 1978: 223)
TT: Sa'd escaped from the battlefield.

Al-Suyūṭī (1969: 187ff) and Lāshīn (1978: 223) maintain that foregrounding of a subject to form a nominal sentence, rather than a verbal sentence, when the predicate is a verbal phrase, can either achieve restriction or signal emphasis, depending on the context. Lāshīn (1978: 225–6) explains that in a structure where the subject is placed before the verb, the verb becomes restricted to the subject. In this case, emphasis stems from the fact that two subjects will exist in the sentence, the preposed subject as well as the subject clitic attached to the verb since Arabic conjugates verbs for the subject. Simultaneously implied will be negation that the action denoted by the verb was carried out by anyone other than the subject (Elimam 2013: 64).

According to the word order of the above example, emphasis is derived from dual reference to the subject, the proper name/subject Sa'd as well as the conjugation of the verb

(فر) 'lit. he escaped'. The negation that someone has performed the action denoted by the verb 'escaped' is implied. In other words, the subject rather than the verb in this sentence is being debated: the speaker is contesting the addressee who claims that the one who escaped is, say, 'Ali, or that both 'Ali and Sa'd escaped from the battlefield (Lāshīn 1978: 223). Given that Arabic has two types of sentence, the problem with the above translation is that it does not differentiate between the nominal word order above and the verbal word order of the same sentence (فر سعد من الميدان) 'escaped Sa'd from the battlefield'. It may be possible in some contexts to use an emphasis-creating technique in order to reflect preference for nominal rather than verbal structure, for example, a typographical device (*Sa'd* escaped from the battlefield) or the use of cleft- structure (It was Sa'd who escaped from the battlefield).

Speaking specifically about realising the function of *restriction* (حصر أو قصر) in negative clauses, Lāshīn (1978: 220ff.) and al-Jurjānī (1976: 153ff.) maintain that if a verb follows the negation particle, the action of the verb is denied to have been performed by the subject, but it remains unsaid whether the action has occurred at all (Elimam 2013: 65).

Ex 4.2: ما ضربت زيدا (al-Jurjānī 1976: 164)
Gloss: not I-hit Zayd
TT: I did not hit Zayd.

On the other hand, if a subject occurs before a verbal predicate, but at the same time after a negation particle, this structure purports restriction: the verbal predicate becomes restricted to the subject.

Ex 4.3: ما زيدا ضربت (al-Jurjānī 1976: 164)
Gloss: not Zayd I-hit
TT: It was not Zayd that I hit.

The above two examples demonstrate the use of the negation particle (ما) (roughly 'not') before an unmarked verbal sentence order and a marked nominal sentence, the latter featuring the foregrounding of the object before the verb and subject (Elimam 2013: 65).

The meaning clearly differs depending on the element which follows the negation particle. In the example above, (ضربت) 'I hit', which acts as both verb and subject, occurs after (ما) 'not'). The effect of this word order on meaning is that the speaker denies having hit Zayd, but it remains unsaid whether 'Zayd' was hit at all. In the example above, the object 'Zayd' occurs before (ضربت) 'I hit', acting as verb and subject, but after the negation particle. Through this marked word order, the speaker emphasises that he or she has hit someone, but denies it was Zayd that he or she has hit (al-Jurjānī 1976: 164, quoted in Elimam 2013: 65).

Strelkova (2012: 43) explains that failure to deal with the source language syntax effectively often leads to an 'awkward' translation. She adds that a translator 'should look for the reason(s) behind the function of the SL structures, then, starting with the function, translate the thought into the TL'. To explain, syntactic aspects should be treated 'as an aid to comprehension. If the particular SL structure provides a discursive function like emphasis, for example, the translator should find an equivalent and natural TL manner (lexical or semantic) to reproduce this function to the target readers' (ibid. 13).

As can be seen from the above discussion, words can imply extra meanings through the manner/structures in which they are strung together. It is the translator's job to understand not only the author's individual words, but his or her intention as well, and then communicate the meaning in the manner he or she deems best according to TL norms and target readers' expectations. Marked word order in one language may not be mirrored in the TL if the result would be awkward according to the grammatical features or rules of usage in that language. However, other target language resources can be deployed to compensate for the lost effect and/or meaning. Below I provide examples to illustrate how Arabic word order variations can be used to imply extra meaning.

Ex 4.4: إياكَ نعبدُ وإياكَ نستعين (Qur'an 1: 5)
Gloss: *You we-worship and (to) You we-turn-for-help.*
Ahmed Ali's Translation: You alone we worship, and to You alone turn for help. (1984: 11)

In this example from the Qur'an, the object of a verbal sentence is foregrounded to sentence-initial position, creating a marked word order. To explain, the object (إياك) 'You' is foregrounded before the verbs (نعبدُ) 'we worship' in the first clause and (نستعينُ) 'we turn for help' in the second clause. Note that both verbs are conjugated for pronominal reference and act as both verb and subject at the same time. Foregrounding in both cases realises the discursive function of *restriction*, meaning that both verbs are restricted to the foregrounded object: God (see Lāshīn 1978: 232; al-Suyūṭī 1969: 186; al-Makhzūmī 1966: 91). In other words, the two actions denoted by the verbs are restricted to God and by implication denied (negated) in relation to anyone else. Al-Suyūṭī (1969: 189) writes that most *al-Balāgha* scholars agree that an object, whether a proper name, an adverb or a prepositional phrase, can be foregrounded for *restriction*. He explains that the above word order means that we dedicate our worship and turn for help to God alone. To express the effect of this structure on the meaning of the *ayah*, Ahmed Ali also foregrounds the object 'You' and 'to You' respectively, and also uses a lexical strategy; he inserts the word 'alone'.

Ex 4.5: فريقاً هدى (Qur'an 7: 30)
TT: Some He has guided. (A. Y. Ali 1996: 351)

The verse above also features an example of foregrounding of the object for *restriction* (Ibn Hishām 1963: 186). The object (فريقاً) 'some' or 'group', comes before the verb (هدى) 'He-guided'. The effect on the meaning of this word order is that 'guidance' is *restricted* to 'some', meaning that emphasis is placed on the fact that guidance was only given to some. Negation of the possibility that this guidance has been given to all is simultaneously implied. Al-Zamalkānī (1974: 214–5) argues that the above example involves foregrounding the object in order, first and foremost, to draw attention to it, and secondly to emphasise it. These are not necessarily contradictory explanations since *al-Balāgha* scholars agree that lexical foregrounding always involves drawing attention and assigning more (عناية) 'care' to the foregrounded element. Unlike the example above, where Ahmed Ali uses both marked word order and a lexical strategy, A. Y. Ali here opts for mirroring the word order of the original insofar as the grammar of English allows him: he foregrounds the object 'some' by placing it in initial position in the clause, a similarly marked choice in English, which realises what is sometimes called 'contrastive focus', on the preposed element (see, for example, Tavangar 2003; Li and Xu 2003; Quirk 1997: 1377–8; Green 1982: 124–8).

To elaborate, Dahlgren (1998: 36) considers that focus 'presents what is relatively the most important or salient information in the given setting'. He also discusses new focus and contrastive focus: the former 'presents new information in declarative sentences to fill an information gap on the part of the listener' while contrastive focus has two subtypes: parallel and counter presupposition. Sandt and Bosch (1999: 298) adopt a rather complicated division of focus, which they divide into the following three types (1) psychological focus – entities in a discourse that both speaker's and addressee's attention is currently focused on; (2) semantic focus – information that is being predicated in relation to the topic; and (3) contrastive focus – imposed salience on a given constituent (often, but not necessarily, a topic) that the speaker wants to call the addressee's attention to in order to contrast it with other potential members of a relevant 'contrast set'. Under 'Emphasis', Swan (2005: 183–4) discusses focus and divides it into (1) emotive focus, which shows that we feel strongly about what we are saying (for instance, 'You do look nice today!') and (2) contrastive focus, which shows a contrast between true and false, or present and past, or a rule and an exception (for example, 'I don't do much sport now, but I did play football when I was young').

Cantarino (1974: 28) argues that the element to which more emphasis is given in the Arabic sentence is preposed to the sentence-initial position. The following is an example of a predicate being foregrounded for emphasis (see also Martín-Asensio 2002).

Ex 4.6: وَآيَةٌ لَّهُمُ اللَّيْلُ (Qur'an 36: 37)
Muhammad Ali's Translation: And a sign to them is the night. (1920: 860)

In this example, the predicate, (آية لهم) 'a sign for them', is foregrounded before the subject, (الليل) 'the night'. This word order places emphasis on the foregrounded predicate (Ibn Hishām 1963: 124). Here too, Muhammad Ali manages to reflect the same word order of the *ayah* and arguably realises the same function of foregrounding in his translation. He preposes the complement 'And a sign to them' before the subject 'the night', an equally marked word order in English.

Importance is another function of markedness identified in the literature on *al-Balāgha*. Al-*Balāgha* scholars maintain that speakers foreground what they consider more important. The subject may be foregrounded before the verb, that is to the initial position in a verbal sentence (al-Makhzūmī 1966: 91) and the predicate before the subject (ibid. 150) if they are assigned specific importance by the speaker/writer, or for attention-setting (al-Jurjānī 1976: 143ff.). For example, a verbal structure is used if the speaker/writer considers the action denoted by the verb more important than the doer himself/herself. As is the case with specification and restriction, the difference between emphasis and importance seems to be rather subtle. The speaker may choose to start with an element because he or she thinks it is more important than other elements, while placing emphasis on a certain element may be required if the speaker is, say, being challenged and thinks that he or she needs to emphasise a specific element in the relevant context. For example, to tell a story, the speaker is more likely than not to start with the element which orients the audience as to the way the story is structured. If the story is about a certain character, then the character's name, as well as pronominal references to it, are likely to occur in sentence-initial position, while if the actions around which the story evolves are more important, verbs are likely to come in sentence-initial position for importance rather than emphasis.

Ex 4.7: عندَ الامتحانِ يُكرمُ المرءُ أو يُهانُ (al-Makhzūmī 1966: 91)
Gloss: At the test, honoured the person or humiliated
TT: When put to the test, one is (either) honoured or humiliated.

This is an example of foregrounding an adverbial phrase complement to signal *importance*. The complement (عندَ الامتحان) 'when put to the test' is preposed before (يُكرمُ المرءُ أو يهانُ) 'one is (either) honoured or humiliated', where both (يُكرمُ) 'is honoured' and (يُهانُ) 'is humiliated', are verbs in the passive voice, while (المرءُ) 'one' is subject (or rather 'agent'). In my proposed translation, I managed to keep as close as possible to the word order of the Arabic sentence. Baldick (1991: 113) considers adverbial phrase foregrounding one of three forms of inversion in English. Preposing the adverbial phrase ('When put to the test' in this example) before the main clause sounds less marked in English than the above structure in Arabic.

4.2.2 Marked word order in English

The term covers word order inversion, quotation inversion, argument-reversal, shifting, preposing and postposing, *there*-insertion, and cleft and pseudo-cleft structures, which all result in marked word order. Note that marked word order in English is a catch-all term which means any form of word order other than subject-verb-complement. Markedness is achieved through 'foregrounding', which is the placement of an unexpected item in a certain position in the sentence (see Swan 2005; Birner and Ward 1998, Quirk 1997; Birner 1996). Halliday (1974: 112) defines foregrounding as 'prominence that is motivated ... [which] contributes to the writer's total meaning'. He argues that patterns of prominence can be found in poems or prose texts in the form of regularities in the sounds, words or structures that 'stand out in some way' (1974: 112). Cuddon (1991) suggests that foregrounding is used for aesthetic reasons or to attract the reader's attention not to what is being said but to the way it is said. Similarly, Fowler (1993: 98), defines foregrounding as a poetic device of linguistic deviation. Green (1982: 125) explains that foregrounding allows for more important information to appear first. She adds that this type of inversion is available for literary narratives but not conversational narratives.

Similarly, Baldick (1991: 113) explains that word order variation can help a poet to 'preserve the rhyme scheme or the metre of a verse line, or to place special emphasis on particular words'. Along these lines, Sandt and Bosch explain that markedness places focus on a specific item and define focus as a device which relates an utterance to a certain context 'by suggesting that the context provides salient alternatives for the expression in focus' (1999: 171). Halliday (1971/2002: 99) uses the term 'prominence' rather than focus and defines it as 'the name for the phenomenon of linguistic highlighting, whereby some linguistic feature stands out in some way'. Dahlgren (1998: 36) considers that focus 'presents what is relatively the most important or salient information in the given setting'.

In his discussion of the relationship between syntax and focus/prominence, Quirk agrees with the literature that cleft and pseudo-cleft sentences are devices for giving prominence to a certain item by 'more elaborate grammatical means, involving the division of the sentence into two clauses, each with its own verb' (1997: 1383). He rightly considers cleft sentences the most flexible in what it permits to be fronted: its structure makes it natural to place focus on any item in the sentence. He maintains that the cleft sentence indicates 'divided focus and which of the two focused items is new will depend on the context' (ibid. 1384).

In short, the literature on English syntax agrees that marked word order in English is used to achieve a stylistic function which they call attention-setting, emphasis, focus, prominence, amongst others. Below I illustrate the issue of markedness with examples featuring different types of word order variation.

Ex 4.8: His face not many admired, while his character still fewer could praise. (Quirk 1997: 1377–8)
TT: أما وجهه فلم يعجب الكثيرون، وأما شخصيته فلم تعجب إلا القليلون

Back translation: As for his face, (it) did not appeal to many, and as for his character, (it) only appealed to few.

This example features the preposing of the direct objects in both clauses. This marked word order draws attention to the direct object in both clauses. The translation sounds equally marked in Arabic.

Ex 4.9: Traitor he has become and traitor we shall call him.
TT: خائنا أصبح وخائنا سنسميه.

Back translation: Traitor he became and traitor we will call him.

According to Quirk (ibid. 1377–8), this example features the preposing of subject complement and object complement, respectively. The same items are also preposed in my translation for emphasis.

Ex 4.10: In London I was born and in London I shall die.
TT: في لندن ولدت وفي لندن سوف أموت
Back translation: In London I was born and in London I will die.

This example features the foregrounding of the predication adjunct (ibid.). Quirk explains that the fronting of the predication, common in journalism, seems to aim at giving end-focus to the subject and, at the same time, using the early part of the sentence to 'set the scene'. Note that Arabic mirrors the same word order to realise the same function.

Ex 4.11: They have promised to finish the work, and finish it they will (ibid.).
TT: لقد وعدوا بإنهاء عملهم وسوف ينهونه بالتأكيد
Back translation: They have promised to finish the work and will certainly finish it.

This example features the foregrounding of the predication 'finish it'. Mirroring this word order in Arabic is not possible due to the use of object and subject pronouns in the same clause. Note that Arabic conjugates a verb for subject and object pronouns and that the latter will appear as a clitic attached to the end of the verb, making it impossible to mirror this marked word order which requires splitting the verb and object. However, I propose compensating lexically for the lost stylistic effect of emphasis via the addition of (بالتأكيد) 'certainly'.

Ex 4.12: Often did she visit the inhabitants of that gloomy village. (no source indicated in Green 1982: 125)
TT: عادة كانت تزور سكان هذه القرية الكئيبة
Back translation: Often she visited the inhabitants of this gloomy village.

Green discusses this example as an instance of inversion after some adverbs, 'often' in this case. What matters in my view here is the preposing of the adverb, rather than the inversion of the auxiliary and subject 'did she'. My proposed translation mirrors the marked word order resulting from the preposing of the adverb in the original sentence but not the auxiliary subject reversal since the verb (كانت) 'she-did' is conjugated for the subject and they cannot be separated from each other.

Ex 4.13: Of more probable concern to Crane's followers is a feeling Crane didn't come off too well in the first debate. (*Champaign-Urbana Courier*, quoted in Green 1982: 127)
TT: ولعل أكثر ما أقلق أنصار كرين هو شعورهم بأنه لم يبل بلاء حسنا في أول حوار
Back translation: Probably what most concerned Crane's followers was their feeling that he did not do well in the first debate.

This example features 'inversion after preposed abstract prepositional phrase' (Green 1982: 127). Similarly, the translation follows the same word order of the original but does not actually sound marked. This is because the adjective 'probable' is rendered into Arabic as a verb (لعل), which is unmarked in Arabic.

Theorists agree that cleft/pseudo-cleft structures are an example of marked word order, whereby emphasis is placed on a certain element of the sentence. Aarts and Aarts explain that cleft structures follow the pattern: it + be + emphasised constituent + who/that ... and define them as: 'a construction which makes it possible to put special emphasis on a particular constituent' (1988: 97). In addition, they explain that pseudo-cleft structures are similarly used to give special emphasis to a certain constituent of the sentence and describe them as 'subject-predicator-subject-attribute sentences, in which the subject is realised by a what-clause, the predicator by a form of be and the subject attribute by a noun phrase, an infinitive or an –ing' (1988: 98). Similarly, Dryer maintains that clefted sentences 'give prominence to the clefted element' (1995: 107). Theorists, by and large, agree that it is the element which follows 'be' that is emphasised in cleft structures. As such, in the following examples (adapted from Halliday 1994: 59), 'the queen', 'my uncle' and 'that chair', respectively, are emphasised.

Ex 4.14: It was the queen who sent my uncle that chair.
TT: إن الملكة هي من أرسل لعمي ذاك الكرسي

Ex 4.15: It was my uncle the queen sent that chair.
TT: إن عمي هو من (ذاك الذي) أرسلت له الملكة ذاك الكرسي

Ex: 4.16: It was that chair the queen sent to my uncle.
TT: إن ذاك الكرسي هو ما أرسلت الملكة لعمي

The translations above equally adopt marked work order, placing emphasis on the same constituents emphasises in the original sentences.

Finally, marked word order need to be identified, and, more importantly, the function it realises in the source text needs to be communicated to the target readers. This can be achieved via adopting an equally marked work order, or through the use of other strategies, including lexical compensation, as demonstrated above. Failure to communicate the functions of markedness results in loss of meaning. For a detailed examination of the notion of marked word order in Arabic and English see Elimam (2010; 2013).

4.3 Passive structure (أسلوب البناء للمجهول)

A passive structure features the shift of the left-hand and right-hand noun phrases, which leads to placing the object in the subject position (e.g. Fowler 1991: 77). This structure is used in Arabic only when the subject is not known or not mentioned in the sentence. According to El-Farahaty (2015: 41, 74), 'Arabic seeks accuracy and precision by avoiding obscurity of agents.' Similarly, Rosenhouse (1988: 92) states that 'Arabic is known to avoid passive verb forms and not to favour much use of them on its sentences.' If, however, the subject or agent is mentioned in the sentence, an active structure should be used instead and the original emphasis created through the use of the passive structure can be realised in a different way. However, Arabic journalistic writing seems to use the passive a lot more frequently. The reason, I argue, is that a lot of the news read in Arabic is produced through translation from English, and journalists seem to stay too close to the English sentence structure.

English, on the other hand, uses the passive structure to place more emphasis on the object by placing it in sentence-initial position, when the subject is less important than the object, or to obscure the agent (El-Farahaty 2015: 23). The use of the passive can be particularly common in journalistic writing to avoid laying the blame or pointing the finger at a specific subject to avoid the potential legal implications thereof. There is also a special set of verbs both in Arabic and English which allows language users to promote the object to the status of the subject (see also word order variation above and Almanna 2016: 86–7).

Furthermore, Baker (1992/2011: 112–3) argues that the use of the passive has become the norm in technical English writing. This is also true of Arabic, notwithstanding the discussion above. The reason is that English is the language of technology at the moment, and most translations are carried out from English into other languages including Arabic. In other words, English structure has a strong influence on Arabic technical writing which is mostly translated from English.

Ex 4.17: The building was designed by the architects in 2010.
TT: صمم المهندسون المبنى في 2010
Back translation: The architects designed the building in 2010

The translation will sound natural if the sentences are rendered using an active Arabic structure since the sentence features the subject 'the architects'.

Ex 4.18: The wire was cut off.
TT: قُطِع السلك

This is a passive structure in English which does not feature the subject of the verb and can, therefore, be directly translated into an Arabic passive structure. Both sentences imply the existence of an unmentioned subject/agent which has caused the wire to be cut off.

Ex 4.19: The wire snapped.
TT: انقطع السلك

This verb form implies that the wire is the agent of the action, meaning that it caused itself to be cut off, and simultaneously negates the possibility of an external subject. The Arabic translation sounds equally natural and close to the original structure, featuring the 'wire' as the subject or agent of the verb.

Ex 4.20: وَلَئِن مـتُّمْ أَوْ قـتِلْتـمْ لإِلى اللهِ تُحْشَرُون (Qur'an 3: 158)
Gloss: And whether you die or are killed to Allah you will be gathered.
Abdel Haleem's translation: whether you die or are killed, it is to God that you will be gathered. (2004: 46)

This is an example featuring the foregrounding of a complement, that is placing it before the verb. The complement (إلى الله) 'to God' is foregrounded before the verb (تُحْشَرُون) 'are gathered', which is in the passive voice. The effect of this foregrounding on the meaning is that emphasis is placed on God as the only One before whom we will be 'gathered', and at the same time negating that we can be 'gathered' before anyone else is implied (al-Suyūṭī 1969: 189). The translator opts to stay as close as possible to the original by using a cleft structure (*it*-structure), which allows him or her to front the complement 'to God' to realise contrastive focus, in addition to using a passive verb form.

4.4 *Iḍāfa* (الإضافة), roughly translated as 'construct/genitive structure'

This Arabic-specific structure does not have a direct equivalent English structure. It can, however, be used to translate English possessive and compound structures. The *iḍāfa* is made up of two or more lexical units, only the last of which is definite, rendering the whole structure definite.

Ex 4.21: سيارة أحمد

This *iḍāfa* construction can be rendered into English as 'Ahmed's car'. It is worth noting that the ('s) does not have a direct Arabic equivalent, but its function has been reproduced through the *iḍāfa,* which features the use of (سيارة *sayyāra*) as an indefinite noun together with Ahmed, a definite noun since it is a proper name.

Ex 4.22: باب السيارة

This *iḍāfa* can be rendered roughly as 'the car door', 'the door of the car' or 'the car's door'. In this *iḍāfa* construction, the noun (باب) 'door' is placed before the definite noun (السيارة) 'car'.

Ex 4.23: باب سيارتي

This *iḍāfa* can be translated as 'the door of my car', 'my car door' or 'my car's door'. Here, the noun (باب) 'door' is attached to (سيارتي) 'my car', a definite noun due to the existence of a possessive pronoun.

In all three previous examples, the translators will decide which version he or she will use: whether to use the compound structure with or without 'of' or the possessive 's' based on the rules of natural language usage.

4.5 Grammatical gender (التذكير والتأنيث)

In Arabic, words can either be masculine or feminine. Feminine words, generally speaking, bear a grammatical ending: the sound /t/ or /h/, spelt as (ت) or (ة), which identifies their gender. Masculine words are identified by lack of such ending. This feature can be particularly challenging when translating from English into Arabic (see Baker 1992/2011: 99ff.).

Ex 4.24: The pronoun 'It'

This is a neutral pronoun which can be translated as (هو) or (هي), which means 'he' and 'she', and also as (هذا) or (هذه), meaning 'this' for masculine and feminine, respectively, especially when referring to animals and inanimate objects.

In addition, English has started using neutral forms, such as 'their', or both genders, for example, s/he (alternatively, he or she), as a form of 'political correctness'. This is not possible in Arabic because verbs, nouns, adjectives and pronouns are either masculine or feminine and it would be extremely cumbersome to inflect all of these items twice (for both genders) in every sentence. Thus, in most cases, only one gender can be used at a time. However, it is worth noting that in Arabic, as in some other languages, the 'masculine' form is a general form of reference. It refers to both masculine and feminine simultaneously. In cases where only masculine, rather than both genders, is addressed, (a) lexical item(s) can be used to make this clear to the addressee, as the following example shows (see also Elimam 2013: 36).

Ex 4.25: على المدرسين فقط التوجه إلى القاعة
TT: (male-)teachers only have to go to the hall

Here 'only' marks the fact that only male teachers are being addressed. Note that losing it can generalise the meaning implied by (المدرسين) 'teachers' to both male and female teachers in the right context, meaning where male and female teachers work in the same place.

4.6 Grammatical number (الإفراد والتثنية والجمع)

In English, words can be either singular or plural while in Arabic there is yet one more category, which is 'dual', referring to two items, reserving the 'plural' category to three or more items. This difference in dealing with number requires that the exact number which the pronominal 'they' refers to be identified (be it dual or plural), and the corresponding Arabic dual pronominal be used in order to avoid confusion and achieve accuracy. Clues as to the exact number that 'they' refers to may be identified from the co-text or context. Newmark (1988/2003: 85) discusses the change in grammar from SL to TL under the term 'shift', which he borrows from Catford, and 'transposition'. Baker (1992/2011: 88) proposes either omitting the 'relevant information on number' or expressing this information 'lexically' by using English words which can express the notion of duality such as 'two' or 'both'. Baker, however, warns against exaggeration in reflecting this and other idiosyncratic grammatical features as this could result in an unnatural target text. In other words, duality can be rendered only when it is meaningful and necessary for achieving accuracy.

In addition, Arabic also features the use of the plural when addressing one person as a sign of respect. Royal plural can also be used by speakers of high social status, like kings and queens, to refer to themselves (see Baker 1992/2011: 105). Note that although I discuss below some examples of individual words, the decision to discuss the issue of number under sentence level rather than word level is that the grammatical number has implications across clauses and sentences because, as I have already mentioned, verbs, nouns, pronouns and adjectives have to be inflicted according to the number of the subject.

Ex 4.26: parents

This word can be rendered into Arabic in the dual form (أبوان *abawān*) if it refers to two parents, or in the plural form (آباء *ābā'*) when referring to more than two.

Ex 4.27: children

This can be translated using either dual or plural words in Arabic, as the case may be in the relevant context: (طفلان *ṭiflān*) 'two-children' and (أطفال *aṭfāl*) 'plural-children', that is three or more children.

Ex 4.28: God

When featuring the upper case 'G' and used in the singular form, this word refers in English to the supreme Deity, which can be an 'equivalent' to Allah in Arabic. On the contrary, 'god' in English can be used in the plural form to refer to other deities, beings or items of worship (إله).

4.7 Definiteness (التعريف والتنكير)

The use of definiteness or indefiniteness differs across the two languages in question. 'The' is directly translated as (الـ /al/) in Arabic, but the usage of each article is language-specific, as summarised in the table below.

As can be seen from Table 4.1, (الـ) can be prefixed to countable nouns to make them definite. Furthermore, 'a' and 'an' have no equivalent in Arabic, and an indefinite noun is used on its own instead. (الـ) is prefixed to some words even if the English counterparts are not preceded by 'the', especially if the SL words are uncountable.

4.8 Collocations (المتلازمات اللفظية)

This term is defined as 'the habitual juxtaposition of a particular word with another word or words with a frequency greater than chance, a pair or group of words that are habitually juxtaposed'.[1] For instance, English speakers always say a 'cup of coffee' rather than a 'glass of coffee'. There is no grammatical restriction on the use of the words 'glass' and 'coffee', but 'cup' and 'coffee' are put together for the consideration of habitual use. Not only do words collocate with specific collocates in a specific language, but also the same word can change its meaning when in collocation with a different collocate, as is the case with 'heavy' below. Collocation 'presupposes a semantic relation of some sort between the elements. Unfortunately, this relation is not always transparent as it may be figurative' (Husni and Newman 2015: 2). It is worth noting that collocations do not

Table 4.1 Comparison between the use of definite articles in Arabic and English

English (the)	Arabic (الـ)
'the' + lexical item: Ex: the boy	lexical item+ (الـ) Ex: الولد *al-walad*
a/an + lexical item: Ex: a boy	no article Ex: ولد *walad*
no article + lexical item Ex: literature	lexical item+ (الـ) Ex: الأدب *al-adab*

form a fixed set of a language; new collocations are being created every day due to the need to express new meanings as well as the creative use of language (see also the use of collocation to coin new meanings in Chapter 3). According to Dickins et al. (2002: 71), 'the translator has to be able to recognise and render ST collocative meanings. But it is just as important to avoid unwanted collocative clashes in the TT.' They draw on Leech and Short (1981: 17) to illustrate this idea by explaining how 'pretty' collocates with 'girl', 'boy', 'woman' and 'flower' while 'handsome' collocates with 'man', 'boy' and 'vessel', although both adjectives have a shared meaning of being good-looking. Furthermore, some theorists see the relationship between collocations as arbitrary while others do not and provide restrictions when trying to explain this relationship (see McCawley 1968: 35, and Leech 1966).

Collocations can be divided into different types based on the angle you look at them. Here I provide two categorisations of collocations based on the grammatical categories of the words involved in the collocation in each language followed by another categorisation which may be challenging to translators, namely, marked vs unmarked collocations.

4.8.1 Grammatical collocations

The first type of collocations involves the grammatical categories of words which can be strung together to form collocations. I discuss and illustrate with examples these types for English and Arabic below.

A. Grammatical collocations in English[2]

- noun + noun

  Ex 4.29: a surge of anger (نوبة من الغضب), literally 'a fit of anger'

- verb + noun

  Ex 4.30: commit suicide (ينتحر), this one word/verb communicates the meaning of the two-word collocation

- adjective + noun

  Ex 4.31: excruciating pain (ألم رهيب)

- adverb + adjective

  Ex 4.32: completely unsatisfied (غير راض إطلاقا)

- noun + verb
  Ex 4.33: lions roar (تزأر الأسود)

- verb + expression with preposition
  Ex 4.34: burst into tears (انفجر في البكاء)

- verb + adverb
  Ex 4.35: wave frantically (يشير بشكل محموم), literally 'wave in a frantic manner'

B. Grammatical collocations in Arabic (see Husni and Newman 2015: 8; Ghazala 2008/2014: 106ff.):

- noun + noun
  Ex 4.36: (غروب الشمس) 'sunset' (literally, the setting of the sun)

- verb + noun
  Ex 4.37: (غربت الشمس) 'the sun went down'

- adjective + noun
  Ex 4.38: (طويل الأناة) 'very patient'

- noun + adjective
  Ex 4.39: (رجل وسيم) 'a handsome man'

- noun + [prep] + noun
  Ex 4.40: (جماعة من السمك) 'school of fish'

  Ex 4.41: (شريحة من اللحم) 'slice of meat/meat steak'

4.8.2 Translation strategies for grammatical collocations

To render each set of these types into the TL, the translator needs to bear the TL collocational restrictions and rules of natural usage in mind. Abiding by the grammatical type of words in the source language is only secondary, in this case, to meaning. In fact, type shifts (Catford 1965/1978) are likely to occur while translating collocations. In other words, there are not necessarily one-to-one equivalent grammatical structures between the two languages in question here. For instance, (commit suicide) is rendered as a verb in Arabic: (ينتحر); see also 'sunset' above.

Ex 4.42: 'Break the law' is a perfect collocation in English, while in Arabic, the law cannot be 'broken' but 'opposed' or 'deviated from', that is (يخالف القانون).

Ex 4.43: 'Heavy smoker' can be translated into Arabic as (يدخن بشراهة), 'smokes excessively', 'heavy drinker' as (مدمن خمر), 'alcohol addict', and 'heavy rain' as (مطر غزير), 'pouring rain'. 'Heavy' is translated in three different ways, which all share the meaning of 'excessiveness' (see Baker 1992/2011: 55).

4.8.3 Marked vs unmarked collocations (المتلازمات اللفظية المألوفة وغير المألوفة)

The second type of classification of collocations, which is probably more challenging due to the relevant effect on the ST style, is whether the collocation is marked or unmarked.

1. Unmarked collocations: these refer to words which are expected to occur together; in other words, typical collocation which does not attract the readers' attention as such.

   Ex 4.44: 'A glass of milk' is a regular, unmarked English collocation and its close translation as (كوبا من الحليب/كوب حليب) is equally unmarked.

2. Marked collocations: these are a combination of words which defy regularity and foreground the meaning due to the untypical occurrence of the collocational components.

   Ex 4.45: 'A cup of milk' is marked in English since the two words are not used together regularly. The close Arabic translation (فنجان حليب) is equally marked for the same reason.

Identifying whether a collocation is marked or unmarked can also be challenging as the translator needs to bear in mind their respective registers of occurrence. The register is an important factor in deciding whether a word or collocation is marked or unmarked.

Ex 4.46: Describing people as 'yellow' is unmarked in a specialist medical register where it refers to a medical condition, 'jaundice', but can be marked, or even a racist remark, in a non-specialist register.

4.8.4 Translation strategies of marked vs unmarked collocations

Having identified a collocation as marked, the next challenge will be representing the meaning of the collocation in the TT. This challenge can occur as a result of rendering the SL collocation closely without paying special attention to language-specific rules of collocation or the nuances of meaning of the relevant words.

> Ex 4.47: 'In fact, the money came from the Sultan of Brunei, a naïve individual, easily romanced and seduced by the *oily charm* of Mohamed Fayed' (Baker 1992/2011: 63)

The translator rendered 'oily charm' as (سحر زائف), meaning 'false charm'. According to Baker (1998/2011: 63), 'oily charm' in English means not only someone who is insincere, but also that there is something unpleasant, even sickening, in the way they show excessive politeness, while 'false charm' in Arabic only suggests someone who appears charming at first glance but turns out to be not as good as they claim to be. The TT is toned down for no apparent reason, probably due to the lack of understanding of the SL collocation on the part of the translator who could have used (خبث) or (مكر) 'cunningness'. On the other hand, however, the Arabic rendering flows well and does not jar upon the potential readers of the text.

In rendering marked collocations, the translator may have to choose between reproducing 'accuracy' or 'naturalness', if both cannot be achieved at the same time. An 'accurate', meaning close TL rendering, may help reflect the flavour of the ST to the readers, while a natural, but not necessarily close TL rendering, may reproduce the same effect on the TL readers, though it misses out on the nuances of the ST meaning. The following are examples of unmarked collocations in English and their renderings, which also sound unmarked in Arabic.

> Ex 4.48: 'Rich colours' can be rendered as (ألوان باهرة), which means 'dazzling colours', in order to achieve naturalness. Note that literal translation of the SL unit as (ألوان غنية) sounds unnatural in Arabic. Another Arabic collocation can be (كثير الألوان) 'with/having many colours'. Obviously, the final selection of translation depends on the meaning of the SL collocation in context (see Baker 1992/2011: 61).

> Ex 4.49: 'Crisp writer': according to Baker (1992/2011: 61), rendering this collocation as (كاتب أحد قلما) 'sharp-pen writer' does not reproduce the correct meaning as the Arabic equivalent is usually used to describe the style of a 'fierce critic'. Therefore, I suggest rendering the SL collocation as (كاتب ناضج/رائع الأسلوب), 'writer with a mature/an excellent style', which captures the sense of the SL counterpart.

Ex 4.50: 'Play a role': the Arabic translation of this colocation is (يؤدي دورا), literally 'carry out a role'. However, through the effect of calqued translation, (يلعب دورا), literally 'play a role', has become commonly used. Dickins et al. (2002: 30) argue that some calqued expressions have become a standard TL equivalent of SL expressions. This actually comes at the expense of naturalness in Arabic.

To summarise collocation translation strategies:

1. Use a TL equivalent to reproduce the meaning and structure:

   Ex 4.51: 'Sooner or later' (عاجلا أو آجلا), which is a very close rendering of the SL unit.

   Ex 4.52: 'For better or for worse' (في السراء والضراء), which literally means 'in ease and distress'.

2. Use a TL equivalent to reproduce the meaning only:

   Ex 4.53: (بقوة وحماس), literally, 'with power/might and enthusiasm', can be rendered as 'with might and main'.

3. Omission:

   Ex 4.54: (بلا قيد أو شرط), literally 'without restriction or condition', can be rendered as 'unconditionally'.

   Ex 4.55: (تهديد ووعيد), literally, 'threat and menace', can be rendered as 'threats'.

Note also that some would argue that the above examples can be considered fixed expressions. This is because there is an area of overlap between fixed expressions and collocations (see more on idioms in Chapter 5).

4.9 Conclusion

This chapter has discussed some of the most common translation issues that occur at sentence level. Word order variations, resulting in marked word order, in both Arabic and English have been examined and illustrated with plenty of examples to demonstrate how to deal with the issue of markedness due to its influence on the meaning implied by the relevant marked structures. The chapter has also covered the passive structure, (الإضافة *iḍāfa*), roughly translated as 'construct/genitive structure', grammatical gender, grammatical number, definiteness and collocations. In all cases, examples were provided from Arabic and English in order to demonstrate how each language differs in its use of these structures and the translation strategies available to deal with the issue in question. Below is a summary of the translation issues and their viable strategies.

Word order translation issue:

- marked word order is used to place 'focus', 'prominence' or 'emphasis' on a specific item in the sentence.

Word order translation strategies:
This markedness or its effect on meaning needs to be dealt with in the translation through the following:

- opting for a corresponding target language marked word order,
- using unmarked word order plus a lexical compensation, or
- omission by using unmarked word order only.

Passive structure translation issue:

- in English, a passive structure is used when the subject is not known or not important.
- in Arabic, a passive structure cannot be used if the subject is known.

Passive structure translation strategies:

- where the subject is known, change a source text passive to an active structure in the translation into Arabic to produce a smooth-reading translation.
- change some active into passive structures when translating into English to produce a smooth-reading translation.

Iḍāfa (الإضافة) translation issue:

- no directly equivalent English grammatical structure exists.

Iḍāfa (الإضافة) translation strategies:

- use ('s) or compound structure, with or without 'of', in English.

Grammatical gender translation issue:

- in Arabic, words are either masculine or feminine, which is not the case in English.
- Arabic does not have the neutral pronoun 'it' and a pronoun with the correct gender must be used.

- English uses neutral forms, such as 'their', or he or she, which is not possible in Arabic because verbs, nouns, adjectives and pronouns are either masculine or feminine, which places restrictions on the use of both genders simultaneously in all sentences.

Grammatical gender translation strategy:

- abide by the rules of natural usage in both languages.

Grammatical number translation issue:

- in terms of number, words in Arabic are singular, dual or plural.
- Arabic conjugates words for number which can be problematic due to the lack of a dual category in English.

Grammatical number translation strategy:

- use the plural for dual when translating into English, unless this would change the meaning.
- use of the dual category as appropriate when translating into Arabic.

Definiteness translation issue:

- the use of the definite article in both languages differs significantly.

Definiteness translation strategy:

- abide by the rules of natural grammar usage.

Collocations translation issue:

- grammatical collocations: the grammatical categories of words which can be strung together to form collocations.
- marked and unmarked collocations: typical collocation which does not attract the readers' attention versus the untypical occurrence of the collocational components.

Collocations translation strategies:

- grammatical collocations: bear the collocational restrictions and rules of natural usage in mind.
- unmarked collocations need to be reproduced by unmarked collocation according to TL norms.
- marked collocations need to be rendered by marked translations to reproduce the same effect.

The next chapter will examine some common stylistic issues that occur at text level, namely, idioms and fixed expressions, metaphors, similes, puns and cohesion.

4.10 Exercises

4.10.1 All the exercises in Chapters 1, 2 and 3 feature several of the issues discussed in this chapter. Read these passages again and identify some of these issues and decide whether or not you would translate them differently now that you have been introduced to their respective translation strategies.

Tips: For instance, Chapter 1, exercise 1.8.2 (كان ذلك زمن الحرب. الحرب؟) and (كنا نقاتل من أجل الأكل) feature structural issues. Speaking specifically of the use of 'the', how would you translate (الأكل) and (الحرب)? With respect to grammatical number and gender, how would you render (someone's feet were getting longer every day), noting that body parts which come in two are always feminine in Arabic, which warrants a different way of dealing with the issue here compared to the following exercise? Other issues include *iḍāfa*, for instance, (زمن الاشتباك), and collocations, for example, (ذكور شديدو المراس).

Another example is exercise 3.5.2 in Chapter 3, which features the issue of grammatical gender. Consider how you rendered (المعلمة) 'female teacher' and (طالباً) 'male pupil' into English, and how you would deal with them now after being introduced to some relevant translation strategies.

Tips: In this exercise, you may decide to communicate the gender of either character or both to the target readers if you think this is important to the development of the story or in line with the translation approach you are adopting. However, if this is not the case, and you think that this information does not add to the story, you may want to use a neutral gender instead.

One further example is from Chapter 3, exercise 3.5.1, which features the use of a marked word order in the first sentence: 'Usually when my dad is banging on about "good old days . . ."' Revisit your translation and decide whether you want to reflect the same word order in your translation or to adopt a regular word order, and whether your decision is in line with your overall approach.

Tips: Arabic uses marked word order to place emphasis, amongst other functions, on the foregrounded element. In this example, would you follow the same SL word order to give a 'taste' of the SL structure to the target readers, or would you start with the subject, i.e. 'My dad', featuring a regular word order?

4.10.2. The following excerpt is the introductory paragraphs of (موسم الهجرة إلى الشمال) 'Season of Migration to the North' by the Sudanese novelist Tayeb Salih. Read the passage and try to identify some of the challenges discussed in this chapter and decide how you would deal with them.

عدت إلى أهلي يا سادتي بعد غيبة طويلة، سبعة أعوام على وجه التحديد، كنت خلالها أتعلم في أوروبا. تعلمت الكثير، وغاب عني الكثير، لكن تلك قصة أخرى. المهم إنني عدت وبي شوق عظيم إلى أهلي في تلك القرية الصغيرة عند منحنى النيل. سبعة أعوام وأنا أحن إليهم وأحلم بهم، ولما جئتهم كانت لحظة عجيبة أن وجدتني حقيقة قائما بينهم، فرحو بي وضجوا حولي، ولم يمض وقت طويل حتى أحسست كأن ثلجا يذوب في دخيلتي، فكأنني مقرور طلعت عليه الشمس. ذاك هدف الحياة في العشيرة، فقدته زماننا في بلاد "تموت من البرد حيتانها". تعودت أذناي أصواتهم، وألفت عيناي أشكالهم من كثرة ما فكرت فيهم في الغيبة، بيني وبينهم شيء مثل الضباب، أول وهلة رأيتهم. لكن الضباب راح، واستيقظت ثاني يوم وصولي، في فراشي الذي أعرفه في الغرفة التي تشهد جدرانها على ترهات حياتي في طفولتها ومطلع شبابها وأرخيت أذني للريح. ذاك لعمري صوت أعرفه، له في بلدنا وشوشة مرحة. صوت الريح وهي تمر بالنخل غيره وهي تمر بحقول القمح. وسمعت هديل القمري، ونظرت خلال النافذة إلى النخلة القائمة في فناء دارنا، فعلمت أن الحياة لا تزال بخير، أنظر إلى جذعها القوي المعتدل، وإلى عروقها الضاربة في الأرض، وإلى الجريد الأخضر المنهدل فوقها هامتها فأحس بالطمأنينة . أحس إنني لست ريشة في مهب الريح، ولكني مثل تلك النخلة ، مخلوق له أصل ، له جذور له هدف.

Tips: (موسم الهجرة إلى الشمال) is widely acclaimed as one of the best Arabic novels in the twentieth century. With this in mind, which translation approach would you adopt? Who is your intended target readership? The passage above features some of the issues discussed in this chapter. For example, 'تموت من البرد حيتانها' features the foregrounding of the complement/prepositional phrase before the subject. How would you deal with this issue and similar ones?

Note that some of the issues you will come across in the above passage will be dealt with in the next chapter, for example, similes and metaphors.

4.10.3 The following excerpt is from Aldous Huxley's *Brave New World* (1947). Identify the structural translation issues you would come across if you were to translate this passage.

Tips: how would you deal with the marked word order of the first sentence? Do you think this sentence would have to be restructured in Arabic or can it be followed closely? How about 'For of course some sort of general idea they must have'? How would you deal with collocations such as 'scarcely breathing silence', 'soliloquizing hum' and 'a troop of . . . students'?

Note that 'Straight from the horse's mouth' is an idiom; a translation issue which will be discussed in the next chapter.

Bent over their instruments, three hundred Fertilizers were plunged, as the Director of Hatcheries and Conditioning entered the room, in the scarcely breathing silence, the absentminded, soliloquizing hum or whistle, of absorbed concentration. A troop of newly arrived students, very young, pink and callow, followed nervously, rather abjectly, at the Director's heels. Each of them carried a notebook, in which, whenever the great man spoke, he desperately scribbled. Straight from the horse's mouth. It was a rare privilege. The D. H. C. for Central London always made a point of personally conducting his new students round the various departments. 'Just to give you a general idea', he would explain to them. For of course some sort of general idea they must have, if they were to do their work intelligently – though as little of one, if they were to be good and happy members of society, as possible. For particulars, as everyone knows, make for virtue and happiness; generalities are intellectually necessary evils. Not philosophers but fretsawyers and stamp collectors compose the backbone of society.

Notes

1. <https://en.oxforddictionaries.com/definition/collocation> (last accessed 7 August 2021)
2. <https://www.englishclub.com/vocabulary/collocations.htm> (last accessed 7 August 2021)

CHAPTER 5
TEXTUAL TRANSLATION ISSUES AND STRATEGIES

5.1 Introduction

This chapter discusses issues relating to translating some of the most common textual issues (مشكلات الترجمة على مستوى النص واستراتجياتها). In particular, this chapter will cover the challenges relating to the translation of idioms and fixed expressions (الأقوال المأثورة والتعابير الاصطلاحية), metaphor (الاستعارة), similes (التشبيه) and puns (التورية), being the most commonly used metaphoric devices, as well as the issue of cohesion (سبكة النص أو تماسك النص). Note that 'metaphor' is used as a general term to imply allegory (مجاز), metonymy (كناية) and personification (تشخيص). Similar to the previous two chapters, I will start by explaining the issue under discussion before proposing translation strategies to be used in dealing with the relevant challenges that these stylistic issues pose for the translator. The discussion will also be illustrated with examples from both English and Arabic. As is the case with the translation issues discussed in the previous two chapters, there is no one fit-for-all-situation translation strategy, but the choice of how to deal with the issue at hand has to be informed by the overall translation approach adopted by the translator and what he or she wants to communicate to the readers, amongst other issues.

5.2 Idioms and fixed expressions (الأقوال المأثورة والتعابير الاصطلاحية)

An idiom is defined as 'an expression in the usage of a language that is peculiar to itself either grammatically (as *no, it wasn't me*) or in having a meaning that cannot be derived from the conjoined meanings of its elements (as *ride herd on* for "supervise")'.[1] Husni and Newman (2015: 26) define an idiom as a 'fixed expression with figurative or metaphorical meaning, whereas "the essential feature of an idiom is its non-literal, metaphorical meaning"'. It is important to note that most idioms resist variation, but some allow for slight variations, for instance, 'the ball is in their court' as opposed to 'the ball is a *little/firmly* in their court', (Baker 1992/2011: 67ff.). Therefore, understanding the meaning of an idiom can be tricky and requires linguistic and cultural knowledge on the part of the translator. An idiom can be long or short and may even seem ill-formed grammatically (ibid. 69). Some idioms are metaphoric, and some are not (see more in Abdou 2012). Note also that the meaning of an idiom almost always differs from the aggregate meaning of its individual lexical items.

This challenge can be even more accentuated in the case of metaphoric idioms. To translate an idiom appropriately, a decision which takes into consideration several issues is required, including when and how to use a TL idiom.

5.2.1 The difficulties of translating idioms

These include the following, according to Baker (1992/2011: 71ff.):

- The difference in meaning between the SL and corresponding TL idiom: the SL idiom may have a seemingly close, but different in meaning, TL idiom.

  Ex 5.1: 'Pull someone's leg' is an idiom which implies the meaning of 'lying', in a joking sense, in English, while a close Arabic counterpart, (يسحب رجله), implies tricking someone into talking about a secret (ibid. 70).

- The existence of no TL equivalent idiom: this can be because of the culture-specific or metaphoric references embedded in the SL idiom.

  Ex 5.2: 'Bringing (or carrying) coal(s) to Newcastle' features a cultural reference to the fact that Newcastle, UK, was known for the coal industry and cannot be maintained in a translation by an Arabic idiom.

  Ex 5.3: 'At the end of the day' can be rendered in Arabic closely. However, the translation would not communicate the meaning implied by the SL idiom. This idiom is sometimes rendered as (في نهاية المطاف), which literally means 'at the end of the turn'. It is also sometimes rendered more communicatively as (على أي حال) 'at any rate' or 'anyway'.

- The difference in context and frequency of the usage of idioms between the SL and the TL. For example, spoken English seems to use more idioms than spoken Arabic while written Arabic, especially literary Arabic, uses more idioms than written English. This difference in the language's use of idioms needs to be taken into consideration, especially if naturalness, rather than 'literalness', is the aim of the translation.

5.2.2 Strategies for translating idioms

The order in which the strategies below are presented should not be taken to impart some kind of importance to particular strategies over others. It is rather used for convenience since the appropriate strategy always depends on several contextual factors, including the translation *skopos* and the frequency of the use of idioms, as stated above.

A. Direct translation (الترجمة المباشرة أو المتداولة)

By 'direct translation' I mean the use of an available, used or established rendering, that is a TL idiom commonly used to translate the SL idiom in question. This strategy is alternatively called 'use of a TL idiom of similar meaning and form' by Baker (1992/2011: 76). This option of translation by a direct TL equivalent may not be available with respect to the majority of Arabic and English idioms due to grammatical and cultural differences between the two languages. The existence of such idioms depends on how close the languages and cultures in question are. The examples below show a rare occasion where there is a direct/equivalent Arabic idiom for an English one.

Ex 5.4: You make my blood boil with your bad manners.
TT: إنك تجعل الدم يغلي في عروقي بسوء أخلاقك (Ghazala 2008/2014: 128)

Ex 5.5: She cannot believe her eyes/ears.
TT: لا تستطيع أن تصدق عينيها – أذنيها (ibid.)

Ex 5.6: Turn something on its head.
TT: يقلبه رأسا على عقب (Baker 1992/2011: 77)

Ex 5.7: To fish in troubled water.
TT: يصطاد في الماء العكر

Ex 5.8: The ball is in their court.
TT: الكرة في ملعبهم

Note that the final expression above involves a standard metaphor, implying 'it is up to them to make the next move' (*OED*). This metaphor can also be adapted as follows: 'the ball is a little in their court' (Newmark 1988/2003: 111), which can also be rendered closely into Arabic as (الكرة في ملعبهم لحد ما).

Ex 5.9: يصطاد عصفورين بحجر واحد
Gloss: To catch two sparrows with one stone.
TT: To kill two birds with one stone.

This expression can also be considered as a direct translation, even though 'sparrow' is a hyponym of 'birds'.

B. Cultural substitution (المقابل أو المرادف أو البديل الثقافي)

This strategy is alternatively called 'use an idiom of similar meaning but dissimilar form' by Baker 1992/2011: 78). If the image used in the idiom cannot be rendered into the TL, replace the expression by a culturally equivalent TL expression; one that communicates the meaning – even if the image involved is different – provided it is equally frequent. It should be noted though that spoken English features more idioms than spoken Arabic, but written Arabic features more idioms than written English. This issue of frequency – frequency of using the particular idiom and of using idioms in general – is an important difference to bear in mind because it may entail that not every Arabic idiom should be rendered into an idiom in English or vice versa. Using a culturally equivalent idiom arguably maintains the same 'wit' and concise style and equally packs more meaning in few words.

Ex 5.10: It is raining cats and dogs.
TT: تمطر كأفواه القرب
Back translation: It's raining like (it is coming from) waterskins' mouths.

This TL idiom communicates the meaning but features an image different from the TL one.

Ex 5.11: Beauty is skin deep.
TT: الجمال جمال الروح
Back translation: Beauty is the beauty of the soul.

This TL cultural substitution renders the same meaning of the SL idiom, but features a different image, using 'soul' instead of 'skin'.

Ex 5.12: The cat has got his tongue.
TT: لم ينبس ببنت شفة
Back translation: He did not utter a word. (Lit. 'the daughter of a lip'.)
The original image, of the cat having one's tongue, cannot be maintained in the translation and, therefore, a cultural equivalent can be used to render this idiom.

Ex 5.13: Don't wash your dirty linen in public.
TT: إذا بليتم فاستتروا
Back translation: If you have a problem, hide it.

Here the ST phrase has been replaced by a TT phrase with a religious connotation appropriate to the TL culture.

Ex 5.14: bringing coals to Newcastle

TT: يبيع المياه في حارة السقايين

Back translation: He sells water in the alleyway of those who distribute free water.

As explained above, this ST idiom has a cultural reference which cannot be communicated in Arabic. Therefore, another TL idiom, which can be described as a cultural substitution, may be used instead. This TL idiom recreates the same concept of trying to do something in an inappropriate context but uses a TL-specific reference instead. The use of this substitution strategy arguably achieves a similar effect on the TL readers; it reproduces the meaning in a concise/idiomatic manner and sounds natural to the TL readers.

Ex 5.15: at the end of the day

TT: (على أي حال) or (في نهاية المطاف)

Back translation: 'at any rate' and 'at the end of the turn', respectively.

This ST idiom does not have an Arabic idiom equivalent in meaning and form, therefore, the above two expressions, which reproduce the meaning, can be used instead. Note that (على أي حال) 'at any rate' sounds more natural than (في نهاية المطاف) 'at the end of the turn'.

Ex 5.16: إن شاء الله

TT: 'Hopefully' or 'God willing'.

This is a ST cultural (religious) expression which can be rendered through cultural substitution as 'Hopefully'. This translation involves the loss of the religious reference packed in the Arabic expression, but sounds more target-oriented than the close rendering 'God willing' which is not commonly used in English.

Ex 5.17: الحمد لله

TT: 'Thankfully' or 'Thank God'.

Here too is a cultural (religious) expression that can be rendered as 'thankfully', which is more communicative than the literal 'Thank God'. This is because the ST expression is used more commonly in Arabic than the literal translation is in English. Note also that 'thankfully' is used on a daily basis in English but not in a religious sense as a sign of relief.

C. Literal translation (الترجمة الحرفية)

This strategy is called 'borrowing' by Baker (1992/2011: 79). Literal translation can be used when the SL idiom does not exist in the TL, and the translator decides to communicate the essential meaning packed in the SL idiom by staying close to it. This strategy is particularly recommended if the literal rendering

1. communicates the meaning and image intended by the ST idiom;
2. does not sound too weird for TL readers; and/or
3. if the translator aims to bring the TT readers closer to the SL.

Many English idioms have found their way into Arabic through this strategy. The idiom 'the ball is in someone's court' mentioned above is a good example of this.

Further, to prepare the TT readers for the new meaning or image, the translator may decide to render the ST idiom into the TT preceded by a phrase that warns them they that they are about to read something new, such as 'as they say in English' (كما يقولون بالإنجليزية) or 'as the English saying goes' (كما يقول المثل الإنجليزي) or something similar. The opposite is also true: an Arabic idiom can be translated closely into English and introduced by an introductory statement, as mentioned above. This solution can be particularly helpful if the translator's aim is to reflect some of the SL idiosyncratic features in the translation in order to bring the TL readers closer to the SL culture.

Ex 5.18: Better late than never.
TT: كما يقول المثل الإنجليزي 'لأن تأتي متأخرا خير لك من ألا تأتي'
Back translation: As the English saying goes, 'to come late is better for you than not coming at all'.

Ex 5.19: All is fair in love and war.
TT: كما يقول المثل الإنجليزي 'كل شيء مباح في الحب والحرب'
Back translation: As the English saying goes, 'everything is allowed in love and war'.

D. Paraphrase (الشرح)

This seems to be one of the most common strategies used in dealing with idioms, especially if producing a naturally sounding TT is the aim. Losing both the image and form and unpacking the meaning of the SL idiom will help communicate the meaning across to TT readers clearly (see Elimam 2010 and Baker 1992/2011: 80). This loss also includes the ST writer's witty and concise style. In other words, the translations below lose the form of the expression and feature the meaning in a non-idiomatic format instead.

Ex 5.20: 'More or less' and 'plus or minus'.
TT: تقريبا
Back translation: Approximately

Ex 5.21: Blow the gaff.

TT: يفشي السر

Back translation: To tell the secret.

Ex 5.22: Achilles' heel.

TT: نقطة ضعف

Back translation: A point of weakness

Ex 5.23: Blown a microchip or two.

TT: جُن أو فقد عقله

Back translation: Gone mad.

Ex 5.24: Caught red-handed.

TT: ضُبط متلبسًا/تم ضبطه متلبسًا

Back translation: Caught committing (the crime).

In all these examples, the source language idioms are too language-specific to have equivalent TL idioms in terms of meaning and form or form only. The translations, therefore, reproduce the meaning and lose the idiomatic form/image.

Note that the translator may decide to not use a direct translation of an idiom and use a paraphrase of its meaning instead for one reason or another. For instance, 'there and then' can be rendered by the directly available Arabic idiom, which reproduces the meaning and the image of the ST idiom, 'في التو واللحظة' or paraphrased as 'فورا' which means 'immediately'.

E. Literal translation plus a paraphrase, an in-text gloss or a footnote (الترجمة الحرفية بالإضافة إلى الشرح أو إضافة معلومات بين قوسين أو حاشية سفلية)

Another possible strategy is for the translator to use literal translation and paraphrase the meaning or add either an in-text gloss, that is bracketed information within the body of the translation, or a footnote to explain the meaning of an idiom. This can be used should the translator find a particular idiom to be crucial to the dialogue or the plot in a literary work and that omitting, paraphrasing or literal translation alone would result in a great loss of meaning. For instance, in example 5.14 above, 'bringing coals to Newcastle' can be rendered literally as (يجلب الفحم إلي نيوكاسل) together with the relevant explanation of the meaning of the SL idiom in brackets or in a footnote as follows: (يفعل شيئ عديم الجدوى) 'to do something pointless' or (كان إقتصاد مدينة نيوكاسل قائما على بيع الفحم) 'The economy of the city of Newcastle was dependent on selling coal.'

F. Omission (with or without compensation) (الحذف مع التعويض أو بدونه)

The translator may decide to omit the idiom completely because there are no similar TL equivalents in meaning and/or form and because they are too complex to paraphrase, or due to the difference between the SL and TL in terms of the frequency of using idioms. The translator may also decide to compensate for the lost meaning or function through the use of other means. These can include adding an idiom in the TL where the ST features no idiom.

5.3 Metaphors: common vs new (الاستعارات الشائعة أو الجديدة)

A metaphor, according to *Oxford Reference*, is a 'figure of speech in which a word or phrase is applied to an object or action to which it is not literally applicable'.[2] Metaphors are used by writers to help the readers create a mental picture of what is being talked about. Metaphors can also help the readers understand concepts by drawing an analogy between these concepts and other factors that the readers can relate to better. Metaphors make writing more interesting and attractive to the readers, and all writers use them intentionally or unintentionally as ordinary usage of language, almost any language, features many metaphors. Some theorists see metaphors as a cognitive process that involves a comparison between two entities. This comparison involves two elements: 'the vehicle', which is the existing entity to which the other entity, called the 'target', is compared to achieve a specific purpose (Lakoff and Johnson 1980: 7–9). A metaphor consists of an image and a meaning drawn from that image, and the ultimate aim of the translator is to communicate both if possible.

There are several classifications of metaphors, see Dickins et al. (2002), Newmark (1988/2003), Larson (1984), to name but a few. A metaphor can involve one word, two words (collocation), an idiom or fixed expression, or a clause. It can be a simple metaphor or an extended metaphor; *Animal Farm* is a good example of the latter. For the purpose of this guide, I propose to categorise metaphors under two types: common metaphor and new metaphor. Common metaphors cover those metaphors which do not strike the readers' attention as metaphors either at all, because they are overused, or straight away because they are commonly used by language speakers. The second type is new metaphors, which pertains to newly used or coined metaphors whether or not the creator of this metaphor is known. These are particularly challenging to translate because they betray something about the author's writing ability and sophistication of style. This classification takes into consideration the fact that what makes a difference in the context of translation is whether a metaphor is common or new. This difference needs to be taken into consideration by the translator because of the different effect on the meaning and, therefore, on the reader/receiver associated with each type.

5.3.1 Challenges in translating metaphors

Translating a metaphor is challenging for several reasons. Firstly, metaphors are probably the most common stylistic feature used by authors, and identifying whether what is at hand is a common or new metaphor (see below) is also troublesome. Secondly, establishing whether the available ST metaphor has the same currency of the ST metaphor is arduous but a prerequisite for producing a good translation; a common ST metaphor needs to be rendered by an equally common TT metaphor. Thirdly, it is also important to bear in mind the meaning, rather than just the image, being communicated. Finally, it is important that the translator identifies the ground for comparison, or where the deep meaning differs from the surface meaning when rendering a metaphor. This is important because the translator will need to reproduce the deep meaning since producing both surface meaning and deep meaning is unlikely to be possible across different cultures. In other words, metaphors are derived from one's culture and therefore may not be easy to translate across cultures which are different from each other.

5.3.2 Strategies of translating common metaphors

As is the case with all metaphors, these metaphors can be rather efficient in delivering a lot of meaning in a few words. Some of them allow for adaptation by the user; some do not. There are usually available translations of common metaphors; however, the challenge in this case is to find these available translations, while taking the translation approach and text type into consideration. Here, too, the order in which the strategies are presented does not imply obligation or preference since the choice of strategy is a contextual issue left to the translator to decide upon.

A. Direct translation (الترجمة المباشرة أو المتداولة)

Reproducing the ST metaphor is a good option if the TL has a comparable metaphor in terms of image and meaning, which is commonly used to render the metaphor in question. The translator should also make sure the TL metaphor has a comparable frequency or currency of usage to the ST metaphor. The other issue to bear in mind is that some images can imply different meanings across languages.

Ex 5.25: You light up my life.
TT: (أنت تنير حياتي) or (أنت نور حياتي)
Back translation: 'You light up my life' and 'You are the light of my life', respectively.

Ex 5.26: الحياة رحلة

TT: Life is a journey.

Ex 5.27: كان أسدا في الميدان

TT: He was a lion in the battlefield.

The common metaphors in all three SL and TL examples above are very close in terms of the image and the meaning communicated.

Ex 5.28: He has the heart of a lion.

TT: (قلبه كقلب الأسد) or (قلبه قلب أسد)

Back translation: 'His heart is like the lion's heart.' Or 'His heart is a lion's heart.'

These two renderings, the first featuring a simile and the second a metaphor, reproduce the same SL meaning and image. The SL metaphor can also be reproduced into Arabic as (هو أسد) that is 'he is a lion', which is a frequently used Arabic metaphor implying courage. This translation maintains the SL meaning and image even though some words were omitted from the original. In other words, a common metaphor is used to reproduce a common ST metaphor.

Ex 5.29: 'Pigs' are seen as nice animals by some people in the West but not so in Arab and Muslim countries, where Islam forbids rearing or consuming them. However, if the word 'pig' is used as a swear word, it can be easily reproduced in English-Arabic translation without much difficulty, albeit with more strength in Arabic than in English due to the same reason mentioned above (see more on translating 'pig' below).

B. Cultural substitution (المقابل أو المرادف أو البديل الثقافي)

According to this strategy, alternatively called 'replacing the SL image with a TL image', the translator can use a comparatively different TL image that maintains the same SL meaning and has equal frequency. Note that colloquial metaphors have an emotional impact and changing the image may affect the overall impact on the target readers. This may be an inevitable loss if both image and meaning cannot be reproduced simultaneously. This strategy will be more viable between close languages and cultures if a direct translation is not possible.

Ex 5.30: 'Lamb of God' is a metaphor referring to the Prophet Jesus, which was rendered as the 'seal of God' (and sometimes as 'pup of God')[3] in the language of the Eskimo, as their culture does not feature lambs and because they depend on the 'seal' for their sustenance.

Ex 5.31: 'Pig' can be rendered into Arabic as 'lamb' or 'cow' in the right context, not only to avoid the pejorative sense the SL word has in Arabic culture, but also to maintain the same level of frequency of usage. It is interesting to note that in English cooking programmes subtitled into Arabic, a 'pork cooking recipe' is usually rendered as 'lamb cooking recipe' to appeal to the target viewers.

Ex 5.32: 'Dragon' is seen as a benevolent and kind animal in the Far East but as a violent, fire-spitting animal in the West and in Arab countries, making it easier for the Arabic-English translator to maintain the same metaphor but the case is different for translating between Arabic or English and Chinese.

C. Paraphrase (الشرح)

When used to render a metaphor, this strategy is alternatively called 'demetaphorisation' by Newmark (1998/2003) and 'reducing the ST metaphor to sense' by Baker (1992/2011). It can be used if the image cannot be maintained in order to render the implied meaning only. Although it unpacks the meaning of the original metaphor, this strategy results in the loss of the emotive or pragmatic effect of the ST metaphor. In addition, metaphors can be used to talk about sensitive topics and the meaning may become harsher when it is reduced to sense. Furthermore, similar to the case with idioms, paraphrasing involves the loss of the witty style created through the use of metaphors.

Ex 5.33: Oil prices hit rock bottom.
TT: وصلت أسعار النفط لأدنى مستوياتها
Back translation: Oil prices reached their lowest level.

This translation renders the meaning of the original metaphor but loses the image, namely, oil prices are like a sunken ship, which cannot be communicated in Arabic due to its language norms.

Ex 5.34: The weeks crawled by until we met again.
TT: مرت الأسابيع ببطء شديد حتى تقابلنا مرة أخرى
Back translation: The weeks passed slowly until we met again.[4]

Here too, the image of the weeks 'crawling' like a slow animal cannot be maintained and the meaning has been paraphrased, meaning explained, instead.

Ex 5.35: My big brother is a couch potato.
TT: أخي الأكبر كسول للغاية
Back translation: My older brother is very lazy.[5]

The original metaphor likens someone who 'watches a lot of television and does not have an active life'[6] to a potato. This image cannot be communicated into Arabic and therefore a paraphrase of the intended meaning of being 'lazy' is rendered instead. The translator may also incorporate the implied, but not explicitated, idea of watching television all day in the rendering.

5.3.3 Strategies for translating new metaphors

As has been mentioned, this type covers newly coined metaphors or 'metaphorical neologism', as Newmark (1998/2003) calls it. These metaphors are usually anonymously coined, although in literary works the author can be identified. In the latter case, these metaphors reveal something about the writer's style and have a great effect on meaning; hence, the need to reproduce them in the translation.

A. Literal translation (الترجمة الحرفية)

This strategy is supposed to convey the SL metaphor, image and meaning, closely to the target readers. This is because these new metaphors are also equally new in the SL and usually have no readily available equivalents or corresponding translations to use. Literal translation is used for the purpose of attempting to offer the target readers a feel of the author's style.

Ex 5.36: Brain drain.
TT: استنزاف العقول

This metaphor is rendered into Arabic literally, which is an equally recent metaphor.

Ex 5.37: Greenback.
TT: ورق أخضر
Back translation: green bills/notes.

This SL metaphor is used to refer to the USD, and a similar Arabic equivalent is used to translate it, (ورق أخضر), which is also a literal translation of the SL term.

Ex 5.38: فمنذ أن كانت تضاء بأنوار القناديل الخافتة قبل غزو الكهرباء

TT: Ever since it had been lit by the light of subdued lamps – before the invasion of electricity (Rolph 1995: 13, quoted in Dickins et al. 2002: 152).

Ex 5.39: ولا القمر يستدير بطنه في سمائنا بصورة طبيعية

TT: And the belly of the moon does not grow round in our sky naturally (Rolph 1995: 13, quoted in Dickins et al. 2002: 152).

In examples 5.38 and 5.39, the underlined source words were rendered literally into English, see also examples 5.40 and 5.41 below.

B. Paraphrase (الشرح)

As has been mentioned, this strategy is also called 'demetaphorisation' when used to render metaphors (see Newmark 1998/2003) and 'reduce the ST metaphor to sense' (see Baker 1992/2011). If the new SL metaphor is too language-specific to render via literal translation because it involves an idiosyncratic structure or a culture-specific image, paraphrase, which implies losing the image but unpacking the meaning, can be used instead. Looking at the final two examples above, the translator can reduce them to sense if the context allows for this strategy.

Ex 5.40: فمنذ أن كانت تضاء بأنوار القناديل الخافتة قبل غزو الكهرباء

Gloss: Ever since it had been lit by the light of subdued lamps – before the invasion of electricity (Rolph 1995: 13, quoted in Dickins et al. 2002: 152).

TT: Ever since it had been lit by the light of subdued lamps – before the advent of electricity.

Here the metaphor packed in the underlined word 'invasion' was reduced to sense through the use of 'advent' (دخول).

Ex 5.41: ولا القمر يستدير بطنه في سمائنا بصورة طبيعية

Gloss: And the belly of the moon does not grow round in our sky naturally (Rolph 1995: 13, quoted in Dickins et al. 2002: 152).

TT: And the moon does not grow into a full moon in our sky naturally.

Here the metaphor 'belly of the moon' was paraphrased to 'grow into a full moon'.

Ex 5.42: مصر تشعر نحو سوريا الشقيقة بأنها قطعة من قلبها

Gloss: Egypt feels towards Syria that it is a piece of its heart.
TT: Egypt feels a strong affinity and deep affection towards Syria (adapted from Dickins 1999: 7, quoted in Dickins et al. 2002: 245).

A literal rendering of the above metaphor does not communicate the right meaning in the TT and, therefore, paraphrase is required to disambiguate the meaning.

Ex 5.43: ولقد انتظر طويلا أن تبزغ فوق صحرائه أنثى
Gloss: He had been waiting for a long time for a woman to appear over his desert.
TT: He had been waiting for a long time for a woman to dawn over the desert of his life (St. John 1999, quoted in Dickins et al. 2002: 155).

The issue with the following two metaphors is that they are colloquial, and the translation is written in standard Arabic, losing not only the image but also the colloquialism of the original metaphor. Note that Arabic writing is almost always associated with formal register for which standard rules of writing are used.

Ex 5.44: skint
TT: مفلس
Back translation: penniless

The original metaphor is an informal British metaphor implying 'having little or no money'.[7] It can be paraphrased as (مفلس) (penniless) or something similar.

Ex 5.45: stoned
TT: تحت تأثير المخدرات
Back translation: under the influence of drugs

This British metaphor implies someone who is 'under the influence of drugs, especially cannabis'.[8] It can be paraphrased, as shown above.

C. Literal translation plus paraphrase, an in-text gloss or a footnote (الترجمة الحرفية بالإضافة إلى الشرح أو إضافة معلومات بين قوسين أو حاشية سفلية)

Another strategy is for the translator to use literal translation to render the new metaphor closely and paraphrase it or add either an in-text gloss or a footnote to explain its meaning. Similar to the case of idioms, discussed above, this strategy can be used where the translator finds a new metaphor too significant to be omitted or otherwise lost in the translation.

For instance, (قبل غزو الكهرباء) discussed above can be rendered closely as 'before the invasion of electricity' together with an in-text gloss or a footnote paraphrasing the meaning as follows: 'advent or invention of electricity'.

D. Omission (with or without compensation) (الحذف مع التعويض أو بدونه)

This is not a recommended translation strategy, especially in dealing with new metaphors. It is, nonetheless, an available strategy should the translator find the new metaphor too culture- or language-specific to be dealt with in any of the above strategies. However, the translator may also decide to compensate for the lost meaning or function through adding a novel metaphor elsewhere in the TL where the ST features no metaphor. This strategy can help the target readers appreciate the creative aspect of the original author's style better compared to omission without compensation. Creating a new TL metaphor, however, is a demanding strategy indeed on the part of the translator.

5.4 Simile

A simile is 'a figure of speech that makes a comparison, showing similarities between two different things. Unlike a metaphor, a simile draws resemblance with the help of the words "like" or "as." Therefore, a simile is a direct comparison.'[9] It introduces vividness into what we write or say. Writers make use of this literary device to express their feelings and thoughts clearly through word pictures drawn via these comparisons. Structurally, a simile consists of 'tenor' or 'topic' known in Arabic as (مشبه *mushabba*) 'likened', 'vehicle' (مشبه به *mushabba bih*('likened to', similarity feature (وجه الشبه *wajhu al-shabah*) 'point of similarity' and the similarity marker (أداة التشبيه *adatul tashbīh*).

Some authors argue that[10]

- Using similes attracts attention and appeals directly to the senses of listeners or readers, encouraging their imaginations to understand what is being communicated. Also, it brings rhythm, life-like quality in our daily speech and the characters in fiction or poetry.
- Simile allows readers to relate the feelings of a writer or a poet to their personal experiences. Therefore, the use of similes makes it easier for readers to understand the subject matter of a literary text, which may have been otherwise too demanding to comprehend. Like metaphors, similes also offer variety in our ways of thinking and offer new perspectives on the world.

The relevant literature discusses types of similes, that is conventional, encyclopaedic and compressed (see Almanna 2016: 113). However, what matters here most is how to render similes between Arabic and English.

5.4.1 Strategies for translating similes

Newmark (1993: 19) claims that 'similes present no translation issues, and are translated literally in any type of text, however improbable or bizarre they may be. As they state a supposition rather than a fact, the translator has no cause to intervene [if the text is literary].' I argue, however, that direct translation is not possible all the time, particularly when the meaning being communicated is too culture- or language-specific to come across through literal translation, see example 5.50 below.

A. Direct translation (الترجمة المباشرة أو المتداولة)

Using a commonly used corresponding translation should be the preferred strategy in order to communicate the features of the literary work or the particular author's style to the target readers. However, this strategy can only be used if the available (direct) translation communicates the meaning packed in the original simile. The English examples below have directly available translations into Arabic.

Ex 5.46: Our soldiers are as brave as lions.
TT: جنودنا شجعان كالأسود

Ex 5.47: Her cheeks are red like a rose.
TT: خديها حمراوان كالزهر

Ex 5.48: He is as cunning as a fox.
TT: هو ماكر مثل الثعلب

Ex 5.49: He eats like a pig.
TT: يأكل مثل الخنزير

The translations above reproduce the meaning and image in all four examples. Note that in the final example, in particular, the translation reproduces the original simile's image and negative meaning; the latter is clearly intended since another neutral alternative in English would be 'to eat like a horse'.

B. Cultural substitution (المقابل أو المرادف أو البديل الثقافي)

The use of a TL culture- or language-specific image to reproduce the original similarity feature helps reproduce the meaning of the simile. In the following example, the simile, which is also a metaphoric expression, can be replaced with a TL image. Although the two images are different, the meaning is the same: both similes emphasise the dryness of the well through comparing it to a 'bone' in English and the to the 'rocks' in Arabic.

Ex 5.50: The water well was as dry as a bone.
TT: كان البئر جافا كالصخور
Back translation: The well was as dry as rocks.

C. Literal translation (الترجمة الحرفية)

Opting for a literal rendering of the ST simile can be used should the translator consider the original image to be new or important, provided the meaning can be gleaned in the translation. If the meaning cannot be understood, one of the following two strategies may be used instead.

Ex 5.51: As shiny as a new pin.
TT: يلمع/لامع مثل الدبوس الجديد
Back translation: As shiny as/shines like a new pin.

Ex 5.52: As blind as a bat.
TT: أعمى كالوطواط
Back translation: As blind as a bat.

The above two examples are rendered literally into Arabic. Although the image in both cases is not Arabic-specific, the Arabic reader will be able to figure out the meaning of the similes in both cases.

D. Literal translation plus paraphrase, an in-text gloss or a footnote (الترجمة الحرفية بالإضافة إلى الشرح أو إضافة معلومات بين قوسين أو حاشية سفلية)

If the translator decides to use literal translation but knows that the original meaning of the simile does not come across, using literal translation followed by a paraphrase, an in-text gloss or a footnote can be used to help the reader not only to appreciate the original stylistic feature but also to understand the intended meaning.

Ex 5.53: Shall I compare thee to a summer's day?

Thou art more lovely and more temperate. (Shakespeare, Sonnet 18)

Considering that summer days are a lot hotter in Arab countries than in the UK, some of the published translations of this sonnet rendered the likened to element, that is 'summer's day', as 'winter's day' in Arabic. However, Newmark argues against this particular translation, stressing that the Arabic readers must make the effort to 'find out the truth of the simile' (1988/2003: 164). One strategy, in this case, can be to use the literal translation of the simile and add a footnote explaining the difference in the weather between the UK and Arab countries in summer. Another strategy would be to use literal translation plus paraphrase of the deep meaning as follows: (هل أقارنك بيوم صيف جميل) 'shall I compare you to a beautiful summer's day', where 'beautiful' brings the meaning closer to the target readers.

E. Paraphrase (الشرح أو الحذف مع التعويض أو بدونه)

If the literal translation strategy does not communicate the meaning in cases where the original image is too language-specific, paraphrase can be used. The following two examples, respectively, feature losing the image and unpacking the meaning of the original simile because 'monkeys' are not seen as funny in Arabic, nor are bones 'dry'. In other words, paraphrasing the original similes below loses the image and the structure but retains the meaning.

Ex 5.54: He is as funny as a monkey.
TT: هو مرح
Back translation: He is funny.

Ex 5.55: The well was as dry as a bone.
TT: كان البئر جافا تماما
Back translation: The well was completely dry.

F. Omission (with or without compensation)

Omission can be used if the ST simile it too culture- or language-specific to be rendered in any of the above strategies. However, the translator may also decide to compensate for the lost image, meaning or function of the original simile through adding another elsewhere in the TT where the ST features no simile. As is the case with rendering metaphors, compensation can help the target readers to appreciate the witty aspect of the original author's style compared to omission without compensation. Adding a simile is not as demanding as creating a new metaphor.

5.5 Puns

Puns, a form of wordplay, are created through the use of one word ('mouse', which can refer to the actual animal or a computer mouse), two words with the same sound ('piece' vs 'peace' and 'speciality' vs 'special tea'), a group of words with the same sound (to, too, two).[11] Polysemic words, words which can have more than one meaning, are used as puns to create laughter because they have more than one meaning. Puns, as a literary device, are used for concentrating meaning or arousing laughter or amusement (see Newmark 1993: 23).

5.5.1 Strategies for translating puns

Puns are very challenging to render due to orthographic and phonemic differences between Arabic and English. This means a literal translation strategy is impossible to use. In fact, most puns are omitted when rendered using one of the lexical meanings involved, as is illustrated below.

A. Literal translation (الترجمة الحرفية)

All puns defy literal translation between Arabic and English. As has been mentioned, the reason is that they are too language-specific, orthographically and phonemically, to have a target language equivalent that reproduces the same set of meanings.

B. Substitution (استخدام تورية بديلة)

In a situation where the use of the ST pun is intended for creating laughter, it needs to be substituted, that is replaced, by another TL pun that reproduces the same effect on the readers or listeners. However, this is quite a demanding option. It is worth mentioning that poetic puns are even more difficult to translate as they are bound by metre and are, therefore, usually sacrificed in the translation process (see Newmark 1993: 23).

C. Paraphrase (الشرح)

Since literal translation and substitution of puns are not readily available options, with the first being more difficult to achieve than the second, in a situation where both senses of a pun/word are important for the context, they both need to be reproduced.

Ex 5.56: وقائل قال وما سنها فقلت وهل لها سن

TT: And someone said, 'How old is she?' I said does she have an age/teeth?

In the above poetic verse, the poet is making fun of his brother who married a very old woman. The pun in 'سن' comes from the fact that it means both 'age' and 'teeth' in Arabic. In other words, the bride is too old and has no teeth. An explanation of the dual meaning of the pun can make the meaning accessible to the target readers.

D. In-text gloss or footnote (إضافة معلومات بين قوسين أو حاشية سفلية)

This is a particularly useful strategy in dealing with puns which cannot be rendered via literal translation, substitution or paraphrase. If the translator decides to explain a particular pun to the reader, extra information can be provided as an in-text gloss or a footnote. In the example below, Hilali and Khan provide the second meaning of the original Arabic pun in brackets. However, lack of explanation of the fact that this is a pun which implies two meanings can be confusing to the readers.

> Ex 5.57: الشَّمْسُ وَالْقَمَرُ بِحُسْبَانٍ (5) والنَّجْمُ وَالشَّجَرُ يَسْجُدانِ (6) (Qur'an 55: 5–6)
> Hilali and Khan's translation: The sun and the moon run on their fixed courses (exactly) calculated with measured out stages for each (for reckoning). And the herbs (or stars) and the trees both prostrate themselves (to Allah . . .). (1977/1998: 631)

The polysemous word (النَّجْمُ) means both 'herbs' and 'stars'. Hilali and Khan provide the two meanings, rendering the word as 'herbs (or stars)'. As 'stars', this word relates to the previous verse, which refers to the 'Sun' and 'Moon', and as 'herbs', it relates simultaneously to the second verse, which refers to 'trees'. No word with corresponding meanings exists in English. The translators can either render only one meaning, resulting in translation loss, alternatively called 'under translation', or use two words to render the SL meaning, thus losing the conciseness of the Qur'an. Hilali and Khan opt for an in-text gloss, presenting both meanings to the target readers to reflect the original pun.

> Ex 5.58: إِنَّ الَّذِينَ كَذَّبُوا بِآيَاتِنَا واستكبروا عنها لا تُفَتَّحُ لَهُمْ أَبْوابُ السَّماءِ وَلا يَدْخُلُونَ الْجَنَّةَ حَتَّى يَلِجَ الْجَمَلُ فِي سَمِّ الْخِياطِ . . . (Qur'an 7: 40)
> Qara'i's translation: Indeed, those who deny Our signs
> And are disdainful of them –
> The gates of the heaven will not be opened for them,
> Nor shall they enter paradise
> Until the camel passes through the needle's eye*
>
> *Footnote: (or, 'until the cable passes through needle's eye') (2004: 210–1)

The word 'الْجَمَلُ' can mean 'camel' or 'thick rope'. The translation above makes use of a footnote in order to reproduce the second meaning.

E. Omission (with or without compensation) (الحذف مع التعويض أو بدونه)

Since puns do not lend themselves easily to translation because they are usually too language-specific, omission is a popular strategy. As is the case with metaphor and idioms above, the translator may decide to compensate for the lost witticism created in the ST through the use of a pun by adding a pun somewhere in the TT where the ST does not feature one. Here too, compensation by adding a TL pun can help the target readers appreciate the witty style of the original author (see more in Delabastita 1996, 1997, 2004; al-Aqad et al. 2017).

The example above, reproduced below for ease of reference, has been dealt with differently by Hilali and Khan.

> Ex 5.59: إِنَّ الَّذِينَ كَذَّبُوا بِآيَاتِنَا واستكبروا عنها لا تُفَتَّحُ لَهُمْ أَبْوابُ السَّماءِ وَلا يَدْخُلُونَ الْجَنَّةَ حَتَّى يَلِجَ الْجَمَلُ فِي سَمِّ الْخِياطِ . . . (Qur'an 7: 40)
>
> Hilali and Khan's translation: Verily, those who believe Our Ayat (proofs, evidences, verses, lessons, signs, revelations, etc.) and treat them with arrogance, for them the gates of heaven will not be opened, and they will not enter Paradise until the camel goes through the eye of the needle (which is impossible). (1977/1998)

The translators miss out on reproducing the pun implied through the word (الْجَمَلُ), which, as explained above, can mean 'camel' or 'thick rope'. They, however, compensate for the lost effect by adding an in-text gloss that unpacks the function of the original pun, namely, 'this is impossible to happen'. Although this strategy compensates for the original function of the pun, the readers will not be aware of the existence of a pun in the ST.

5.6 Cohesion (سبكة النص أو تماسك النص)

I discuss the issue of cohesion as a text level issue because, as is shown below, cohesion-creating devices seem to involve more than one sentence at a time. Furthermore, in Arabic, punctuation marks are not used as often as in English (see Baker 1992/2011: 228). For instance, a full stop may only occur at the end of a whole paragraph in Arabic rather than at the end of what is considered in English to be a full sentence. In other words, Arabic sentence boundaries are not marked by punctuation marks but by meaning, which determines where a sentence starts and ends. In addition, Arabic uses explicit connectors between phrases, clauses and sentences comparatively more than English, which will help readers to identify sentences boundaries.

Cohesion is defined as 'the relationship between sentences' (Newmark 1988/2003: 59). Similarly, Baker (1992/2011: 190) defines cohesion as

> the network of lexical, grammatical, and other relations which provide links between various parts of a text. These relations or ties organise and, to some extent, create a text, for instance, by requiring the reader to interpret words and expressions by reference to other words and expressions in the surrounding sentences and paragraphs. [In other words,] cohesion is a surface relation; it connects together the actual words and expressions that we can see or hear.

It goes without saying that this device can be quite language-specific; languages may act differently in terms of the manner in which (levels of) cohesion is achieved. Halliday and Hasan (1976, see also Ghazala 2008/2014: 72ff; Baker 1992/2011: 190ff.; Newmark 1988/2003: 57, 59) identify the following cohesive devices in English:

- Reference (الضمائر)
- Repetition (التكرار)
- Substitution (الإبدال)
- Ellipsis (الحذف)
- Conjunction (حروف العطف)
- Lexical cohesion (التماسك اللفظي)

Arabic and English, however, use these devices differently, and attention must be paid to how each language makes use of each specific device. The following section explains how these devices work in both languages.

5.6.1 Reference

Halliday and Hasan (1976) use reference to cover the use of pronouns, articles or adverbs to refer back or forward within a text, thereby creating anaphoric or cataphoric cohesion, respectively. According to El-Farahaty (2015: 30), 'this is only effective . . . when the reference and its antecedent are clearly laid out and there is no possibility of ambiguity'. According to Baker (1992/2011: 190ff.), reference is a semantic relationship referring to:

- the relationship between a word and what it points to in the real world; and
- the relationship of identity which holds between two linguistic expressions, in a more restricted sense of the term.

Ex 5.60: Mrs Thatcher has resigned. She announced her decision this morning.
TT: السيدة تاتشر استقالت، وقد أعلنت قرارها هذا الصباح
Back translation: Mrs Thatcher has resigned, and she-announced her decision this morning.

In this example, 'Mrs Thatcher' is a direct reference to a real person in the word, and 'she' refers back to 'Mrs Thatcher', exemplifying the second meaning of reference above. The reader has to retrieve the identity of what is being talked about by referring to another expression in the immediate context (Baker 1992/2011: 191). Note that an Arabic conjunction has to be used between the two sentences for a smooth reading, and that is why I have added (و) 'and' in my translation above.

Reference devices

Reference can be achieved in both Arabic and English in similar but not exact means. I discuss below types of pronouns and repetition, as examples of reference-creating devices.

- Pronouns of different types can be used for referring back or forward to an entity, event or participant. They are probably the most common reference items in English and Arabic. However, they are used differently across the two languages, as the discussion below illustrates.
- Pronominal references in Arabic can be used quite differently from English. Due to verb inflection system, an Arabic verb has to be conjugated for/agree with the subject in terms of its number and gender, in addition to tense. This effectively means that a sentence may not have a free-standing subject but have a verb clitic instead. In the previous example, 'She announced' is translated into one Arabic word, verb cum subject (أعلنت). In terms of function, the use of verb conjugation fulfils the same function of the subject pronoun obtaining in the English sentence.
- Possessive pronouns can similarly differ between the two languages as the following example shows.

Ex 5.61: The boy's socks and shoes
TT: جورب الولد وحذائه
Gloss: The boy's socks and his-shoes

This is a classic example of how Arabic puts possessive pronouns to use. Translation of this example into Arabic features the use of both the *iḍāfa*/genitive structure to render 'the boy's socks' and a possessive pronoun to render 'and shoes'. A close rendering of the English clause, however, would not sound natural in Arabic.

- Demonstrative pronouns establish similar links between expressions in a text, thereby creating cohesion (Baker 1992/2011: 191).

Ex 5.62: Mrs Thatcher has resigned. This delighted her opponents.
TT: السيدة تاتشر استقالت، وهذا أسعد خصومها/وقد أسعد هذا خصومها
Back translation: Mrs Thatcher has resigned, and this delighted her opponents.

In this example, the demonstrative pronoun, which refers to the 'resignation' anaphorically, is reproducible in both form and function in Arabic: 'this' is rendered by the use of an Arabic demonstrative, which similarly refers back to an event in the previous sentence. Here too, an explicit connector, (و), meaning 'and', between the two sentences needs to be added in Arabic for natural usage.

5.6.2 Repetition

This device also achieves textual cohesion. I draw here on Baker (1992/2011: 192–3), who draws on Halliday and Hasan (1976: 283), to illustrate this point. I also provide the Arabic translation of each example to show whether Arabic acts differently or similarly in these particular situations.

Ex 5.63: There is a boy climbing that tree.
TT: هناك ولد يتسلق تلك الشجرة

1. The boy is going to fall if he does not take care. (repetition)
TT: الولد سيسقط إن لم ينتبه (تكرار)

2. The lad is going to fall if he does not take care. (synonym)
TT: الصبي سيسقط إن لم ينتبه (مرادف)

3. The child is going to fall if he does not take care. (superordinate)
TT: الطفل سيسقط إن لم ينتبه (كلمة أعلى رتبة)

4. The idiot is going to fall if he does not take care. (adjective)[12]
TT: المعتوه سيسقط إن لم ينتبه (صفة)

5. He is going to fall if he does not take care. (pronominal reference)
TT: (هو) سيسقط إن لم ينتبه (ضمير فاعل)

All the above examples are easily translatable into Arabic. The translations I provided above feature the same issues under discussion: the use of repetition, synonym, superordinate, general word and pronominal reference (see above for the use of verb conjugation in Arabic).

To elaborate on the function of lexical repetition further, Jawad states that

> lexical repetition assumes the role of organising and rendering the text cohesive in much the same way connectives do. Rhetorically lexical repetition has to do with the expressive meaning that a marked repetitive pattern evokes ... by the recurrence of certain lexical items in a short piece of text, a foregrounded image is projected on the surface of the text signalling a semantic weight that goes beyond the mere senses of the repeated utterances. (Jawad 2009: 754, quoted in El-Farahaty 2015: 45)

The similarity of the English sentences and their respective Arabic translations should not mask the fact that patterns of reference vary across languages and genres within the same language. For example, in advertising and political discourse, names rather than pronominal references to them seem to be preferred in order to fix products or party names into the minds of the receivers (see Cook 1992: 154, quoted in Baker 1992/2011: 193). English is also reported to prefer the use of pronominal references 'in tracing participants' (Baker 1992/2011: 193; see also El-Farahaty 2015: 29–30).

5.6.3 Substitution

This is a grammatical relationship, which features replacing (an) item(s) by another item(s), for example, do, one, the same (see Baker 1992/2011: 196; Halliday and Hasan 1976).

Ex 5: 64: I like movies.	- And I do.
TT: أحب (مشاهدة) الأفلام	وأنا أيضا/كذلك -
Back translation: I like (watching) movies	- And I too.

The use of 'do' cannot be maintained in the Arabic translation due to lack of an equivalent auxiliary, thus, its meaning needs to be unpacked lexically.

Ex 5.65: You think Joan already knows?	- I think everybody does.
TT: تعتقد أن جون تعرف بالفعل؟	أعتقد أن الجميع يعرف -
Back translation: You think Joan already knows?	- I think everybody knows.

In the previous example, 'does' replaces 'knows' in the source text. Here too, 'does' is irreproducible in Arabic and the main verb, (يعرف) 'knows', needs to be repeated.

Ex 5.66: My axe is too blunt. I must get a sharper one. (Baker 1992/2011: 196)
TT: فأسي كليلة جدا، لابد أن أحصل على واحدة أحدّ.
Back translation: My axe is too blunt. I must get a sharper one.

In this example, note that 'one' replaces 'axe' and that the Arabic rendering is quite close to the English version: it reproduces 'one' because this is a semantic rather than a grammatical issue, unlike the previous two examples.

Ex 5.67: I will have two poached eggs on toast, please. - I'll have the same.
TT: سآخذ بيضتين مسلوقتين وخبزا محمصا من فضلك - سآخذ نفس الشيئ
Back translation: I'll have two poached eggs on toast, please. - I will have the same thing.

Note that 'the same' replaces 'two poached eggs on toast' and that (نفس) 'the same' is rendered as the first item in an *iḍāfa*/genitive structure in Arabic, one which requires a definite noun to qualify and cannot stand on its own and, hence, the need to reproduce a noun (الشيء) 'thing'. The issue in this example is grammatical rather than semantic and, thus, the two languages act differently.

To summarise, it seems from the above set of examples that grammatical substitution involving 'do', 'does' and 'the same', cannot be maintained in Arabic, while semantic substitution involving 'one' can. The translator needs to abide by the rules of natural usage in each language rather than try to stay close to the source language structure, which may not produce a smooth reading translation. The shifts here, to use Catford's terminology (1965/1978), are necessary rather than optional.

5.6.4 Ellipsis

This is a grammatical relationship, which involves the omission of an item because it is understood and where the grammatical structure allows for this omission. In other words, 'an item is replaced by nothing' (Baker 1992/2011: 196, see also Beaugrande and Dressler 1981: 49; Halliday and Hasan 1976: 197).

Ex 5.68: Joan brought carnations and Catherine (...) some sweet peas. (Baker 1992/2011: 197)
TT: أحضرت جون ورد القرنفل وأحضرت كاثرين زهور البازلاء
Back translation: Joan brought carnations and Catherine brought some sweet peas.

The English sentence above features the ellipsis of 'brought' while the translation has to repeat the verb, filling in the ellipted item; otherwise, the translation will not be grammatical.

Ex 5.69: Here are thirteen cards. Take any (. . .). Now give me any three (. . .). (Baker 1992/2011: 197)

TT: هذه 13 بطاقة. خذ أيا منها. والآن أعطني أية ثلاث

Back translation: Here are thirteen cards. Take any of them. And now give me any three.

The original sentence features the ellipsis of 'cards' twice. The ellipted items have to be filled in to produce a grammatical rendering in the second clause: (خذ) 'take' is a transitive verb which requires an object. Note also that (منها) 'of them' can be replaced by the original referent itself, 'cards'. The use of the object pronouns, however, is intended to produce a smooth reading version. In the final clause, Arabic can mirror the original word order, with no need to reproduce the ellipted item seeing that (ثلاث) 'three' can stand for the object and the meaning is clear from the context. In other words, reproducing the object in the first case of ellipsis is a grammatical necessity but a stylistic preference in the second case.

Ex 5.70: Have you been swimming? - Yes, I have.

TT: هل كنت تسبح؟ - نعم كنت أسبح

Back translation: Have you been swimming? -Yes, I have been swimming.

The translation requires filling in the ellipted verb (أسبح) 'swimming' to abide by natural and grammatical Arabic usage (see Baker 1992/2011: 197). Of course, a short answer is possible here, but the translation provided is intended to stay as close as possible to the ST.

Ex 5.71: As if!

This ellipted expression implies doubt about something.[13] The ellipted items can be understood from the context and, in Arabic, the translation will have to fill in the ellipted item(s) to sound natural. For example, if someone is trying to lift something up, 'as if' can be used to imply doubt that the person in question can actually carry that item. The Arabic translation will need to unpack this meaning (وكأنك تستطيع حملها) 'As if you can carry it.'

Ex 5.72: If only!

This ellipted expression can mean 'I wish.'[14] Here too, this ellipted structure derives its meaning from the context in English, and the Arabic translation will have to fill in the ellipted item(s) to sound natural. For example, in a situation where the ellipted item is 'I had the money', the translation would be (لو أن عندي المال) 'If only I had the money.' It is noteworthy here that the second part of the conditional structure can equally be ellipted in Arabic because its meaning can be disambiguated from the context.

The need to fill in the ellipted item to render the meaning clearly holds true while translating into the opposite direction: Arabic into English. In other words, supplying the ellipted item(s) may equally be necessary for grammaticality in Arabic into English translations. The following example features a verse from the Qur'an, which involves missing out words, indicated by (. . .), which are necessary for completing the sentence formally but not for understanding its meaning. However, due to differences in the way English employs ellipsis, it is sometimes necessary to add the ellipted words (which usually appear in brackets) to complete a sentence in the translation.

Ex 5.73: وإذ أخذنا ميثاقكم ورفعنا فوقكم الطور . . . خذوا ما آتيناكم بقوة واسمعوا . . .
قالوا سمعنا وعصينا وأشربوا في قلوبهم . . .العجل بكفرهم
قل . . . بئسما يأمركم به إيمانكم إن كنتم مؤمنين
(Qur'an 2: 93)

Close translation: And when We made with you a covenant and caused the Mount to tower above you (. . .): Hold fast by that which We have given you, and hear (. . .), they said: We hear and we rebel. And (. . .) the calf was made to sink into their hearts because of their rejection. Say (. . .): Evil is that which your belief enjoins on you, if you are believers.

Pickthall's translation: And when We made with you a covenant and caused the Mount to tower above you, (saying): Hold fast by that which We have given you, and hear (our Lord), they said: We hear and we rebel. And (worship of) the calf was made to sink into their hearts because of their rejection. Say (to them): Evil is that which your belief enjoins on you, if you are believers. (2005: 14)

The significance of this *al-Balāgha* (rhetorical) linguistic device, which is to engage the readers or listeners even more with the text of the Qur'an as well as achieve conciseness, is arguably lost in the translation. In addition, these additions can provide more room for the expression of ideology and for freer interpretation (see Elimam 2013: 36–7; Ali 1992).

5.6.5 Conjunction

Conjunction is defined as 'the use of formal markers to relate sentences, clauses and paragraphs to each other', and it signals the way in which the text producer wants the receiver to 'relate what is about to be said to what has been said before' (Baker 1992/2011: 200). The most commonly used conjunction in Arabic is probably the (و /wa/). (و) can be used to imply two different meanings: temporal sequence, simultaneous action, semantic contrast, semantic equivalence, and so on (see Ghazala 2008/2014: 72ff; Holes 2004: 234). I provide below types of conjunction and examples of each type in English.

1. additive:
   and, or, also, in addition, furthermore, besides, similarly, likewise, by contrast, for instance
2. adversative:
   but, yet, however, instead, on the other hand, nevertheless, at any rate, as a matter of fact
3. causal:
   so, consequently, it follows, for, because, under the circumstances, for this reason
4. temporal:
   then, next, after that, on another occasion, in conclusion, an hour later, finally, at last
5. continuatives:
   now, of course, well, anyway, surely, after all
   (Halliday and Hasan 1976, quoted in Baker 1992/2011: 200)

It is worth noting here, firstly, that the same conjunction may be used to signal different relations based on the relevant context. Secondly, these types of relations can be expressed in different ways. A temporal relationship can be expressed via the items mentioned above, the use of the verb (follow, precede), or no items at all, for instance, 'I got up early and had breakfast' (see Baker 1992/2011: 200). Thirdly, some English texts make little or no use of conjunctions, and some are more conjunctive than others: religious and fiction texts use more conjunctions which serve to clarify the kind of the inter-sentential and intertextual relationships that exist in the particular piece of writing. Science and journalistic writing on the other hand use fewer (causal) conjunctions because there is 'high level of assumed knowledge' in science between authors and readers (ibid. 205), and 'to give an impression of objectivity . . . and the need to avoid giving overt explanations of reported events which risks the danger of legal suits and liability' (ibid.).

Fourthly, English depends on the use of relatively smaller chunks but fewer inter-sentential connectors to present and organise information. Arabic, on the other hand, uses longer chunks because the use of punctuation is not as common as it is in English, but more inter-sentential connectors are used (which are arguably small in number, according to Jabouri and Knowles 1988, quoted in Baker 1992/2011: 202). 'Sentential' here has to be understood in the Arabic context: in Arabic meaning and grammar can be used to define the sentence while in English punctuation serves this function. Fifthly, adjusting the patterns of conjunctions, that is explicitation of the types of relationships which hold between sentences when translating into Arabic and relying more on implicit connections and the use of punctuation when translating into English, to abide by TL norms affects both the content and the line of argument. Sixthly, (re)chunking long ST sentences into smaller TL ones alters the original level of importance accorded to each unit:

> every option will have its advantages and disadvantages. Following the source-language norms may involve a minimal change in overall meaning . . . On the other

> hand, noticeable deviation from typical target-language patterns of chunking information and signalling relations is likely to result in the sort of text that can easily be identified as a translation because it sounds 'foreign'. (Baker 1992/2011: 210)

For example, Abdel Haleem's translation of the Qur'an divides the undivided, continuous Qur'anic text into paragraphs: '[i]n order to clarify the meaning and structure of thoughts and to meet the expectation of modern readers' (2004/2005: xxxiv). Abdel Haleem also breaks what would otherwise be too long a sentence into smaller units to solve the problem of *iltifaat* [change of addressee] (ibid. xxxv). However, not respecting the division of sentences, for example, by translating two sentences into one or translating one into two, not an uncommon practice in translation, provides more room for interpretation and ideological involvement on the part of the translator. Changing a complete sentence to a clause or vice versa may have a potential implication (loss or addition, for example) for meaning (Bin Salāma 2000: 103).

Ex 5.74: فَلَمَّا فَصَلَ طَالُوتُ بِالْجُنُودِ قَالَ إِنَّ اللهَ مُبْتَلِيكُم بِنَهَرٍ فَمَن شَرِبَ مِنْهُ فَلَيْسَ مِنِّي
وَمَن لَّمْ يَطْعَمْهُ فَإِنَّهُ مِنِّي إِلاَّ مَنِ اغْتَرَفَ غُرْفَةً بِيَدِهِ (Qur'an 2: 249)

Hilali and Khan's translation: Verily! Allah will try you by a river. So whoever drinks thereof, he is not of me; and whoever tastes it not, he is of me, except him who takes (thereof) in the hollow of his hand. (1977/1998: 63)

Bewley and Bewley's translation: Allah will test you with a river. Anyone who drinks from it is not with me. But anyone who does not taste it is with me – except for him who merely scoops up a little in his hand. (2005: 35)

Al-Bayḍāwī (n.d.) and al-Zamakhsharī (n.d.) explain that the context of the verse is that Talut led the Israelites to fight the giants who lived in Palestine. The army, which marched out with Talut during a hot season, asked him to ask God for a river. Talut responded by saying that God would give them a river to test them. The commentators explain that the clause (وَمَن لَّمْ يَطْعَمْهُ فَإِنَّهُ مِنِّي) 'anyone who refrains from tasting it will belong with me', is foregrounded for importance (الأهمية) before the clause (إلاَّ مَنِ اغْتَرَفَ غُرْفَةً بِيَدِهِ) 'except he who takes a handful with his hand', which would regularly occur after the clause (فَمَن شَرِبَ مِنْهُ فَلَيْسَ مِنِّي) 'Whoever drinks from it, he is not of me.' In other words, having divided people into two main categories, those who drink from the water (who do not belong to Talut) and those who do not drink from the water (and who thus belong to Talut), the verse then excludes those who drink only a handful from the first group. Logically, therefore, this exemption should come after the mention of the first not the second group but it is delayed here for foregrounding.

Hilali and Khan's translation above closely follows the word order of the verse, and they do not suggest that the verse features any foregrounding. Bewley and Bewley change the meaning by placing a full stop after the first category, 'Anyone who drinks from it is not with me', and coordinating the second and third categories with a dash indicating interjection, 'But anyone who does not taste it is with me – except for him who merely scoops up a little in his hand.' This structure implies that the third category, meaning those who drink a handful, are excluded from the category of those who did not drink at all, a meaning different from that communicated by the verse according to the commentators above.

5.6.6 Lexical cohesion

Lexical cohesion refers to the role played by the selection of vocabulary in organising relations within a text. Vocabulary creates lexical chaining. For instance, repetition can be an example of lexical cohesion creating devices. Repetition refers to the repetition of the same lexical items (words, phrases, clauses), see El-Farahaty (2015: 29; see also Newmark 1988/2003: 60). This could be a synonym, near-synonym, superordinate, or a general word (Halliday and Hasan 1976: 278). Note that languages differ in the level of lexical repetition they tolerate and, generally speaking, Arabic seems to tolerate more lexical repetition than English.

The following example, (العودة إلى الجذور) 'Going Back to the Roots' by Rashad Abu Shawir,[15] features lexical cohesion, in addition to some of the devices discussed above.

Ex: 5.75

عندما هبت العاصفة دوى صوتها القوي عاليا. خافت الأشجار وأحنت جذوعها وأغصانها ، فمرت العاصفة ولم تتمكن من اقتلاع الأشجار أو تخريب الحقول.

غضبت العاصفة وأخذت تدور حول الحقول مزمجرة متوعدة وصرخت: " أيتها الأشجار! إنك تنحنين احتراما لي . أليس كذلك؟"

ضحكت الأشجار وقالت: "لا أيتها العاصفة، إنما نفعل ذلك لنتفادى جنونك."

زأرت العاصفة متوعدة:" انتظري وسترين كيف سأحطمك!"

لم تأبه الأشجار بتهديدات العاصفة، ظلت تميل بغصونها على التراب. عادت العاصفة وأطلقت كل غضبها، لكنها لم تتمكن من اقتلاع الأشجار .

حاولت العاصفة أن تعرف سر التصاق الأشجار بالأرض فسألت: "أيها الأشجار، قولي لي، لماذا تلوين أغصانك باتجاه الأرض؟

You can see the repetition of (الأشجار) 'the trees'. You can also see how words like (غصون) 'branches' and (حقول) 'fields' are also repeated and relate to the same lexical family.

5.7 Conclusion

This chapter has covered some of the prominent translation issues which can occur at a textual level: idioms and fixed expressions (الأقوال المأثورة والتعابير الاصطلاحية), metaphors (الاستعارة), similes (التشبيه), puns (التورية) and cohesion (سبكة النص أو تماسك النص). To reiterate, I am not implying that the translation process is carried out at text level independently or separately, but the classification is intended to provide a practical way of approaching the translation issues. Issues at any level of the text and the strategies used to deal with them will influence the translator's output and are influenced by his or her overall translation approach, amongst other factors. Below is a summary of the issues and strategies discussed in this chapter.

Idiom translation issues:

- Difference in meaning between the SL and corresponding TL idiom
- The existence of no TL equivalent idiom
- The difference in context and frequency of the usage of idioms between the SL and TL

Idiom translation strategies:

1. Direct (available) translation
2. Cultural substitution
3. Literal translation
4. Paraphrase
5. Literal translation plus a paraphrase, an in-text gloss or a footnote
6. Omission (with or without compensation)

Metaphor translation issues:

- Identifying whether what is at hand is a common or new metaphor
- Establishing whether the available ST metaphor has the same currency of the ST metaphor.
- Focusing on rendering the meaning rather than just the image
- Identifying the ground for comparison or the deep meaning of the metaphor

Common metaphor translation strategies:

1. Direct translation
2. Cultural substitution
3. Paraphrase

New metaphor translation strategies:

1. Literal translation
2. Paraphrase
3. Literal translation plus a paraphrase, an in-text gloss or a footnote
4. Omission (with or without compensation)

Simile translation issue:

- Difference in the use of the image between the two languages or cultures

Simile translation strategies:

1. Direct translation
2. Cultural substitution
3. Literal translation
4. Literal translation plus a paraphrase, an in-text gloss or a footnote
5. Paraphrase
6. Omission (with or without compensation)

Puns translation issues:

- Understanding the meanings implied by the source text word
- Finding an equivalent target language word

Pun translation strategies:

1. Literal translation
2. Substitution
3. Paraphrase
4. In-text gloss or footnote
5. Omission (with or without compensation)

Cohesion translation issues:

- In Arabic, punctuation marks are not used as often as in English
- Arabic uses explicit connectors between phrases, clauses and sentences comparatively more than English

Cohesion creating devices:

- Reference
- Repetition
- Substitution

- Ellipsis
- Conjunction
- Lexical cohesion

Cohesion and cohesion-creating devices translation strategies:

1. produce conjunctives between sentences when translating into Arabic in accordance with Arabic language norms.
2. use more punctuation marks and fewer conjunctives when translating into English and fewer punctuation marks and more conjunctives when translating into Arabic in accordance with TL norms.

5.8 Exercises

5.8.1 The translation exercises in the previous chapters feature some of the issues covered in this chapter. Check your translations and decide whether you would deal with relevant issues differently in line with the strategies discussed in this chapter. For instance, exercise 3.5.1 features several of the issues discussed in the current chapter. Identify as many as possible of the relevant issues and consider how you would translate them now that you have been introduced to the relevant translation strategies.

Tips: Identify your overall translation approach to start with. For example, would you adopt a foreignisation or domestication approach? And bearing this in mind, consider how you would render the stylistic issues you come across: what translation strategies would you use in each case? Note that the informal tone is imbedded throughout this text and cannot be separated from how its stylistic features are employed.

For example, how would you deal with the expression 'good old days'? Would (الأيام الخوالي) or (أيام الشباب) be appropriate translations? Consider what 'take a leaf out of his book' means. Can it be translated literally into Arabic? If not, why? How will you deal with metaphors, for example, 'shrouded in mystery' or 'became glued to our smartphones'?

See also how exercise 4.10.2 features some issues, including metaphors and similes. Read the text again, identify some of the issues discussed above and decide how you would render them into Arabic. In fact, the passage features several similes and metaphors, as well as other textual issues, for example, (حتى أحسست كأن ثلجا يذوب في دخيلتي، فكأنني مقرور طلعت عليه الشمس) features a double simile. How would you render them into Arabic? How would you translate the metaphor in (وأرخيت أذني للريح)? Note that it is important to communicate the intricate style of the author, Taib Salih, of this particular novel to the audience as he is world renown.

5.8.2 The following passage is taken from Ayman Al-Otoom's (ياصاحبي السجن) "Oh Fellow Prisoners" (2012). What textual issues do you think it features and how do you propose to deal with them?

Tips: the passage can be considered an extended metaphor. It tells of the author's experience of having been invited to deliver one of his poems in Ajloun Castle, Jordan, which was built by Salaḥueddin (Saladin in English) in 1184 CE. The visit seems to have haunted the author and hence the series of metaphors involving him and the castle. Note that (فاجعتي) is a metaphor for the poem he delivered on that visit which led him to be jailed.

مر أسبوع على الأقل منذ منتصف شهر آب في العام 1996، التاريخ الذي ألقيت فيه فاجعتي والتقيت فيه رائعتي ، ولا زالت جوارحي معطرة بلقاء القلعة، يرافقني اللقاء حيث أذهب ، أخرج من البيت فيخرج معي، أصعد إلى الباص فيفعل مثلي، أدخل الجامعة فلا يتركني ، وحين أهم بقراءة كتاب ، تخرج ظلاله من بين السطور . . . ولا يختفي ، بل قل لا ينزوي جانبا إلى حين التقى بعض الأصدقاء القدامى أو الزملاء. . . ثم يعاود الظهور مرة أخرى حالما أفارقهم.

5.8.3 The following excerpt is taken from a text which was used by the EU Commission in their annual competition to reward the best young translators in the European Union (2016). Translating this text into Arabic would pose many of the textual challenges discussed in this chapter. Identify as many challenges as possible and consider which translation strategies you would use to deal with them.[16]

Tips: Note how this text reads differently from the one above. Consider how this may influence your translation approach. Remember also that your translation strategies have to be in line with your translation approach.

Translating chance into career

It never fails to amaze me how apparently insignificant events can have such a far-reaching impact on people's lives. In my case, three chance occurrences led me to move from England to three other countries and become a professional translator.

It all started at a rock festival. Towards the end of the final night, with the rain drizzling down as usual, a group of us were approached by three somewhat bedraggled fellow festival-goers, one of whom asked us in faltering English how to get to the station. It emerged that they were from Germany and had been travelling around Europe. My German was fairly basic, and the station was a long way away, so I offered to show them at the end of the show. To cut a long story short, we stayed in touch and I opted to study German at university.

By the time I graduated I had become so fascinated by all things German that I wanted to go and live there. Teaching was the obvious job for me and, only one month after obtaining my degree, I found myself living in Essen, teaching English and translation to students of all ages and backgrounds. It so happened that my boss was Italian, and he had long cherished an ambition to open a language school in his own country. When, two years later, he offered me the chance to go to Pisa as his Head of Languages, it seemed that another adventure was beckoning.

So, off I went, armed with a smattering of Italian and a belief that what I'd done once I could do again. I went on to spend three years teaching English and German in Italy, taking on more and more translation work as my Italian improved.

And this is where the third combination of events came into play. One of the friends who had been at the festival with me was now working in Denmark. He came across an advertisement in the paper – the Internet was a thing of science fiction in those days – for a competition organised by the European Commission for translators with at least two EU languages. I had never thought about becoming a full-time translator before, but now, with my German and Italian, I decided to give it a go.

With few expectations I applied and duly sat the competition in Rome. Much to my surprise, I was subsequently invited to Brussels for the oral test. I passed that as well, and two years later became a fully-fledged translator for the Commission in Brussels.

Notes

1. <https://www.merriam-webster.com/dictionary/idiom> (last accessed 4 September 2019)
2. <https://www.oxfordreference.com//view/10.1093/oi/authority.20110803100153175> (last accessed 24 August 2022)
3. <https://triangulations.wordpress.com/2010/05/05/the-pup-of-god/> (last accessed 4 September 2019)
4. <https://penlighten.com/list-of-similes-metaphors> (last accessed 1 December 2019)
5. <https://penlighten.com/list-of-similes-metaphors> (last accessed 1 December 2019)
6. <https://dictionary.cambridge.org/dictionary/english/couch-potato> (last accessed 1 December 2019)
7. <http://www.oxforddictionaries.com/definition/english/skint> (last accessed 1 December 2019)
8. <http://www.oxforddictionaries.com/definition/english/stoned> (last accessed 1 December 2019)
9. <https://literarydevices.net/simile/> (last accessed 1 December 2019)
10. <https://literarydevices.net/simile/> (last accessed 1 December 2019)
11. <https://literarydevices.net/pun/> (last accessed 15 June 2019)
12. Baker uses 'general word' to describe 'idiot'. I use 'adjective' instead to better describe the function of this word and differentiate it from 'superordinate' which means a 'general word'.
13. <https://www.macmillandictionary.com/dictionary/british/as-if> (last accessed 24 August 2022)
14. <https://dictionary.cambridge.org/dictionary/english/if-only> (last accessed 24 August 2022)
15. <https://www.noor-book.com/?search_for=%D9%86%D8%B5%D9%88%D8%B5+%D8%B9%D8%B1%D8%A8%D9%8A%D8%A9+%D8%B9%D9%85%D8%A7%D8%AF+%D8%AD%D8%A7%D8%AA%D9%85#google_vignette> (last accessed 24 August 2022)
16. <https://ec.europa.eu/info/sites/info/files/file_import/en_english_28.pdf> (last accessed 24 August 2022)

CHAPTER 6
CONTEXTUAL TRANSLATION ISSUES AND STRATEGIES

6.1 Introduction

The previous three chapters have dealt with issues directly related to style at lexical, structural and textual levels. This chapter is dedicated to discussing some of the contextual issues which influence the translation process and product (المشكلات السياقية للترجمة واستراتيجياتها). As has been mentioned, context (السياق العام للنص وعملية الترجمة أو السياق اختصارا) is used as an umbrella term referring to all extra-textual elements which can and do influence the ST, TT or the process/producer of translation. These factors include, but are not limited to, the linguistic conventions in use when the ST and TT were produced, ST and TT cultural context, readers' expectations, and the ST author's and translator's aims, ideology, background knowledge, training, and so forth.

For example, the linguistic context in which an utterance is made determines the range of implicatures that can be driven out (realities of the situation) or filter out inappropriate interpretations (Baker 2006). For instance, describing the room temperature as warm can imply a set of different meanings based on the context. It can mean it is nice and warm as opposed to the cold weather outside, or it is too warm and stuffy and you want the window to be opened or the fan/air conditioning to be switched on. Contextual factors can also explain why a ST is organised the way it is, why certain grammatical structures are used and why certain translation approaches or strategies are opted for. Along these lines, Strelkova (2012: 10–11) argues that

> [c]ontext can help you decide on form, on what words to choose and how to arrange them to best convey the sense. Judging when and how you can change content is a different, but equally, important matter. The context, your background knowledge, and possible information on the intended readership, will contribute to that judgement.

This chapter, therefore, will offer an examination of some contextual factors, namely, the translation approach, target readers' expectations, context of reception and translator's aim, translator's ideology, the commissioner's influence, trends in academia or philosophy, and register, illustrating how these factors directly influence the translator's output.

6.2 The translation approach (أسلوب الترجمة)

The translation approach adopted is a major influential factor in the translation process and product. This is because the overall approach determines the local strategies to be opted for, the relevant loss and gain of the meaning rendered and, therefore, the 'flavour' of the resulting translation. The translation approach needs to be determined by the translator or the translation commissioner before the translation process starts. The selection of the approach is usually carried out in line with several considerations, e.g. the *skopos* of the translation, target readers' expectations and the commissioner's desire to market the translation in a specific market. I discuss below a few examples to illustrate this point clearly.

Ex 6.1: Abdel Haleem's versus Hilali and Khan's translations of the Qur'an

These two translations of the Qur'an adopt different approaches; one is target language-oriented by Abdel Haleem and the other, paraphrastic by Hilali and Khan. Abdel Haleem's *The Qur'an* was first published in 2004. The translator's stated aim is 'to go further than previous works in accuracy, clarity, flow, and currency of language' (2004/2005: xxix). In order to achieve this aim, he opts for 'a modern, easy style, avoiding where possible the use of cryptic language or archaisms that tend to obscure meaning ... to make the Qur'an accessible to everyone who speaks English' (ibid. xxix). In other words, Abdel Haleem wants to offer his target readers an easy read; one can describe it as 'domestication'. Abdel Haleem (2004) explains that his translation avoids literalness in rendering Arabic structures and expressions to avoid producing meaningless translations.

On the other hand, Hilali and Khan's translation of the Qur'an is entitled *Interpretation of the Meanings of the Noble Qur'ān in the English Language*, first published in 1977. This translation is described by Kidwai (1992) as 'a summarized English version of Ibn Kathir's exegesis, supplemented by Tabari's, with comments from Sahih al-Bukhari' (the latter, a collection of the sayings/tradition of the Prophet Muhammad, is recognised by Muslims as the second most authentic book in Islam after the Qur'an). The translation's aim is to offer the reader as much of the meanings of the ST as possible, adopting a source text-oriented approach, which I would describe as 'foreignisation'. To elaborate, the translation features extensive use of in-text glosses and footnotes, which offer additional information and explanations to the reader about many intertextual references. The translators use footnotes and brackets to insert explanations of Islamic terms, which they transliterate rather than translate into English, as well as relevant exegetical comments.

As has been mentioned in Chapter 2, foreignisation means producing a target text which deliberately breaks target language conventions by retaining something of the foreignness of the original (see Venuti 1995: 20). Domestication, on the other hand, is adopted to minimise the strangeness of the foreign text for target language readers.

To illustrate how the two translations are influenced by the approaches they adopt, I discuss an example featuring marked word order (see Chapter 5, and see also Elimam 2020, 2013), a stylistic feature used more often in Arabic than in English and the rendering of which should demonstrate which approach the translation adopts.

Ex 6.2: (Qur'an 64: 1) يُسَبِّحُ لِلَّهِ مَا فِي السَّمَاوَاتِ وَمَا فِي الأَرْضِ لَهُ الْمُلْكُ وَلَهُ الْحَمْدُ

Abdel Haleem's translation: Everything that is in the heavens and the earth glorifies God; all control and all praise belong to Him. (2004/2005: 377)

Hilali and Khan's translation: Whatsoever is in the heavens and whatsoever is on the earth glorifies Allah. His is the dominion and to Him belong all the praises and thanks. (1977/1998: 661)

According to al-Bayḍāwī (n.d.) and al-Zamakhsharī (n.d.), the verse above features two cases of foregrounding, namely the predicate (له) 'to Him', which is foregrounded before the subjects (الْمُلْكُ) 'dominion' and (الْحَمْدُ) 'praise', producing marked word order in Arabic. Abdel Haleem uses unmarked word order in English and does not attempt to compensate for the lost stylistic effect through any other means. Hilali and Khan, on the other hand, foreground 'His' and 'to Him' to clause-initial position to reflect the force of the original. In relation to word order, Abdel Haleem (2008) criticises translations of the Qur'an which adopt a literal approach and follow the original word for word, assuming that they are bringing the source text closer to the target reader, since this, in his opinion, is not possible due to the differences between the two languages, Arabic and English. Hilali and Khan, on the other hand, accord more attention to word order than Abdel Haleem, who is more concerned with producing a smooth and natural target text. As can be seen from this example, the translations of the same verse offer the reader a different 'feel' of the source text and this difference is a result of the translation approach adopted in each translation.

Below is another example to show how the translation strategy used is dictated by the overall translation approach, which itself may be a result of taking target readers' expectations into consideration while deciding on how to render the source text.

Ex 6.3: I will go out with my girlfriend tonight.

TT 1: سأخرج مع صديقتي الليلة

Back translation: I will go out with my girlfriend tonight.

TT 2: سأخرج مع زوجتي الليلة

Back translation: I go out with my wife tonight.

Although this example can be rendered into Arabic using a direct translation strategy (see lexical translation strategies in Chapter 3), a close translation will sound foreign in a culture that does not entertain the idea of having a girlfriend or boyfriend. The second translation, a domesticated version, takes this issue into account and brings the text closer to the receiving culture and its norms. It is evidently clear here that the translation approach adopted has an influence on the resulting translation of micro-level segments.

The following is an example which also features the effect of the translation approach adopted on local strategies and, in turn, the output.

Ex 6.4: ما زلنا نخرج شهداء تحت الارض (Baker 2007: 166)
Back translation: We are still pulling martyrs from under the ground.
English subtitle: We are still pulling victims out of the rubble.

In this example, adopting a foreignising translation approach, and, in turn, a direct lexical translation strategy, produces a concept that is alien in this situation in the target language; the concept of martyrdom will sound rather strange in this context to the English readers. Adopting an overall domesticating approach dictates the selection of certain micro-level strategies, bringing the text closer to the culture of the target reader but loses the religious flavour of the source text.

6.3 Target readers' expectations (توقعات قاريء الترجمة)

The importance of taking the target reader's expectations into consideration before embarking on the translation process cannot be stressed enough. The success or otherwise of a translation depends on how it is received to the extent that, in recognition of how much target readers' expectations can influence translation choices on both macro- and micro-levels, some theorists argue that target readers are the 'actual' translators. The examples below will illustrate how taking target readers' expectations into consideration can have a direct influence on the translator's output.

Ex 6.5: Abdel Haleem's *The Qur'an* (2004/2005)

Abdel Haleem carried out the translation with a specific readership in mind, and he therefore attempted to accommodate their expectations and/or needs, even where this might result in a departure from the layout of the Qur'an or some of its formal features. For, in addition to the use of modern English to accommodate target readers' expectations, he divides the undivided, continuous Qur'anic text into paragraphs to clarify the meaning and offer modern readers an easy read (Abdel Haleem 2004/2005: xxxiv). He uses punctuation in such a way as to make it simpler for readers to follow the text, for example, mark where speakers start and end (ibid. xxxiv–xxxv). Perhaps this is why he makes relatively heavy use of punctuation marks compared to other translators. Abdel Haleem also writes that he prefers shorter sentences to solve the problem of *iltifāt* (change of addressee) (ibid. xxxv), making the translation easier to read.

Further, since Abdel Haleem's intended readership is the lay public, who include non-Arabic speaking Muslims or people interested in the Qur'an and/or learning about Islam, he includes a relatively long introduction, focusing not only on the Qur'an itself, but also on Arabia before and after Islam and on the life of the Prophet Muhammad, in order to contextualise the message of the Qur'an against a backdrop of life in Arabia at the time. With his intended readership in mind and in order to further ease the reading experience for them, Abdel Haleem provides an introduction to each (سورة) '*sūra*, a chapter of the Qur'an' in which he offers some background information about it. His translation thus features introductions both to the whole translation and to each chapter, as well as footnotes, although used only when necessary, to guide the readers (Abdel Haleem 2004/2005). Note that the Qur'an itself does not come with introductions to either the chapters or the whole Book.

Furthermore, correct usage of English is of particular importance in the context of meeting target readers' expectations. Therefore, Abdel Haleem had the translation proofread by native speakers of English who also knew Arabic. The revision would have had some impact on how the target text reads. All else being equal, native speakers of English may prefer a translation which reads fluently. Abdel Haleem himself confirms the effect of revision by native speakers on his translation. He explains that when he first embarked on the task of translating the Qur'an, he translated only one page of the text and had it evaluated and proofread by his Muslim and non-Muslim students at SOAS, who are native speakers of English. Their initial response was that he had used an old-fashioned English style. Abdel Haleem repeated the translation several times, improving the language each time until the students were satisfied with the translation and the language he used. The fact that the translation reads smoothly is thus partly the result of the target readers' feedback and direct involvement.

Ex 6.6: Pickthall's *The Meaning of the Glorious Koran* (1930/2005)

This particular translation features an interesting example of an anticipated clash between the readers' background knowledge and text knowledge. The following quote demonstrates how the translator decides to prepare the target readers for a different read from what they are used to. This quote is not in the source text of the Qur'an but additional information provided by the translator himself or herself.

> Yusuf takes its name from its subject which is the life-story of Joseph. It differs from all other Surahs in having only one subject. The differences from the Bible narrative are striking. Jacob is here a Prophet, who is not deceived by the story of his son's death, but is distressed because, through a suspension of his clairvoyance, he cannot see what has become of Joseph. The real importance of the narrative, its psychic burden,

> is emphasised throughout, and the manner of narration, though astonishing to Western readers, is vivid. (Pickthall 1930/2005: 141)

Another example of taking target readers' expectations into consideration can be seen in how ʿAbduh (1902) translated *Hamlet* into Arabic. The tragedy is given a happy ending, 'with the ghost of the late king appearing in the last scene to hand the throne to Hamlet, who does not die in this version. After granting his forgiveness to the dying Gertrude and Laertes, and sending Claudius cursed to hell, the ghost addresses Hamlet thus in a frequently quoted passage (1902: 110, quoted in Hanna 2005: 171):

> And you may happily live on earth, forgiven by Heaven. Go before me to where your uncle sat; this throne was made but for you (Hamlet ascends the throne, looking admiringly at his father, while the ghost gradually descends into the depths of the earth, smiling at Hamlet).

Theatre translators in late nineteenth- and early twentieth-century Egypt attempted to relate to the world of their audience, reformulating the original plots of the plays they translated in order to relate them to the social reality of their audience (Hanna 2005: 180–1).

6.4 Context of reception and the translator's aim (السياق العام للترجمة وهدف المترجم)

As has been mentioned above, Abdel Haleem opts for 'a modern, easy style ... to make the [translation of the] Qur'an accessible to everyone who speaks English' (2004/2005: xxix). Abdel Haleem's main motivation is his commitment to Islam. Abdel Haleem (2004) tells us how his earlier academic interests were mainly literary. His move into Qur'anic studies occurred in the 1980s when he encountered claims by some orientalists to the effect that the Qur'an was subject to textual change at the hands of early Muslims before it was canonised during the third Hijri decade, which is incorrect from an Islamic point of view. This is because Muslims view the Qur'an as the literal word of God revealed to the Prophet Muhammad and then passed on verbatim to the Muslims who memorised it and the scribes who committed it to writing. They also believe that nothing has been added to or detracted from the original revelation/the original version, which was later reproduced and circulated in the Muslim world. Only then did Abdel Haleem decide to redirect his scholarly efforts away from literature in an attempt to correct the distorted image of the Qur'an in Western academia. Abdel Haleem (2004) states that his translation is part of his effort to propagate Islam; this aim is served by offering readers a text which reads fluently rather than one which sounds archaic or foreign to them. He further wants to make English an 'Islamic language': that is to make Islamic texts written in English as accessible to readers who are native speakers of English as Islamic texts written in Arabic, Turkish and Persian are to their respective readers (2008).

Another source of influence on Abdel Haleem in terms of deciding the aim of his translation is the time in which his translation was produced. Abdel Haleem's translation was produced in an era which features a growing interest in the Qur'an in the West, at both official and personal levels. According to Kidwai (2007: ix), the number of editions of translations of the Qur'an rose from 296 in 1980 to 890 in 2002. The number of Muslim communities living in the West, whose first language is not Arabic and who depend on translations of the Qur'an for a general understanding of the text, has also been on the rise. There is also a large increase in the number of converts to Islam throughout the world, and in Europe and America in particular. In fact, since the events of 9/11, the various translations of the Qur'an have been bestsellers worldwide (Rigonu 2006: 77; see also Elimam 2019).[1]

Another source of influence is that it is an era of 'misunderstanding' Islam and the Qur'an. Being a 'Muslim' or 'Arab' is now sometimes equated with being 'violent' in the media. Abdel Haleem has a tougher task than his predecessors in trying to promote a text which has come to be widely viewed as 'alien' and associated with several negative stereotypes in the world of his English-speaking readers. In addition, little Arabic literature gets translated into the English-speaking world (see Said 1990, and Eagleton et al. 1990), and this, as Baker puts it, 'both reflects and reinforces the gap between the two cultures' (2000: 260). For all of these contextual reasons, Abdel Haleem decides not only to translate the Qur'an into English on his own but also to adopt a smooth, domesticated English style that brings the translation close to the target readers to allow them to read and understand the message of the holy book easily.

As opposed to Abdel Haleem's aim, see how the translator's intention to tarnish the image of Islam can be seen right from the title of the translation given by Alexander Ross to his 1649 translation of the Qur'an: *The Alcoran of Mahomet . . . newly Englished for the satisfaction of all that desire to look into the Turkish vanities*. See more on the issue of ideology below.

Another example of how context can influence the translator's choice of approach is the translation of Sonnet 18, where Shakespeare compares his love to a summer day.

> Ex 6.7: Shall I compare thee to a summer day?
> Thou art more lovely and more temperate:

An Arabic translation of the above poetic verses rendered 'summer' into 'spring', considering how hot summer can be in Arab countries that the reader might find this particular comparison/simile inappropriate (see Newmark 1988/2003: 164).

A further example is how Tanyous 'Abduh labels *Hamlet* as *Riwāya* (1902), meaning 'novel' (Hanna 2005: 19). This is because the genre of plays was not known in the Arab world at the time. In addition, given the context of early twentieth-century Egypt, early drama translations were carried out with a view of being performed by 'singers-cum-actors for an audience for whom singing made good theatre' (Hanna 2005: 185). In other words, theatre translators considered the context of reception of their work and were aware that not taking it into consideration could lead to the failure of their work. With this in mind, translators need to know that staying close to the ST is not the only translation approach available to them and need not worry about having to alter the ST through their work for the TT to fit well into its respective context.

6.5 Translators' ideology (معتقدات المترجم وأفكاره)

The translators' ideology, meaning values and belief system, can naturally influence their output. This is because translators either cannot stop their own understanding from filtering through to their work or because they use translation to propagate their ideology.

Ex 6.8: the translator's religious ideology

The translator's affiliation to a religion or a sect can influence their output in the sense that they sometimes choose one meaning of the source text over the other in line with their own affiliation. Mollanazar and Mohaqeq (2005) discuss the translation of the following verse by Qara'i, a Shi'i, Hilali and Khan, mainstream Sunni Muslims, and Arberry, a Christian orientalist. They argue that the type of religious ideology to which each of the translators subscribes influences his respective translation and they offer the following example to support their argument (ibid. 65–6):

Ex 6.9: وَاعْلَمُواْ أَنَّمَا غَنِمْتُم مِّن شَيْءٍ فَأَنَّ لِلّهِ خُمُسَهُ وَلِلرَّسُولِ وَلِذِي الْقُرْبَى
وَالْيَتَامَى وَالْمَسَاكِينِ وَابْنِ السَّبِيلِ (Qur'an 8: 41)

Hilali and Khan's translation: And know that whatever of war-booty that you may gain, verily one-fifth of it is assigned to Allah, and to the Messenger, and to the near relatives [of the messenger Muhammad], (and also) the orphans, Al-Masakin (the poor) and the wayfarer. (1977/1998: 225)

Qara'i's translation: Know that whatever thing you may come by, a fifth of it is for Allah and the Apostle, for the relatives and the orphans, for the needy and the traveller. (2004: 246)

Arberry's translation: Know that, whatever booty you take, the fifth of it is God's, and the Messenger's, and the near kinsmen's, and the orphans', and for the needy, and the traveller (1955/1998: 173)

The translators differ in relation to rendering the phrase (أَنَّمَا غَنِمْتُم) underlined above. Hilali and Khan render it as 'whatever of war-booty that you may gain', and thus limit the 'fifth' to 'war-booty' in line with the mainstream Sunni understanding, namely that the phrase refers to war booty only. By contrast, in line with Shi'i understanding, Qara'i translates the phrase as 'whatever thing you may come by', which unduly generalises the 'fifth' to all types of earnings, rather than just war booty. Arberry translates word for word and does not even add the word 'war' before 'booty' even though they are strong collocates. Arberry's word-for-word translation, Mollanazar and Mohaqeq (2005) argue, can occasionally be ambiguous. However, on this occasion, it is closer to Hilali and Khan's translation than to Qara'i's. Finally note that the word 'booty' may have a negative connotation, namely 'valuable things that are stolen, especially by soldiers in a time of war'.2 But in the context of the verse, it refers to valuable items soldiers collect, rather than steal, from the battlefield after the end of the battle, that is spoils of war.

6.6 The commissioner's influence (تأثير العميل أو مكاتب الترجمة)

The commissioner of the translation, who can be the author of the ST or the agency providing the translation task, may influence the process/product by imposing the use of a language variety or type of spelling, for instance, American as opposed to British, specific rendering of certain words, and the general translation approach, amongst other factors. They may also decide on important issues relating to the layout of the translation, its title, which they try to make sure sounds attractive to target readers for sales purposes, and even its conclusion and how the plot is resolved.

For example, early translations of the Qur'an were commissioned by the church. These translations were aimed at tarnishing the image of Islam and the Qur'an. According to al-Lāwindī (2001: 19–20), the first Latin translation of the Qur'an was carried out in 1143 by Robert Kent. The church did not allow the translation to be circulated publicly because it did not include a preface outlining a Christian critique of the Qur'an. In other words, the translation was kept for the exclusive use of the clergy and was not circulated because it was considered 'blasphemous' from a Christian point of view since the Qur'an views Jesus as a human and Prophet, not God or the son of God. It was not until 1543 that the translation was first published by Theodor Bibliander, who adds an introduction describing Islam as a satanic religion and warns the readers against the 'dangers' of the Qur'an. The translation was later republished in 1594 by Henkelman and in 1598 by Mariachi (spelt as "Marracci" in Burman 1998: 706; see also Rabaḍāwī 2005).

6.7 Trends in academia or philosophy (التوجهات الأكاديمية أو الأفكار الفلسفية)

Some translations are only a representation of preconceived thoughts, ideas or current trends in academia or philosophy. Rippin reviews Richard Bell's translation of the Qur'an (1937) and concludes that it is influenced both by Bell's negative views on the Qur'an and by a trend then prevalent in academia, namely, the historical approach. An example of this is that while the order of chapters in the Qur'an and of verses within the chapters is taken for granted by Muslims and scholars of the Qur'an, Bell's translation is divided into passages made up of different verses taken from different chapters (in this, his translation is similar to the first version of Dawood's translation). Bell attempts to explain the meaning of the Qur'an in historical terms, in order to 'situate the passage within the life of Muhammad, which then confirms the interpretation of the text, provides some sense of chronology and furnishes evidence of disjunction in Qur'anic passages' (Rippin 1992). To do this, when Bell finds two verses with related meanings in close proximity, he considers one of them to be a 'substitution' for the other and reformulates the intent of the relevant passage to fit it into a different historical situation. For Bell, a parallel passage can provide an indication of where a revision has taken place or where editing has combined originally separate passages. He sometimes attempts to establish which of two parallels the 'original' version is. Moving verses around in this manner is not allowed from an Islamic point of view. And from a linguistic point of view, bin Salāma (2000: 103) points out that not respecting the division of sentences and, in turn, the original relationship between sentences, for example, by translating two sentences as one, or translaṭing one as two, not an uncommon practice in translation, may have an implication for the meaning of the relevant verses, providing more room for interpretation and involvement on the part of the translator, which is not acceptable from an Islamic point of view, given that translators are not qualified scholars/ exegetes of the Qur'an. Rippin (1992) points out that Bell's work reveals its age, as it reflects an ideological climate in which history was believed to provide an explanation for textual phenomena. He concludes that Bell's 'observations are based upon his perception of the meaning of the text' (1992) and that it is a 'distillation' of Bell's thoughts and a representation of the implications of his theories on the Qur'an.

6.8 Register (مستوى رسمية النص)

Register is another factor which can potentially influence the translation. Adopting a simple definition of a formal and informal register, one can see how the translator's choice of words may be affected accordingly, see Table 6.1.

Note that Arabic writing is almost always associated with a formal register (مستوى عال من الرسمية), while spoken Arabic is associated with informal register. This issue, which was discussed in Chapter 1 under components of style, influences how informal texts in English are received in Arabic when they are translated using a formal register.

Table 6.1 Examples of different words used in different registers

Formal register	Informal register
respect	look up to
assemble	put together
encounter	come across

6.9 Conclusion

This chapter aimed to illustrate with relevant examples how, what I called, 'contextual factors' can, and indeed do, influence the translator's output. Translations of the same source text can read differently due to taking some influential factors into consideration, for example, the translation approach, target readers' expectations, context of reception and the translator's aim and ideology, the commissioner's influence, current trends in academia or philosophy, and the register. To recap, it is not difficult to see that who the translation is being produced for can change many things in the process. For instance, a target text produced adopting foreignisation as an approach understandably reads differently compared to using a domestication approach. A source text being rendered for an adult readership will read 'drastically' differently from a rendering which aims at young readers. The aim of the translator, for example, to entertain, educate, inform, persuade the readers, will also dictate the use of certain translation strategies and approaches. For instance, Abdel Haleem aimed at producing a smooth-reading text that provides the meanings of the Qur'an in an accessible manner, and achieving this aim required him to avoid literal translation and to have his translation reviewed and proofread by native speakers of English several times. The translator's ideology, meaning beliefs and values, influences the translation directly and indirectly. Ideology can filter through the translation unconsciously, or a translation can be used to propagate a certain ideology, for instance, translations of the Qur'an by mainstream Muslims and other sectarian translators. Academic ideas can similarly influence the translation since translator's approach the text, any text, with their background, for example, education, reading, training, and bring this to bear on their understanding and, in turn, on their output. Maintaining a formal as opposed to informal register will also dictate the choice of the vocabulary, and sometimes the structures, to be used.

The above is not an exhaustive list of the contextual factors which can influence the translation process and/or product. The discussion above and the examples are only intended to illustrate how not only lexical, structural and textual but also extra-textual factors, which I call contextual, can directly influence the translation and communicate a different meaning and/or feel to the target readers whose needs and expectations can be considered the 'actual' drivers of the translation and whose appreciation of the output can make or break the translator's career.

6.10 Exercises

6.10.1 The following is the method of baking a sponge cake written for adult readership in mind.[3] Translate it for children.

Tips: Consider the issue of children's safety, including using the oven and the electric whisk. Make sure that the children who read the translation find the instructions clear and that they are advised to seek help from an adult to use an electric whisk, turn an oven on/off and take the hot cake out of the oven.

Heat oven to 180C/160C fan/gas 4, butter and line the base of two 20cm spring-form cake tins with baking parchment.

Using an electric whisk beat the butter and sugar together until pale and fluffy. Crack the eggs in one at a time and whisk well, scraping down the sides of the bowl after each addition. Add the lemon zest, vanilla, flour, milk and a pinch of salt. Whisk until just combined then divide the mixture between the two tins.

Bake in the centre of the oven for 25–30 mins until a skewer inserted into the middle of each cake comes out clean. After 10 mins remove the cakes from their tins and leave to cool completely on a wire rack. Fill how you like. My personal favourite is a good dollop of lemon curd and some fresh cream, then dust the top with icing sugar. Will keep for 3 days.

6.10.2 The following is a short story attributed to (جحا) a funny Arabic character which features in many jokes and short stories. Translate it for an English reader who does not know this background.[4]

Tips: consider communicating some background information about (جحا) 'Juha' to the TT readers and the fact that some stories and/or jokes feature him as funny, wise or 'stupid'. Make sure you use punctuation marks in line with English usage, considering that the text below contains some very long sentences which will need dividing up to appeal to the TT readers.

قصة جحا والحمار

أراد جحا أن يشتري حماراً فذهب إلى السوق، توقف عند حمار أعجبه، وقال لصاحبه بعد جدال على الثمن: هذا كل ما معي الآن، فإمّا أن تبيعني الحمار أو أنصرف لحالي، أخيراً وافق الرجل ومشى جحا يجرّ الحمار خلفه، فرآه اثنان من اللصوص، فاتفقا على سرقة الحمار، تسلّل أحدهما بخفة وفكّ الحبل من رقبة الحمار دون أن يشعر جحا بشيء، وربط رقبته هو بالحبل كل ذلك وجحا لا يشعر بما يجري، مشى اللص خلف جحا بينما اللص الآخر بالحمار، وكان المارّة من الناس يرون ذلك ويتعجبون لهذا المنظر ويضحكون، وجحا يتعجب في نفسه ويقول: لعلّ تعجّبهم وضحكهم يرجع إلى أنهم معجبون بحماري. لمّا وصل جحا إلى البيت التفت خلفه إلى الحمار فرأى الرجل، والحبل في رقبته، فتعجب من أمره وقال له: من أنت؟ فتوقف اللص باكياً وأخذ يمسح دموعه قائلاً: يا سيدي أنا رجل جاهل أغضبت أمي، قال جحا: ثم ماذا؟ قال اللص: فدعت أمي عليّ وطلبت من الله أن يمسخني حماراً فاستجاب الله دعاءها، ولما رأى أخي الكبير ذلك أراد ان يتخلص مني فعرضني في السوق للبيع وجئت اشتريتني وببركتك وبفضلك رجعت إنساناً كما كنت، وأخذ اللص يقبّل يد جحا داعياً شاكراً، فصدقه جحا وأطلقه بعد أن نصحه بأن يطيع أمه ويطلب منها الصفح والدعاء ..!! في اليوم التالي توجّه جحا إلى السوق ليشتري حماراً فرأى الحمار نفسه فعرفه، واقترب جحا من الحمار وهمس في أذنه قائلًا: يظهر أنك لم تسمع كلامي، وأغضبت أمك مرة ثانية، والله لن أشتريك أبداً.

Notes

1. <https://www.stylist.co.uk/books/the-all-time-most-popular-books-in-the-world-revealed/127306> (last accessed 1 June 2019)
2. <https://www.oxfordlearnersdictionaries.com/definition/english/booty> (last accessed 24 August 2022)
3. <https://www.bbcgoodfood.com/recipes/sponge-cake> (last accessed 10 April 2020)
4. <https://mawdoo3.com/قصة_جحا_والحمار> (last accessed 24 August 2022)

CHAPTER 7
COMMENTARY WRITING

7.1 Introduction

Translation students writing a commentary on their translations, also known as annotation writing, need to make sure they identify a general translation approach before they start the process of rendering the source text into their target language. As has been mentioned, rendering works by famous writers requires the translator to stay close to the source text in terms of its formal features in order to offer the target readers a 'close-up picture' of the text. This means reproducing the source text's stylistic features, including layout, for example, short paragraphs, drawings, images, as much as possible, even if this is not the norm in the target language. For instance, using short paragraphs in modern English literary works is quite common, and the translator may want to maintain the same layout unless there is a good reason for not doing so. Furthermore, rendering literary works which were selected for translation because of the topic they deal with rather than the fame of the writer or sophistication of style can afford the translator more 'leeway' in terms of how much they can distance themselves from the original style and in deciding to bring the text closer to the target readers through a communicative or domesticating translation.

The overall translation approach largely 'dictates' choice of local strategies. To put this differently, decisions to adopt specific translation strategies need to be in line with the overall approach, generally speaking. This does not mean that if you are adopting a communicative translation approach you cannot use the strategy of literal translation on occasion, or that adopting a semantic translation approach does not allow you to employ the cultural substitution strategy here and there, provided, in all cases, you have a good rationale for your choice of strategy. Rather, it means that most of the micro-level strategies will be in line with your overall approach.

Writing a translation annotation requires, first of all, identifying a translation issue in the source text. This can be any of the issues discussed in Chapters 3 to 6 of this textbook or any other that the translator identifies (see also Baker 1992/2011; Almanna 2016 56ff.). Drawing on Translation Studies literature, the student needs to explain clearly why this is an issue in this particular text, making sure to choose challenging rather than simple issues. The student then needs to choose a translation strategy and justify this choice by, for instance, referring back to the translation *skopos* or approach, translation brief or commissioner's instructions, etc. In addition, if the strategy used to deal with the issue in question is not in line with the adopted translation approach, an explanation is necessary. For example, adopting a foreignisation approach implies a close translation overall. If the translator decided to deviate from this approach and render a source text item, for instance, metaphor or idioms, by paraphrase or cultural substitution, a justification as to why this happened is needed: is this because the source text item cannot be rendered literally or directly, being a source-culture image or metaphor whose close translation does not communicate the meaning, and may therefore confuse the target readers? Or is it because meaning can be communicated better through a target-oriented translation strategy, for instance, paraphrase, cultural substitution and so on? The student can also draw on parallel texts, which are texts or translations in the source or target language featuring the same issue or strategy under discussion, to justify a translation choice. Furthermore, it may be necessary to provide a gloss, which is a word-for-word rendering of the source text to illustrate structural issues, and/or back translation to make sure that the readers can follow the discussion. Finally, *meta* language should be used, that is the terminology used in the Translation Studies literature to discuss translation issues and solutions, to identify the issue and the solution and to elaborate on the loss and gain involved in the strategies used. In the next section I provide examples of annotations to demonstrate some translation issues that can occur with their solutions.

7.2 Example annotations

Writing an annotation of a translation issue requires the student, using *meta* language, to identify the translation issue, explain why it is an issue, choose a translation strategy, and justify such choice by referring to the relevant literature, the translation approach, the translation brief, the translation aim, and/or parallel texts. The student needs to make sure that a gloss and/or back translation into English of the translation is provided. To elaborate, a gloss is a word-for-word translation of the ST or TT to show the readers, for example, structural issues which cannot be communicated through the relevant ST or TT. Back translation refers to the translation into English of your translation (into any other language), and is necessary to give the readers, who can only read English, access to the TT. I provide below sample annotations to demonstrate how this process works.

The issue in the following example is that the ST features a cultural reference, specifically, proper names.

Ex 7.1: Not Harry Potter, but Alan Greenspan.
TT: البطل هنا ليس هاري بوتر (ساحر في فيلم مشهور) لكن ألان جرينسبان
Back translation: The hero here is not Harry Potter (magician in a famous film series)

'Harry Potter' is a cultural bound name which refers to the field of literature in general and cinema in particular. Named after their hero, the films tell the story of a boy called Harry Potter, who discovers he is a wizard with magical powers. As a proper name and title of a series of films and books, *Harry Potter* cannot be simply transliterated in the sentence above because it will lose all these connotations. Here the idea behind referring to 'Harry Potter' is that people think that the new Federal Reserve chairman, Alan Greenspan, can come up with similar magic tricks to put an end to inflation and put the economy back on the road of strong growth, which all seems, from the writer's point of view, 'hogwash'. As some Arabic readers may have not heard about Harry Potter, the addition of extra information in an in-text gloss helps clarify the meaning. If, however, the translator thinks that the in-text gloss is not necessary and that the readers will be familiar with the novels/films, a transliteration strategy of both names will suffice (see Chapter 3).

The following example features a cultural reference and word formation (alliteration) issues.

> Ex 7.2: Unfortunately, this hope is more hogwash than Hogwarts.
> TT: ولكن للأسف هذا الأمل كلام تافه أكثر منه تأثرا بسحر مدرسة هوجوارتز لتعليم السحر و الشعوذة المذكورة في الفيلم.
> Back translation: But unfortunately this hope is hogwash/nonsense more than being affected by the magic of Hogwarts school for teaching magic and wizardry mentioned in the films/books.

One issue with this example is that 'Hogwarts' is a continuation of the analogy drawn earlier (see example 7.1 above), which compares Alan Greenspan to Harry Potter. Hogwarts is a further reference to the movies/books: it is the school of magic which Harry Potter attends. It also may not be known to the Arabic reader and therefore the use of paraphrase strategy is necessary (see Chapter 1). On the other hand, this word is a cohesive device, connecting this sentence with the one mentioned in example 7.1 above. As such, a paraphrase which will serve two purposes at the same time is needed (see Chapter 5).

The second issue is that the sound 'hog', which is featured in the two words 'hogwash' and 'Hogwarts', cannot be kept in the translation according to TL norms because one word will be translated and the second transliterated. Therefore, the clear connection between Hogwarts and Harry Potter in the ST has to be explicitly reproduced in the TT for understanding and coherence purposes. Paraphrasing achieves these through unpacking for the TT reader what Hogwarts is and creating an anaphoric reference to the movies and books.

The sentence below features a cohesion and *iḍāfa* issues, namely, ellipsis.

> Ex 7.3: Not only has Japan's economy actually outperformed Germany's in recent years . . .
> TT: الاقتصاد الياباني لم يكن أداؤه أفضل بالفعل من أداء <u>الاقتصاد الألماني في</u> السنوات الأخيرة وحسب . . .
> Back translation: The Japanese economy <u>did not perform better</u> than the German economy in recent years only . . .

The source text's use of possessive 's' is a challenge since Arabic expresses possession either through the use of pronouns to be affixed to the possessed object or genitive structure (*iḍāfa*) but has no direct equivalent to the English 's (Badawi et al. 2004). In compliance with TL norms, the object of possession, i.e. economy, which is ellipted in the ST, has to be repeated after 'Germany's' to create a genitive structure. The differences between Arabic and English are not only in morphology, but in grammar as well. The ST employs the feature of ellipses in this particular instance, however, to produce a natural TT I have decided to replace the 's with the object of possession, ('اقتصاد') 'economy' (see Chapters 4 and 5).

The following annotation features the issue of a complex structure that needs reformulating in line with TL norms.

> Ex 7.4: Bent over their instruments, three hundred Fertilizers were plunged, as the Director of Hatcheries and Conditioning entered the room, in the scarcely breathing silence, the absentminded, soliloquizing hum or whistle, of absorbed concentration (Huxley 1947).
>
> TT: وعندما دخل الغرفة مدير التفريخ والتكييف كان بها ثلاثمئة ملقح ، منكبون على آلاتهم ومستغرقون في في صمت تكاد تنقطع فيه الأنفاس، ومنهمكون في عملهم أشد الانهماك، عقولهم شاردة ، يناجون أنفسهم وهم يغنون أويصفرون. (Mahmoud 2006)
>
> Back translation: and when the director of hatcheries and conditioning entered the room, there were three hundred fertilizers, focusing on their instruments, consumed in the scarcely breathing silence, and plunged in their work, absent minded, soliloquizing hum or whistle.

This source text poses a structural challenge. A close translation of this sentence would not sound natural in Arabic and would not communicate the intended ST meaning. Therefore, the translator (Mahmoud 2006) decides to restructure his rendering in order to communicate the meaning in line with Arabic grammar. Restructuring this particular sentence successfully reproduced the meaning to the target readers.

Title translation can be challenging due to several reasons including cultural or religious references.

> Ex 7.5: حديث الجنود
>
> Gloss: Talk or story of the soldiers
>
> TT: The story of the soldiers

The Arabic ST (حديث الجنود) is the title of a novel by Ayman Al-Otoom (2014) which narrates how soldiers crushed the university students' demonstrations in Jordan in 1986. The title itself is a quote from the Qur'an (85: 17), which illustrates the story of the soldiers of one of the Pharaohs and Thamud who were destroyed despite their power when they disobeyed

Allah. While the Arabic reader can identify the source of the title easily, and the proposed translation above stays close to the ST, the target reader will not be able to identify the religious reference packed in the ST. The loss here is inevitable considering that this is the title of the novel and use of any other strategies to unpack the reference to the readers would not be appropriate. Considering that quoting verses from the Qur'an is common in Al-Otoom's novels, a note can be added in the foreword or elsewhere in the translation to make this clear to the target readers.

Sentence structure in Arabic versus English is the translation issue discussed in the following example.

> Ex 7.6: With a masterful flick of his wand, our bespectacled hero vanquishes the evil forces that threaten the world.
> TT: بإشارة ماهرة من عصاه السحرية يتغلب البطل وهو يرتدي نظارته على قوى الشر التي تهدد العالم
> Back translation: With a masterful signal from his magical stick vanquishes the hero who is wearing his glasses the forces (of) evil which threaten the world.

Arabic and English are structurally different as languages: Arabic, a Semitic language, belongs to the Afro-Asian family of languages, English, to the Indo-European one. English follows the subject-verb-object (SVO) order in cases of unmarked structure. Arabic, on the other hand, has two word orders: VSO and SVO. Arabic follows the VSO order by default. However, in cases of emphasis, thematic structures, and for other linguistic considerations, SVO may be used (Elimam 2013, 2009; Hatim and Mason 1997: 87). Since the ST does not follow the regular word order of English (SVO) and the language used is generally emotive and evaluative, and the syntax is used for rhetorical purposes as well as to inform, the TT will have to mirror the ST structure to achieve these purposes. The ST above employs a marked structure to achieve a special effect on the readers; namely, to persuade them to see the writer's point of view. Arabic, in turn, has to mirror the same effect through the use of a corresponding marked structure. As such, whereas the unmarked English structure would be:

'Our bespectacled hero vanquishes the evil forces that threaten the world with a masterful flick of his wand', the equivalent unmarked Arabic sentence structure would be:

يتغلب البطل وهو يرتدي نظارته على قوى الشر التي تهدد العالم بإشارة ماهرة من عصاه السحرية

which can be back translated as: 'vanquishes the hero who is wearing his glasses on the forces of evil which threaten the world with masterful signal from his magic stick', a marked Arabic sentence structure which starts with the prepositional phrase (بإشارة من عصاه السحرية) followed by the verb, subject and then object, and is used to achieve the purpose of catching the readers' attention and persuading them to see the writer's point of view.

The following example (from exercise 3.5.1) features the issues of grammatical gender and grammatical number.

> Ex 7.7: 'So, girls, what do you say? Are you up for going Interrailing this summer?'
>
> TT: إذن يافتيات، ماقولكن؟ هل أنتن مستعدات للسفر بالقطار حول أوروبا هذا الصيف؟
>
> Back translation: So, oh girls, what do you say(-feminine/plural)? Are you(-feminine/plural) ready(-feminine/plural) to travel by train across Europe this summer?

The ST sentence features several translation issues. First of all, translating 'girls' poses grammatical number and gender issues. In Arabic nouns can be singular, dual (meaning two), or plural as well as masculine or feminine. Since it is not clear from the context of the story how many girls are involved here, I am going to use the plural form of 'girls' in Arabic rather than the dual. Furthermore, the relevant elements in the two sentences will also conjugate for plural feminine (see Chapter 3). Secondly, 'Interrailing' is a culture-specific term which, in the context of the ST, means travelling from place to place in Europe by train. Translating the term literally as (السفر بالقطار) 'travelling by train' can imply that this is an achievement in and of itself, which is not the case here. Therefore, paraphrasing the meaning and adding (عبر أوروبا) 'across Europe' clarifies the meaning to the TT readers (see Chapter 3).

The following example demonstrates the issue of idiom translation (from exercise 4.10.2).

> Ex 7.8: أحس إنني لست ريشة في مهب الريح ، ولكني مثل تلك النخلة ، مخلوق له أصل ، له جذور له هدف
>
> TT: I feel I am not a feather in the wind, but, like that palm tree, I am a creature with origin, with roots and with aims.

The ST above features an idiom (ريشة في مهب الريح), which literally means 'a feather in the blowing wind'. This idiom can be rendered by a TL idiom that reproduces the same image and meaning: 'a feather in the wind'. Finding a TL equivalent idiom is usually rare between languages as different as Arabic and English (see Chapter 5). The translation here follows the ST closely to reproduce its stylistic features to the readers. This is because both the author and novel are well known and, therefore, the readers would expect to be exposed to the original stylistic features rather than read a completely domesticated/smoothed out TT which does not communicate the flavour of the original (see Chapters 1 and 3).

The sentence below demonstrates the issues of translating metaphor and word order variation (from exercise 4.10.3).

Ex 7.9: Not philosophers but <u>fretsawyers</u> and stamp collectors compose the backbone of society. (Huxley 1947)

Mahmoud's translation: فأساس المجتمع يتألف من <u>النشارين</u> وجامعي الطوابع ولا يتألف من الفلاسفة (2006: 13)

Back translation: The basis of the society is composed of <u>sawyers</u> and stamp collectors and is not composed of philosophers.

My translation: فليس الفلاسفة وإنما من ينشرون الخشب لصناعة الألعاب وجامعي الطوابع هم من يمثلون العمود الفقري للمجتمع

Back translation: Not philosophers but <u>those who saw wood to make toys</u> and stamp collectors are the ones who represent the backbone of the society.

In my translation above I attempt to stay close to the order of the ST sentence. I also paraphrase the meaning of 'fretsawyers' in order to convey the same sarcastic tone of the original author. Translating this term as (النشارين) 'sawyers', as is the case with the published translation, sounds ambiguous and loses reference to what the sawed wood is used for. Furthermore, translating the metaphor 'the backbone of society' closely into Arabic as (العمود الفقري للمجتمع) reproduces both the meaning and the image involved, as opposed to the paraphrase strategy used, unnecessarily, in the published translation (see Chapter 5).

The following example features the issue of translating abbreviations, and accuracy and naturalness as reasons for re-translation.

Ex 7.10: The D.H.C. for Central London always made a point of personally conducting his new students round the various departments. (Huxley 1947)

Mahmoud's translation: وكان مدير التفريخ والتكييف هذا لمنطقة مركز لندن يهتم أشد الاهتمام دائما بمرافقة طلبته الجدد خلال الأقسام المختلفة (2006: 13)

Back translation: and this hatcheries and conditioning director for centre London paid a lot of attention to accompany his new students round the various departments

My translation: وكان مدير التفريخ والتكييف لمنطقة وسط لندن يحرص على مرافقة طلبته الجدد بنفسه في جولة على الأقسام المختلفة

Back translation: and the hatcheries and conditioning director for central London was keen to accompany his new students personally in a tour around the various departments.

In the above example, the abbreviation D.H.C. poses a translation issue because Arabic tends to not use abbreviations. To solve this issue, the relevant words are written out in full. In addition, overall, my proposed translation reads more accurately and naturally than the published translation. For example, (مركز لندن) 'the centre of London' does not sound correct in this context and that is why I translated it as (وسط لندن) 'central London' (see Chapters 1 and 3).

Similar to the example above, the following sentence has an issue with translating abbreviations, in addition to verb conjugation and collocation issues (from exercise 6.10.1).

Ex 7.11: Bake in the centre of the oven for 25–30 mins.
TT: ضعي قالب الكيكة في وسط الفرن من خمسة وعشرين إلى ثلاثين دقيقة
Back translation: Put(feminine) the cake tin in the centre of the oven for 25 to 30 minutes.

The ST features 'mins' rather than 'minutes', and, as has been explained above, Arabic does not support the use of abbreviations. Therefore, a full word (دقيقة) 'minute' has to be used instead. Note also that the TT word is in the singular rather than plural form in compliance with Arabic norms. The second issue in the above example is the gender of the verb: the TT employs the feminine, rather than the masculine, form of the verb in line with parallel texts. In other words, according to Arabic norms, cooking recipes are usually written in the feminine form; hence my choice of the verb conjugation above. Finally, restructuring the sentence was necessary to produce a smooth reading Arabic translation: 'bake' can be translated literally into Arabic as (إخبزي) but it would not sound natural in this location as it collocates with bread not with 'cake'. I decided, therefore, to use another verb and repeat the subject which was mentioned in the preceding sentence. This is also in line with how parallel texts are written (see Chapters 3 and 6).[1]

The following example relates to translating the title of a literary work.

Ex 7.12: ياصاحبي السجن
TT: Oh, Fellow Prisoners!

Ayman Al-Otoom frequently uses verses from the Qur'an, or parts thereof, as titles for his novels and for chapters within the novels. The above ST, which is part of the Qur'an (12: 39), is the title of one of his novels. Although my proposed translation above is quite close to the original, it does not communicate the connotations, that is the fact that this is a quote from the Qur'an, packed in the original title and recognisable by ST readers. In order to compensate for this inevitable loss, and to make sure that the TT readers understand the religious references embedded in the novel's title and also the analogy between the Qur'anic chapter (Chapter 12, Joseph) in which the verse is embedded, and the story of the novel, a foreword can be written by the translator to explain this issue; otherwise, the Islamic flavour of the title will be lost. If the link between the novel's title and the Qur'anic chapter is lost, a great deal will also be lost, albeit the fact that, like Prophet Joseph, the author was unjustly imprisoned in Jordanian jails (see Chapters 1 and 3).

The example below deals with the issues of translating metaphor and word formation.

Ex 7.13: to keep the post-bubble economy afloat

TT: إبقاء اقتصاد ما بعد حالة تفاقم الأسعار طافيا

Back translation: to keep economy after state of sharp increase in prices afloat

The translation issues here are the prefixation of 'post' to 'bubble' and the figure of speech in 'bubble'. The phrase makes use of a linguistic feature widely used in English which is the affixation system, that is word formation rules, and is further complicated by the metaphor in 'bubble', which refers to a situation where prices rise so high that they create a price explosion. Since Arabic does not employ this feature of affixation, paraphrase is used instead. On the other hand, the word 'bubble' cannot be translated literally as (فقاعة) since this meaning does not fit in the context and, therefore, paraphrase is chosen. In other words, the sense is kept but the image is lost, which is called 'demetaphorisation' in Newmark's terms. However, there is an inevitable loss of the semantic correlation between 'bubble' and 'afloat' to produce an acceptable translation (see Chapters 1 and 5).

The passage below from *Brave New World* features the issue of cohesion.

Ex 7.14: Impulse arrested spills over, and the flood is feeling, the flood is passion, the flood is even madness: it depends on the force of the current, the height and strength of the barrier. The unchecked stream flows smoothly down its appointed channels into a calm well-being. The embryo is hungry; day in, day out, the blood-surrogate pump unceasingly turns its eight hundred revolutions a minute. The decanted infant howls; at once a nurse appears with a bottle of external secretion. Feeling lurks in that interval of time between desire and its consummation. Shorten that interval, break down all those old unnecessary barriers.

TT: وبعدما تتدفق القطرات المحبوسة، التي تسبب الانفعال ، ينبثق فيض من الشعور، أو فيض من العواطف، أو حتى من الجنون. فإن ذلك يتوقف على قوة التيار، وعلى ارتفاع الحاجز وقوته، فالتيار الذي لا يقف في سبيله شي يتدفق بيسر خلال مجاريه المعينة فيكون الهناءة والهدوء. والجنين جائع، والأيام تتوالى ومضخة الدم تدور بغير انقطاع دورتها الثمانمائة كل دقيقة. ويصيح الطفل في القارورة فتظهر في الحال مربية ومعها زجاجة من الإفراز الخارجي. ويكمن الشعور في تلك الفترة من الزمن التي تقع بين الرغبة وإنجازها. وإذا قصرت تلك الفترة حطمت كل تلك الحواجز القديمة غير الضرورية.

Back translation: Impulse arrested spills over, and the flood is feeling, or the flood is passion, or the flood is even madness. As it depends on the force of the current, and on

> the height and strength of the barrier, because the unchecked stream flows smoothly down its appointed channels into a calm well-being, and the embryo is hungry; and day in, day out, and the blood-surrogate pump unceasingly turns its eight hundred revolutions a minute, and the decanted infant howls; so at once a nurse appears with a bottle of external secretion, and feeling lurks in that interval of time between desire and its consummation. And if that interval is shortened, it breaks down all those old unnecessary barriers.

The issue of cohesion is presented in the ST above. Cohesion is 'the transparent linking of sentences' (Dickins et al. 2002: 128). English connects sentences and/or paragraphs rather implicitly and the reader is, therefore, left to figure out the relationship between the sentences and the paragraphs. In contrast, in Arabic, sentences and paragraphs have to be linked explicitly in order for the translation to read smoothly. One way of achieving better cohesion is through the addition of connectors such as (و), 'and', which means: in addition to, plus, then, or is simply used as a connector with a grammatical function such as conjunction (Hatim 2001: 19). In the above examples, each of the ST sentences interconnects with the preceding one implicitly, which are typical English norms, unlike Arabic norms which require the use of explicit connectors (Baker 1992/2011: 190). Without the addition of this explicit connector (و) and (ف), underlined in the above example, the TT sentences will not connect properly or read naturally in Arabic. In other words, there will be cohesion gaps in between these sentences and the preceding ones since Arabic handles cohesion rather explicitly by spelling out the connector (see Chapter 5).

Similar to the previous example, the annotation below features the issue of cohesion.

> Ex 7.15: With a masterful flick of his wand, our bespectacled hero vanquishes the evil forces that threaten the world. Not Harry Potter, but Alan Greenspan.
>
> TT: بإشارة ماهرة من عصاه السحرية يتغلب البطل وهو يرتدى نظارته على قوى الشر التي تهدد العالم. البطل هنا ليس هاري بوتر (ساحر في فيلم مشهور) وإنما آلان جرينسبان
>
> Back translation: With a masterful signal from his magical stick vanquishes the hero who is wearing his glasses the forces of evil which threaten the world. The hero here is not Harry Potter (magician in a famous movie series) but Alan Greenspan.

The connection between these two sentences is quite clear in English. ST readers can easily identify the relationship between the magic referred to in the first sentence and Harry Potter in the second. However, literal translation of these two sentences sounds unnatural in Arabic and the translator has to intervene to achieve a natural rendering. A restructuring of the first phrase of the second sentence as well as the addition of more information is necessary to achieve a natural sounding TT through phrase restructuring plus in-text glosses. In other words, the relationship, obvious in the minds of the ST readers, needed to be disambiguated in the TT for the translation to read smoothly. In this concern, some theorists argue that the translation is bound to be less ambiguous than its original, which is called the explicitation universal (see under 2.5 in Chapter 2).

The ST below features a word order issue and two metaphors which are challenging to translate (see also example 4.10.2).

Ex 7.16: وأرخيت أذني للريح. ذاك لعمري صوت أعرفه، له في بلدنا وشوشة مرحة

Gloss: And I relaxed my ears to the wind. That is I swear is a sound I know. It has in our village a happy whisper.

TT: I listened to the wind. This is definitely the sound I know; the wind has such a happy whisper in our village.

In the source text above, (أرخيت) literally means 'relaxed', which does not sound natural in this context and, therefore, I paraphrased the meaning of the metaphor as 'listened'. (وشوشة مرحة) was translated closely as 'happy whisper', which communicates both the meaning and image of the original to the target readers. Restructuring was also necessary for the translation to read well. For example, the last clause of the TT reproduces the noun 'the wind', and is connected with the previous clause with a semicolon for considerations of natural usage (see Chapter 4).

Ex 7.17: The word 'stupid' exhibits the issue of associated meaning discussed under 3.2.1 in Chapter 3. This word is often rendered into Arabic through direct translation as (غبي). However, taking into consideration the associated meaning in this case (المعنى المتلازم أو المقترن أو المرتبط), in line with Dickins et al. (2002: 68), another translation needs to be used. This is due to the fact that the TL word is being associated with more negativity than the SL word. In fact, the direct Arabic rendering mentioned above can be considered a swear word in Arabic unlike the SL word.

Ex 7.18: The term 'head hunting' is a recent coinage which can be rendered into Arabic in different ways. It can be translated almost literally as (إصطياد العقول), which can be back translated as 'brain hunting'. It can also be translated using paraphrase as (البحث عن الموظفين), which can be back translated as 'searching for employees'. It can further be rendered using a cultural substitution strategy as (اجتذاب الكفاءات), which can be back translated as 'attracting competencies'. The first rendering sounds negative, the second is neutral, while the third is arguably positive. Selecting which strategy to use depends on the overall translation approach (see the discussion of rendering new coinages under 3.2.14 in Chapter 3).

Note

1. <https://akhbarak.net/blog/18/طريقة-عمل-الكيك/> (last accessed 14 April 2020)

FINAL REMARKS

I hope that the foregoing discussion has made it clear to the readers that translation is a decision-making process from beginning to end and that what seems to be a 'direct' translation of a source-text item, whether a word, a sentence, a metaphor or an idiom, requires a decision to be made on its suitability in each translational context. It is important to note that the translation strategy used to render any ST item affects the meaning communicated to the target readers and that no two translators' output will read the same, as translators take different decisions at all levels of the text, not least because of their respective writing styles. Furthermore, even the same translator will deal with the same translation issue differently depending on many factors, textual and/or contextual. Translating a short story to be published in a literary supplement of a newspaper, for instance, would require producing easy-to-read versions considering that the potential readers of this type of publication are people 'on the go'. Compare this to translating the same short story to be published in a literary collection of short stories or something similar; here, the receivers are likely to be more avid and attentive readers of literature, and the translator, in this case, can afford to use a more sophisticated style than in the previous case.

This guide hoped to provide a comprehensive coverage of translation issues and strategies specifically related to translating literary texts, which are usually expressive (Newmark 1988/2003: 39–40): the authors express their views, feelings and emotions, and the translations are expected to communicate these meanings clearly, and in a comparatively similar style to the target readers. It is worth noting that the more established the writer and the more sophisticated the style, the less liberty in dealing with the text the translator will have. This is because the choice of the source text in these cases will be prompted to a large extent by the fame of the source-text author and the sophistication of his or her style. In other words, the translator's aim in this situation would be to offer the target readers a feel of the original work. Furthermore, some literary works primarily fulfil an aesthetic function. The language of these works is designed to please the senses through actual or imagined sounds, metaphors, rhyme and rhythm, balance/contrasts of sentences, clauses and words, amongst others. In fact, sound effects play a major part in poetry in general and children's literature in particular (see more in Newmark 1988/2003: 39–40). This means that a literary translator needs to be as creative as the ST author to be able to recreate the latter's style successfully for the target audience.

The classification of translation issues and strategies to four levels adopted here, namely, lexical, structural, textual and contextual, allows for the examination of translation issues in detail and provides a sense of organisation to this book. In addition, this classification is more practical than structuring this textbook around the taxonomy of strategies since this guide is organised along the lines of the translation process where issues are encountered before strategies are sought. Furthermore, knowledge of the types of translation that abound in a particular text type, and the ability to theorise on them in terms of how they come about and what they result from, in addition to whether it is a text, genre and/or language-related problem, is also an essential requirement for a successful translation. Although organising the coursebook around translation issues rather than strategies may result in some degree of repetition when strategies are being discussed, this is inevitable seeing that the same strategy can be used to deal with a translation issue at lexical, structural, textual or even contextual level. Finally, the use of strategies inevitably results in what can be described as 'meaning manipulation', as some parts of the ST may be lost in the process. In line with their overall translation approach, translators selectively and subjectively use these strategies in a goal-oriented manner in order to solve the translation issues they come across (see Chesterman 1997). As mentioned earlier, knowledge of translation theory can help make the selection of strategies consistent, informed and less subjective (see more in Owji 2013). The decision to assign translation issues to four different levels should not be taken to imply that the translation process takes place at each of these levels individually. Rendering the meaning and/or form of literary texts, and in fact, any text for this matter, requires taking many factors into consideration simultaneously. Note also that although the examples provided here are in Arabic and English, the issues raised and the strategies proposed can lend themselves to other language combinations.

Finally, note that there are several contextual factors that can help the translator determine how to translate and which strategies are more appropriate in which context. The translator needs to decide the *skopos* or purpose of the translation and determine the readership since the assumed knowledge level of the target text readers influences the overall translation approach to be adopted and, in turn, which strategies to select. The translation brief, real or mental, will help with the selection of approach and strategies since it establishes the right context for the translator. It will identify who is going to read the translation and, therefore, help the translator determine the level of knowledge and, more importantly, the readers' expectations.

Glossary

a word's range of meaning	نطاق معاني الكلمات أو الألفاظ
acronyms	اختصارات
adaptation	تكييف أو تطويع الترجمة الترجمة الملائمة أو المعدلة
aesthetic qualities	سمات جمالية
allegory	مجاز
allusions	تلميحات
annotation/commentary	شرح مشكلات الترجمة أو التعليق عليها
associated meaning	معنى متلازم أو مقترن أو مرتبط
borrowing	استعارة الكلمة أو العبارة من لغة أخرى
brevity	إيجاز
cohesion	سبكة أو تماسك النص
collocations	متلازمات لفظية
commissioner	العميل أو كاتب النص
communicative translation	ترجمة تواصلية وتركز على نقل المعنى السياقي للنص
compensation	تعويض
complex lexical items	كلمات أو ألفاظ معقدة
conjunction	حروف العطف
connotative meaning	معنى ضمني أو كامن أو نفسي
context	السياق العام لعملية الترجمة أو سياق النص
context-dependent words	كلمات أو ألفاظ يعتمد معناها على السياق
context-free words	كلمات أو ألفاظ معناها مستقل عن السياق
co-text	سياق الجملة أو السياق اللغوي وهي الجمل السابقة و/أو اللاحقة للجملة المعنية
conventional and non-conventional writing	الكتابة بإسلوب تقليدي/مألوف أو غير تقليدي/غير مألوف
cultural equivalent/cultural substitution	مقابل أو مرادف أو بديل ثقافي
culture-specific words/ loaded words	كلمات أو ألفاظ خاصة بالثقافة
definiteness	التعريف والتنكير
descriptive equivalent	مقابل أو مرادف وصفي
dialect	لهجة محلية لمنطقة ما
diction	أسلوب التعبير

difference in interpersonal or physical perspective	اختلاف المنظور الشخصي أو المادي
direct translation	ترجمة مباشرة أو متداولة
domestication	توطين الترجمة
dynamic translation	ترجمة تأويلية أو تكافؤ التأثير
economical diction	الإيجاز في التعبير
ellipsis	حذف
eponymy	صفة النسبة أو مسمى على اسم
euphemism	تلطف في التعبير
euphony	عذوبة الصوت
expansion	توسع في نقل المعنى
expansive diction	إسهاب في التعبير
explicitation	وضوح أو توضيح
faithful translation	الترجمة الأمينة
false friends/'faux amis'	"أصدقاء مزيفون" - كلمات من لغتين أو أكثر تتشابه في الكتابة أو النطق وتختلف في المعنى
figures of speech	مجاز أو صور بلاغية
footnotes	حاشية سفلية
foreign/loan words	كلمات أجنبية أو مستعارة من لغات أخرى
foreignisation	تغريب الترجمة
formal equivalence translation	ترجمة شكلية أو تكافؤ شكلي
forms of address	صيغ المخاطبة أو استخدام الألقاب
free translation	ترجمة حرة
functional equivalent	مقابل أو مرادف وظيفي
gestures	إشارات أو إيماءات
grammatical gender	التذكير والتأنيث
grammatical number	الإفراد والتثنية والجمع
grammatical structures	تراكيب لغوية
humour	دعابة أو فكاهة
hyponym/specific word	استخدام لفظ مندرج أو خاص
iḍāfa construct/genitive structure	إضافة
ideology	معتقدات المترجم وأفكاره
idiolect	لهجة شخصية أو فردية
idiomatic translation	ترجمة اصطلاحية
idioms and fixed expressions	أقوال مأثورة وتعابير اصطلاحية
interlingual translation	نقل نص مكتوب بلغة ما إلى لغة أخرى

intersemiotic translation	الترجمة من نظام لغوي إلى نظام لغوي آخر مثل نقل نص مكتوب إلى لغة الإشارة
intertextuality	التناص أو إشارة النص إلى نصوص أخرى
in-text glosses	إضافة معلومات بين قوسين لتقريب المعنى
intralingual translation	إعادة كتابة النص باستخدام نفس اللغة كشرح النص بنفس لغته الأصلية لكي يفهمه القاريء
layout	نسق النص
less expressive word	كلمة أقل تعبيرا عن المعنى
lexical cohesion	تماسك لفظي
lexical/denotative meaning	معنى إشاري أو حقيقي أو معجمي
lexical simplification	تبسيط الألفاظ
literal translation	ترجمة حرفية
literal translation, through-translation, calque	ترجمة حرفية
literary language	لغة الأدب أو اللغة الأدبية
literary style	أسلوب أدبي
literature	الأدب
loanword	كلمة مستعارة من لغة أخرى
marked word order	التقديم والتأخير
meta language of translation	مصطلحات علم الترجمة
metaphor	استعارة
metonymy	كناية
modulation	تعديل
naturalisation	تطويع أوتطبيع النطق أو الكتابة لقواعد لغة الترجمة
neologism	كلمات أو ألفاظ جديدة أو مستحدثة
neutral word	كلمة محايدة
normalisation	تعديل أو تطبيع أو تنميط
nominalisation	تراكيب اسمية
omission	حذف
paraphrase	شرح
passive structure	أسلوب البناء للمجهول
personification	تشخيص
phrasal verbs	أفعال مركبة
pun	تورية
reduction	اختزال المعنى
register	مستوى رسمية النص
repetition	تكرار

semantic translation	ترجمة دلالية
sentence structure	بناء أوتراكيب الجمل
simile	تشبيه
simplification	تبسيط
skopos	الهدف أو الغرض
source text/ST	النص الأصلي
strategy	استراتيجية
style	أسلوب الكتابة أو أسلوب الكاتب
stylistic features	سمات أسلوبية
stylistics simplification	تبسيط الأسلوب
substitution	إبدال
superordinate/general word	لفظ شامل أوعام
syntactic simplification	تبسيط التراكيب
target text system	منظومة النص المترجم
target text/TT	الترجمة أو النص المترجم
tense and chronology	الزمن والتسلسل الزمني
tone	نبرة الكاتب أو الكتابة
transference	نقل الكلمة من لغة أخرى
translation approach	أسلوب ترجمة النص بشكل عام
translation brief	عقد تنفيذ الترجمة
translation process	عملية الترجمة
translation strategy	استراتيجية ترجمة كلمة أو عبارة
translation studies	علم الترجمة
translation theory	نظريات الترجمة
transliteration	نسخ صوتي
verbal structures	تراكيب فعلية
vocabulary	مفردات
word formation	صياغة الكلمة
word-for-word translation	الترجمة بإسلوب كلمة مقابل كلمة
words with competing translations	كلمات ذات ترجمات متعارضة أو متباينة

References

Aarts, F. G. A. M and J. Aarts (1988) *English Syntactic Structures.* 1st edn. New York and London: Prentice Hall.

Abdel Haleem, M. A. S. (2008) "ترجمة القرآن ليست قرآنا" (*A Translation of the Qur'an is not the Qur'an*). <https://www.quranicthought.com/wp-content/uploads/post_attachments/5fe22f66311e5.pdf> (date last accessed 30 August 2022).

Abdel Haleem, M. A. S. (2004/2005) *The Qur'an*. Oxford: Oxford University Press.

Abdel Haleem, M. A. S. (2004) "محمد عبد الحليم. . .حامل لنور القرآن في بريطانيا" (*Muhammad Abdel Haleem, Bearer of the Qur'anic Light in Britain*). <http://www.islamonline. net/arabic/famous/2004/06/article05.SHTML> (date last accessed 1 October 2019).

Abdou, A. (2012) *Arabic Idioms.* 1st edn. London: Routledge.

Al-Aqad, M. H., K. Kaur, A. A. Bin Sapar, A. K. Kadhim and N. H. M. Salleh (2017) 'Translation of Selected Pun Words from the Holy Quran into English', *TOJET: The Turkish Online Journal of Educational Technology.* <https://files.eric.ed.gov/fulltext/ED599926.pdf> (date last accessed 30 August 2022).

Al-Bayḍāwī, N. A. A. (n.d) أنوار التنزيل وأسرار التأويل (*The Lights of Revelation and the Secrets of Interpretation*). <https://waqfeya.com/book.php?bid=10388> (date last accessed 30 August 2022).

Al-Jurjānī, A. Q. (1976) دلائل الإعجاز *(Signs of Inimitability) with Comments and Explanations by Mohamed A. Khafaji.* Cairo: Maktabat al-Qāhira.

Al-Lāwindī, S. (2001) إشكاليات نرجمة معاني القرآن (*The Problems of Translating the Meanings of the Qur'an*). Cairo: Maṭba'at Markaz al-Haḍara al-'Arabiya.

Al-Makhzūmī, M. (1966) في النحو العربي: قواعد وتطبيق على المنهج العلمى الحديث (*On Arabic Grammar: Rules and Application of a Modern Methodology*). Cairo: Maktabat wa Maṭba'at Muṣṭafa al-Babī al-Halabī.

Al-Otoom, A. (2014) حديث الجنود (*The story of the soldiers*). Beirut: al-Mu'asasa al-'arabiya lil-dirasāt wa al-nashr.

Al-Otoom, A. (2012) يا صاحبي السجن (*Oh, Fellow Prisoners*). Beirut: al-Mu'asasa al-'arabiya lil-dirasāt wa al-nashr.

Al-Suyūṭī, J. A. (1969) معترك الأقران في إعجاز القرآن (*Peers' challenge in Qur'an's Inimitability*), edited by Ali Mohamed Al-Bagawi. Cairo: Dār al-Fikr al-'Arabī.

Al-Zamakhsharī, F. K. O. (n.d.) المفصل في علم اللغة العربية (*The Detailed Book on the Science of the Arabic Language*). 2nd edn. Lebanon: Dār Al-Jīl.

Al-Zamalkānī, 'A. A. (1974) البرهان الكاشف عن إعجاز القرآن (*The Revealing Evidence about the Qur'an's Inimitability*), edited by Khadijah al-Ḥadithi Aḥmad Maṭlab. Baghdad: Ri'asat Diwān al-Awqāf.

Ali, A. (1984) *Al-Qur'an, A Contemporary Translation.* Princeton: Princeton University Press.

Ali, A.Y. (1996) *The Meaning of the Holy Qur'an. New Edition with Revised Translation, Commentary and Newly Compiled Comprehensive Index.* Beltsville, MD: Amana Publications.

Ali, M. (1920) *The Holy Quran.* 2nd edn. Woking and London: Unwin Brothers; The Gresham Press.

Ali, S. S. (1992) 'Misrepresentation of Some Ellipted Structures in the Translation of the Qur'ān (Analytical Study)', *Meta: Journal des traducteurs* 37(3), pp. 487–90.

Almanna, A. (2016) *The Routledge Course in Translation Annotation.* London: Routledge.

Arberry, A. J. (1998) *The Koran Interpreted, Translated with an Introduction.* Oxford: Oxford University Press.

Badawi, E. M., M. G. Carter and A. Gully (2004) *Routledge Comprehensive Grammars.* London and New York: Routledge.

Baker, M. (1992/2011) *In Other Words*. 2nd edn. London: Routledge.

Baker, M. (2007) 'Reframing Conflict in Translation', *Social Semiotics* 17(2), pp. 151–69.

Baker, M. (2006) 'Contextualization in Translator- and Interpreter-Mediated Events', *Journal of Pragmatics* 38(3), pp. 321–37.

Baker, M. (2000) 'Towards a Methodology for Investigating the Style of a Literary Translator', *Target* 12(2), pp. 241–66.

Baker, M. (1993) 'Corpus Linguistics and Translation Studies: Implications and Applications', in *Text and Technology: In Honour of John Sinclair*, edited by Mona Baker, Gill Francis and Elena Tognini-Bonelli. Amsterdam and Philadelphia: Benjamins Publishing Co., pp. 233–50.

Baldick, C. (1991) *The Concise Oxford Dictionary of Literary Terms*. Oxford and New York: Oxford University Press.

Bassnett, S. and A. Lefevere (1990). *Translation, History and Culture*. London: Printer Publishers.

Bassnett-McGuire, S. (1980) *Translation Studies: Theory and Practice*. London: Methuen.

Beaugrande, R. de and W. U. Dressler (1981) *Introduction to Text Linguistics*. London: Longman.

Bell, R. (1937) *The Qur'an. Translated, with a Critical Re-arrangement of the Surahs, 2 Vols*. Edinburgh: Edinburgh University Press.

Bell, R. T. (1991) *Translation and Translating*. London: Routledge.

Bewley, A. and A. Bewley (1999/2005) *The Noble Qur'an-A New Rendering of its Meaning in English*. Rev. edn. Norwich: Bookwork.

Bin Salāma, R. (2000) 'الترجمة والمحو' (Translation and Omission), in J. Asfour (ed.) قضايا الترجمة وإشكالياتها (*Issues and Problems of Translation*). Cairo: Al-Majlis al-Aʿlā lil-Thaqāfa, pp. 97–112.

Birner, B. J. (1996) *The Discourse Function of Inversion in English*. London and New York: Routledge.

Birner, B. J. and G. L. Ward (1998) *Information Status and Noncanonical Word Order in English*. Amsterdam: John Benjamins Publishing Co.

Boase-Beier, J. (2006) *Stylistic Approaches to Translation*. 1st edn. Manchester: St Jerome Publishing.

Bolinger, D. and D. A. Sears (1968) *Aspects of Language*. New York: Harcourt Brace Jovanovich Inc.

Burman, T. E. (1998) 'Tafsir and Translation: Traditional Arabic Qur'an Exegesis and the Latin Qur'ans of Robert of Ketton and Mark of Toledo', *Speculum* 73(3), pp. 703–32.

Cantarino, V. (1974) *Syntax of Modern Arabic Prose: The Simple Sentence, vol I*. Bloomington and London: Indiana University Press.

Carter, R. (2004) *Language and Creativity: The Art of Common Talk*. London and New York: Routledge.

Catford, J. C. (1965/1978) *A Linguistic Theory of Translation*. London: Oxford University Press.

Chesterman, A. (1997) *Memes of Translation: The Spread of Ideas in Translation Theory*. London and New York: John Benjamins Publishing Co.

Constantine, P. (2020) 'Literary Translation Pedagogy in the United States: New Trends, *Translation Review*' 106(1), pp. 10–14.

Cronin, M. (2013) *Translation in the Digital Age*. London: Routledge.

Cuddon, J. A. (1991) *The Penguin Dictionary of Literary Terms and Literary Theory*. London: Penguin Books.

Dahlgren, S. (1998) *Word order in Arabic*. Göteborg: Acta Universitatis Gothoburgensis Göteborg.

Delabastita, D. (2004) 'Worplay A translation Problem: A linguistic perspective', *Uberstzung Translation Traduction* 1(1), pp. 600–6.

Delabastita, D. (1997) *Traductio*. 1st edn. Manchester: St Jerome Publishing.

Delabastita, D. (1996) 'Introduction: Studies in Intercultural Communication: Special Issue on wordplay and translation', *The Translator* 2(2), pp. 127–39.

Dickins, J., S. Hervey and I. Higgins (2002) *Thinking Arabic Translation*. 1st edn. London: Routledge.

Dik, S. C. (1997) *The Theory of Functional Grammar*. 2nd rev. edn. Berlin: Mouton de Gruyter.

Dryer, M. S. (1995) 'Frequency and Pragmatically Unmarked Word Order', in M. Noonan and P. A. Downing (eds) *Word Order in Discourse*. John Benjamins Publishing Co., pp. 105–35.

Dubois, J. et al. (1973) *Dictionnaire de Linguistique*. Paris: Larousse.

Eagleton, T., F. Jameson and E. W. Said (1990) *Nationalism, Colonialism, and Literature*. New edition. Minneapolis: University of Minnesota Press.

El-Farahaty, H. (2015) *Arabic-English-Arabic Legal Translation*. London: Routledge.

Elimam, A. S. (2020) 'Translating Word Order Variations in the Qur'an: A Qualitative and Quantitative Assessment', *Journal Of critical Studies in Language and Literature* 1(4), pp. 1–12.

Elimam, A. S. (2017) 'Translating the Qur'an into English: Target Readers' Expectations', *Skase Journal of Translation and Interpretation* 11(1), pp. 85–76.

Elimam, A. S. (2019) 'Media, Translation and the Construction of the Muslim Image: A Narrative Perspective', *International Journal of Comparative Literature & Translation Studies* 7(2), pp. 24–32.

Elimam, A. S. (2013) *Marked Word Order in the Qur'ān and its English Translations: Patterns and Motivations*. Newcastle upon Tyne: Cambridge Scholars Publishing.

Elimam, A. S. (2010) 'Paraphrase in Translating Business Texts from English into Arabic', *'Ayn* 3(5), pp. 7–32.

Elimam, A. S. (2009) 'Marked Word Order in the Qur'ān: Functions and Translation', *Across Languages and Cultures* 10(1), pp. 109–29.

Elimam, A. S. (2008) 'هندسة المتطلبات: خريطة طريق', *Journal of Computer Science and Engineering, in Arabic* 2(1).

Elimam, A. S. (2007) 'The Impact of Translation Memory Tools on the Translation Profession', *Translation Journal* 11(1).

Fawcett, P. (1997) *Translation and Language*. 1st edn. Manchester: St Jerome Publishing.

Fowler, R. (1993) *A Dictionary of Modern Critical Terms*. 5th edn. London and New York: Routledge.

Fowler, R. (1991) *Language in the News*. London: Routledge.

Ghazala, H. (2008/2014) *Translation as Problems and Solutions: A Textbook for University Students and Trainee Translators*. Riyadh and Jeddah: Konooz Al-Marifa Company for Printing and Publishing.

Green, G. M. (1982) 'Colloquial and Literary Uses of Inversions', in D. Tannen (ed.) *Spoken and Written Language: Exploring Orality and Literacy*. Norwood, NJ: Ablex Publishing Corporation, pp. 119–54.

Gutt, E. (2000) *Translation and Relevance: Cognition and Context*. Manchester: Routledge.

Halliday, M. A. K. (1971/2002) *Linguistic Studies of Text and Discourse*. London and New York: Continuum.

Halliday, M. A. K. (1994) *An Introduction to Functional Grammar*. 2nd edn. London: Edward Arnold.

Halliday, M. A. K. (1974) *Explorations in the Functions of Language*. 2nd edn. London: Edward Arnold.

Halliday, M. A. K. and R. Hasan (1976) *Cohesion in English*. London: Edward Arnold.

Hanna, S. F. (2005) 'Hamlet Lives Happily Ever After in Arabic', *The Translator: Bourdieu and the Sociology of Translation and Interpreting* 11(2), pp. 167–92.

Hatim, B. (2001) *Teaching and Researching Translation*. 1st edn. Harlow: Longman.

Hatim, B. and I. Mason (1997) *The Translator as Communicator*. London and New York: Routledge.

Hatim, B. and J. Munday (2004) *Translation*. 1st edn. London and New York: Routledge.

Hilali, M. T. and M. M. Khan (1977/1998) *Interpretation of the Meanings of the Noble Qur'an in the English Language: A Summarized Version of At-Tabari, Al-Qurtubi, and Ibn Kathir with Comments from Sahih-Al-Bukhari*. Riyadh: Darusalam Publishing.

Holes, C. (1995/2004) *Modern Arabic*. Rev. edn. Washington DC: Georgetown University Press.

Holmes, J. S. (1972/1988). 'The Name and Nature of Translation Studies', in *Holmes, Translated: Papers on Literary Translation and Translation Studies*. Amsterdam: Rodopi, pp. 67–80.

Husni, R. and D. L. Newman (2015) *Arabic-English-Arabic translation*. London and New York: Routledge.

Huxley, A. (1947) *Brave New World*. New York: HarperCollins.

Ibn Hishām, A. (1963) شرح قطر الندى وبل الصدى (*Explanation of the Drops of Mist and Wetting of the Dry Surface*). Cairo: Maṭbaʿat al-Saʿāda.

Ibrahim, Y. (2003) *The Translation of Collocation into Arabic Problems and Solutions*. University of Leeds: Unpublished PhD dissertation.

Jackendoff, R. (1972) *Semantic Interpretation in Generative Grammar*. Cambridge, MA: MIT Press.

Jakobson, R. (1959) 'On Linguistic Aspects of Translation', in R. Brower (ed.) *On Translation*. 1st edn. Cambridge, MA: Harvard University Press, pp. 232–9.

Kidwai, A. R. (2007) *Bibliography of the Translations of the Meanings of the Glorious Qur'an in English, 1649–2002*. Al-Madinah al-Munawwarah: King Fahd Qur'an Printing Complex.

Kidwai, A. R. (1992) 'English Translations of the Holy Qur'an, An Annotated Bibliography'. <http://www.cyberistan.org/islamic/quranetr.htm> (last date accessed 30 August 2022).

Koller, W. (1995) 'The Concept of Equivalence and the Object of Translation Studies', *Target: International Journal of Translation Studies* 7(2), pp. 191–222.

Lakoff, G. and M. Johnson (1980) *Metaphors We Live By*. 1st edn. Chicago: University of Chicago Press.

Larson, M. (1984) *Meaning-based Translation*. Lanham, MD: University Press of America.

Lāshīn, A. F. (1978) المعاني في ضوء اساليب القرآن (*Meaning in Light of the Quranic Style*). 3rd rev. edn. Cairo: Dār al-Maʿārif.

Laviosa-Braithwaite, S. (2001) 'Universals of Translation', in M. Baker (ed.) *Routledge Encyclopaedia of Translation Studies*. London and New York: Routledge, pp. 288–91.

Leech, G. N. (1966) 'Linguistics and the Figures of Rhetoric', in *Essays on Style and Language: Linguistic and Critical Approaches to Literary Style*, edited by Roger G. Fowler. London: Routledge and Kegan Paul, pp. 135–56.

Leech, G. N. and M. Short (1981) *Style in Fiction*. London: Longman.

Li, J. and S. Xu (2003) 'Foregrounding as a Criterion for Translation Criticism', *Babel* 49(4), pp. 302–9.

McCawley, J. (1968) 'The Role of Semantics in a Grammar', in E. Bach and R. Harms (eds), *Universals in Linguistic Theory*. New York: Holt, Rinehart, and Winston, pp. 125–70.

Mahmoud, M. (2006) (العالم الطريف) (translation) *Brave New World* by Aldous Huxley (1947), Cairo: Dār Al-kātib Al-Maṣrī.

Malmkjær, K. (2011) 'Translation Universals', in K. Malmkjær and K. Windle (eds), *The Oxford Handbook of Translation Studies*. Oxford: Oxford University Press.

Malmkjær, K. (2004) 'Translational Stylistics: Dulcken's Translations of Hans Christian Andersen', *Language and Literature* 13(1), pp. 13–24.

Malmkjær, K. and K. Windle (2011) *The Oxford Handbook of Translation Studies*. 1st edn. Oxford: Oxford University Press.

Marco, J. (2004) 'Translating style and styles of translating: Henry James and Edgar Allan Poe in Catalan', *Language and Literature* 13(1), pp. 73–90.

Martín-Asensio, G. (2002) *Transitivity-based Foregrounding in the Acts of the Apostles*. Sheffield: Sheffield Academic Press.

Mauranen, A. and P. Kujamäki (2004) *Translation Universals: Do they Exist?* Philadelphia: John Benjamins Publishing Co.

Melby, A. K. and C. Foster (2010) 'Context in Translation: Definition, Access and Teamwork', *Translation & Interpreting* 2(2), pp. 1–15.

Merriam-Webster's Collegiate Dictionary (2004) 11th edn. Springfield, MA: Merriam-Webster, Inc.

Millán-Varela, C. (2004) 'Hearing voices: James Joyce, narrative voice and minority translation', *Language and Literature* 13(1), pp. 37–54.

Mollanazar, H. and S. M. Mohaqeq (2005) 'The Holy Qur'an: Translation and Ideological Presuppositions', *Translation Studies* 3(11), pp. 59–66.

Munday, J. (2008) *The Routledge Companion to Translation Studies*. Rev. edn. London: Routledge.

Munday, J. (2001) *Introducing Translation Studies: Theories and Applications*. London: Routledge.

Murtisari, E. T. (2016) 'Explicitation in Translation Studies: The Journey of an Elusive Concept', *Translation & Interpreting* 8(2), pp. 64–81.

Newmark, P. (1988/2003) *A Textbook of Translation*. 8th edn. New York: Prentice Hall.

Newmark, P. (1993) *Paragraphs on Translation*. Clevedon, Philadelphia and Adelaide: Multilingual Matters.

Nida, E. A. (1964/1995) *Toward a Science of Translating*. 2nd edn. Leiden: Brill.

Nida, E. A. and C. R. Taber (1969/1982) *The Theory and Practice of Translation*. Repr. edn. Leiden: Brill.

Nord, C. (2007) 'The Phatic Function in Translation: Metacommunication as a Case in Point', *Belgian Journal of Linguistics* 21(1), pp. 171–84.

Nord, C. (1997) *Translating as a Purposeful Activity: Functionalist Approaches Explained*. 1st edn. London and New York: Routledge.

Nord, C. (1991) *Text Analysis in Translation. Theory, Methodology, and Didactic Application of a Model for Translation-Oriented Text Analysis*. Translated from the German by Christiane Nord and Penelope Sparrow. Amsterdam and Atlanta: Rodopi.

Owji, Z. (2013) 'Translation Strategies: A Review and Comparison of Theories', *Translation Journal* 17(1).

Parks, T. (2007) *Translating style: a literary approach to translation, a translation approach to literature*. 1st edn. London and New York: Routledge.

Paul, G. (2009) *Translation in Practice*. 1st edn. Champaign: Dalkey Archive Press.

Pickthall, M. M. (1930/2005) *The Meaning of the Glorious Qur'an: An Explanatory Translation, New Modern English Edition*. 2nd edn. London: I.D.I.C.

Qara'i, Q. (2004) *The Qur'an, with a Phrase-by-Phrase English Translation*. London: ICSA Press.

Quirk, R. (1997) *A Comprehensive Grammar of the English Language*. 14th edn. London: Longman.

Quirk, R., S. Greenbaum, G. Leech and J. Svartvik (1985) *A Comprehensive Grammar of the English Language*. New York: Longman.

Rabaḍāwī, M. (2005) 'أهداف ترجمات القرآن وأهدافها عبر التاريخ (Aims and Approaches of Translating the Qur'an Through History)', *Mijalat al-Turāth al-'Arabī*.

Reiss, K. (1989) 'Text Types, Translation Types and Translation Assessment', in A. Chesterman (ed.), *Readings in Translation Theory*. Helsinki: Finn Lectura.

Reiss, K. and H. J. Vermeer (1984) *Towards A General Theory of Translation Action. Skopos Theory Explained*. Translated by Christiane Nord. Tübingen: M. Niemeyer.

Rigonu, I. (2006) 'Islamic Features in British and French Muslim Media', in E. Poole and J. E. Richardson (eds) *Muslims and the News Media*. London: I. B. Tauris, pp. 74–86.

Rippin, A. (1992) 'Reading the Qur'an with Richard Bell', *Journal of the American Oriental Society* 112(4), pp. 639–47.

Rosenhouse, J. (1988) 'Occurrence of the passive in different types of text in English, Hebrew and Arabic', *Babel* 34(1), pp. 90–103.

Said, E. W. (1990) 'Embargoed Literature', *The Nation* 251(8), pp. 278–80.

Sandt, R. A. van der and P. Bosch (1999) *Focus: Linguistic, Cognitive, and Computational Perspectives*. Cambridge: Cambridge University Press.

Sayadi, F. (2011) 'The Translation of Neologism', *Translation Journal* 16(2).

Shuttleworth, M. and M. Cowie (1997) *Dictionary of translation studies*. 1st edn. Manchester: St Jerome Publishing.

Strelkova, N. (2012) *Introduction to Russian-English translation*. New York and Leicester: Hippocrene Books.

Swan, M. (2005) *Practical English Usage*. 3rd fully rev. edn. Oxford: Oxford University Press.

Tavangar, M. (2003) 'Lexical Foregrounding: A Perennial Problem in Translating Literary Communication', *Babel* 49(2), pp. 164–84.

Venuti, L. (1995) *The Translator's Invisibility*. 1st edn. London: Routledge.

Vermeer, H. (1987) 'What does it Mean to Translate', *Indian Journal of Applied Linguistics* 13, pp. 25–33.

Vinay, J. and J. Darbelnet (1958/1995) *Comparative Stylistics of French and English: A Methodology for Translation*. 2nd edn, yranslated and edited by J. Sager and M. J. Hamel. Amsterdam and Philadelphia: John Benjamins Publishing Co.

Yusuf, F. (2005) (مسرحية عن مسرحية حلم ليلة صيف) 'A Play Based on A Midsummer Night's Dream'. Cairo: Ministry of Information, Public Authority for Information.

Index

CPSIA information can be obtained
at www.ICGtesting.com
Printed in the USA
JSHW061203240323
39309JS00005B/11